W9-CYZ-570

JOHNSON WITHOUT BOSWELL

JOHNSON

WITHOUT BOSWELL

A Contemporary Portrait of

SAMUEL JOHNSON

EDITED BY

HUGH KINGSMILL

1941 *Alfred A. Knopf* NEW YORK

TO
HESKETH PEARSON

INTRODUCTION

The unqualified praise given by both Macaulay and Carlyle to Boswell's *Life of Johnson* obscured for a long time its limitations as a record of fact and also as a portrait of its subject. Leslie Stephen was, I think, the first to point out that a great deal of Johnson lay outside Boswell's view; Sir Walter Raleigh developed this suggestion in an essay which is the more convincing because of his enthusiasm for the incomparable personal scenes in Boswell, and since Raleigh's death many readers of Boswell have come to feel that his Johnson is too static, a character and an oracle rather than a human being whose life changed from year to year, and whose nature felt desire and experienced frustration.

The aim of this volume is to provide an account of Johnson from contemporary sources outside Boswell, including Johnson's own letters, private meditations and fragmentary reminiscences of his childhood. I have tried to arrange the extracts in such an order as to give a reasonably connected and self-explanatory narrative, but some details about the chief contributors are necessary.

Sir John Hawkins knew Johnson in the years of his obscurity, and remained his friend till his death. Horace Walpole writes of him — " Sir John Hawkins was originally bred a lawyer, in which profession he did not succeed. Having married a gentlewoman who by her brother's death proved a considerable fortune he bought a house

at Twickenham, intending to give himself up to his studies and music, of which he was very fond. He now commenced a justice of peace; and being a very honest moral
man, but of no brightness, and very obstinate and con-
tentious, he grew hated by the lower class and very
troublesome to the gentry, with whom he went to law
both on public and private causes, at the same time collecting materials indefatigably for a History of Music."

Hawkins's *Life of Johnson,* to which Boswell devoted
many pages of disparagement, is a rambling and largely
irrelevant volume, but though inaccurate in many small
details it is written with the sincerity of a narrow self-
opinionated man, attracted to Johnson by a strain of real
feeling, and genuinely perplexed and dismayed by Johnson's carelessness about his own interests. A reluctant
admirer is often more convincing than a slavish disciple,
and even in Boswell there is no scene which brings Johnson more vividly before one than Hawkins's account of
the party at the Devil Tavern.

Mrs. Thrale, daughter of a Welsh baronet, was thirty
years younger than Johnson. Married to a wealthy
brewer, to whom she bore twelve children, she sustained
with great good humour and patience the double burden
of looking after Johnson during sixteen years and acting
as hostess to the distinguished persons her husband
wished to associate with. There can be no doubt that
by far the greater part of such happiness as Johnson got
out of life was due to her care of him in her Streatham
home. Her light rather shallow nature, and quick intelligence, were complementary to his repressed melancholy,
and profound and brooding intellect. When she broke
away from him after her husband's death, and made what
proved an unusually happy marriage, with the Italian
musician Piozzi, he abandoned his lifelong struggle with

his inborn melancholia, dying within five months of her marriage. It was one of those tragedies inherent in the nature of life, and it is useless to blame any of those concerned in it.

Her account of Johnson was written some years after his death, by which time her genuine affection for him had revived, and the charms of the prudent and honourable Piozzi perhaps lost a little of their glow. There is a spontaneity and sincerity in her reminiscences which much more than atone for their unimportant inaccuracies. Johnson confided in her more freely than in any one else, and she has given us the most human picture we have of him.

She also kept a diary during his lifetime, and in the following pages it will be noticed that the extracts from the diary (Mrs. Thrale) are in a different tone from the reminiscences (Mrs. Piozzi), written under the softening effect of memory.

The *advocatus diaboli* in this book is Anna Seward, who lived at Lichfield and was well known as a poetess. Sir Walter Scott, who knew and liked her, suggests that, as a member of the best society in Lichfield, she was annoyed at the fame gained by a son of a local tradesman. There is something in this, but since even nowadays there are plenty of persons who dislike Johnson, it seems fairer to Anna Seward to assume that Johnson jarred on her chiefly for other than social reasons. She had a great deal of intelligence and feeling, and as she was unusually honest and sincere there is no reason to question the authenticity of the dialogues she reports, or the reasonable accuracy of the gossip she records. Johnson fascinated as well as repelled her, and one scene from her pen (A Quaker Convert) surpasses any other account of Johnson in a rage.

To supply links in the narrative which would otherwise have been missing I have used a short biography by Arthur Murphy, a genial Irishman, of whom Johnson was very fond. I have also included a few items from published material drawn upon by Boswell.

Contents

JOHNSON WITHOUT BOSWELL

Chapter I

CHILDHOOD, YOUTH, AND MARRIAGE
1709–1737

Johnson's Parents

Samuel Johnson was the son of Michael Johnson, a bookseller at Litchfield, in Staffordshire; a very pious and worthy man, but wrongheaded, positive, and afflicted with melancholy, as his son, from whom alone I had the information, once told me: his business, however, leading him to be much on horseback, contributed to the preservation of his bodily health, and mental sanity; which, when he staid long at home, would sometimes be about to give way; and Mr. Johnson said, that when his workshop, a detached building, had fallen half down for want of money to repair it, his father was not less diligent to lock the door every night, though he saw that any body might walk in at the back part, and knew that there was no security obtained by barring the front door. "*This* (says his son) was madness, you may see, and would have been discoverable in other instances of the prevalence of imagination, but that poverty prevented it from playing such tricks as riches and leisure encourage." Michael was a man of still larger size and greater strength than his son, who was reckoned very like him, but did not delight in talking much of his family — " one has (says he) *so* little pleasure in reciting the anecdotes of beggary."

One day, however, hearing me praise a favourite friend
with partial tenderness as well as true esteem; "Why do
you like that man's acquaintance so?" said he. "Because,"
replied I, "he is open and confiding, and tells me stories of
his uncles and cousins; I love the light parts of a solid
character." "Nay, if you are for family history," says Mr.
Johnson good-humouredly, "*I* can fit you: I had an uncle,
Cornelius Ford, who, upon a journey, stopped and read
an inscription written on a stone he saw standing by the
way-side, set up, as it proved, in honour of a man who had
leaped a certain leap thereabouts, the extent of which
was specified upon the stone: 'Why now,' says my uncle,
'I could leap it in my boots'; and he did leap it in his
boots. I had likewise another uncle, Andrew, continued
he, my father's brother, who kept the ring in Smithfield
(where they wrestled and boxed) for a whole year, and
never was thrown or conquered. Here now are uncles for
you, Mistress, if that's the way to your heart." Mr. Johnson was very conversant in the art of attack and defence
by boxing, which science he had learned from this uncle
Andrew, I believe; and I have heard him descant upon
the age when people were received, and when rejected,
in the schools once held for that brutal amusement, much
to the admiration of those who had no expectation of his
skill in such matters, from the sight of a figure which pre-
cluded all possibility of personal prowess; though, because he saw Mr. Thrale one day leap over a cabriolet
stool, to show that he was not tired after a chace of fifty
miles or more, *he* suddenly jumped over it too; but in a
way so strange and so unwieldly, that our terror lest he
should break his bones, took from us even the power of
laughing.

Michael Johnson was past fifty years old when he married his wife, who was upwards of forty; yet I think her

son told me she remained three years childless before he
was born into the world, who so greatly contributed to
improve it. In three years more she brought another son,
Nathaniel, who lived to be twenty-seven or twenty-eight
years old, and of whose manly spirit I have heard his
brother speak with pride and pleasure, mentioning one
circumstance, particular enough, that when the company
were one day lamenting the badness of the roads, he
enquired where they could be, as he travelled the country more than most people, and had never seen a bad
road in his life. The two brothers did not, however, much
delight in each other's company, being always rivals for
the mother's fondness; and many of the severe reflections
on domestic life in " Rasselas," took their source from its
author's keen recollections of the time passed in his early
years. Their father Michael died of an inflammatory
fever, at the age of seventy-six, as Mr. Johnson told me:
their mother at eighty-nine, of a gradual decay. She was
slight in her person, he said, and rather below than above
the common size. So excellent was her character, and
so blameless her life, that when an oppressive neighbour
once endeavoured to take from her a little field she possessed, he could persuade no attorney to undertake the
cause against a woman so beloved in her narrow circle:
and it is this incident he alludes to in the line of his
" Vanity of Human Wishes," calling her

" The general favourite as the general friend."

(MRS. PIOZZI)

An Old Man's Child

At the age of two years Mr. Johnson was brought up to
London by his mother, to be touched by Queen Anne
for the scrophulous evil, which terribly afflicted his child-

hood, and left such marks as greatly disfigured a countenance naturally harsh and rugged, besides doing irrepa-
rable damage to the auricular organs, which never could
perform their functions since I knew him; and it was
owing to that horrible disorder, too, that one eye was
perfectly useless to him; that defect, however, was not
observable, the eyes looked both alike. As Mr. Johnson
had an astonishing memory, I asked him, if he could remember Queen Anne at all? " He had," he said, " a confused, but somehow a sort of solemn recollection of a lady
in diamonds, and a long black hood."

The christening of his brother he remembered with all
its circumstances, and said, his mother taught him to spell
and pronounce the words *little Natty*, syllable by syllable,
making him say it over in the evening to her husband and
his guests. The trick which most parents play with their
children, that of showing off their newly-acquired accomplishments, disgusted Mr. Johnson beyond expression; he
had been treated so himself, he said, till he absolutely
loathed his father's caresses, because he knew they were
sure to precede some unpleasing display of his early abilities; and he used, when neighbours came o' visiting, to
run up a tree that he might not be found and exhibited,
such, as no doubt he was, a prodigy of early understanding. Yet he always seemed more mortified at the recollection of the bustle his parents made with his wit, than
pleased with the thoughts of possessing it. " That (said
he to me one day) is the great misery of late marriages;
the unhappy produce of them becomes the plaything of
dotage: an old man's child, continued he, leads much
such a life, I think, as a little boy's dog, teized with awkward fondness, and forced, perhaps, to sit up and beg, as
we call it, to divert a company, who at last go away complaining of their disagreeable entertainment." In conse-

quence of these maxims, and full of indignation against
such parents as delight to produce their young ones early
into the talking world, I have known Mr. Johnson give a
good deal of pain by refusing to hear the verses the children could recite, or the songs they could sing; particularly one friend who told him that his two sons should
repeat Gray's Elegy to him alternately that he might judge
who had the happiest cadence. " No, pray Sir," said he,
" let the dears both speak it at once; more noise will by
that means be made, and the noise will be sooner over."
He told me the story himself, but I have forgot who the
father was.

(MRS. PIOZZI)

Cornelius Ford

Mr. Johnson's mother was daughter to a gentleman in the
country, such as there were many of in those days, who
possessing, perhaps, one or two hundred pounds a year
in land, lived on the profits, and sought not to increase
their income: she was therefore inclined to think higher
of herself than of her husband, whose conduct in money
matters being but indifferent, she had a trick of teizing
him about it, and was, by her son's account, very importunate with regard to her fears of spending more than
they could afford, though she never arrived at knowing
how much that was; a fault common, as he said, to most
women who pride themselves on their œconomy. They
did not however, as I could understand, live ill together
on the whole: " my father (says he) could always take his
horse and ride away for orders when things went badly."
The lady's maiden name was Ford; and the parson who
sits next to the punch-bowl in Hogarth's " Modern Mid-
night Conversation" was her brother's son. This Ford

was a man who chose to be eminent only for vice, with
talents that might have made him conspicuous in literature, and respectable in any profession he could have
chosen: his cousin has mentioned him in the lives of Fenton and of Broome; and when he spoke of him to me it
was always with tenderness, praising his acquaintance
with life and manners, and recollecting one piece of advice that no man surely ever followed more exactly: " Obtain (says Ford) some general principles of every science; he who can talk only on one subject, or act only in
one department, is seldom wanted, and perhaps never
wished for; while the man of general knowledge can often
benefit, and always please." He used to relate, however,
another story less to the credit of his cousin's penetration,
how Ford on some occasion said to him, " You will make
your way the more easily in the world, I see, as you are
contented to dispute no man's claim to conversation excellence, they will, therefore, more willingly allow your
pretensions as a writer."

(MRS. PIOZZI)

Chesterfield and Cornelius Ford

In the life of Fenton, Johnson says, that " his (Cornelius
Ford's) abilities, instead of furnishing convivial merriment to the voluptuous and dissolute, might have enabled him to excel among the virtuous and wise." Being
chaplain to the earl of Chesterfield he wished to attend
that nobleman on his embassy to the Hague. Colley
Cibber has recorded the anecdote. " You should go," said
the witty peer, " if to your many vices you would add one
more." " Pray, my lord, what is that?" " Hypocrisy, my
dear doctor."

(ARTHUR MURPHY)

Early Religious Questionings

Dr. Johnson first learned to read of his mother and her old maid Catharine, in whose lap he well remembered sitting while she explained to him the story of St. George and the Dragon. I know not whether this is the proper place to add, that such was his tenderness, and such his gratitude, that he took a journey to Litchfield fifty-seven years afterwards to support and comfort her in her last illness; he had inquired for his nurse, and she was dead. The recollection of such reading as had delighted him in his infancy, made him always persist in fancying that it was the only reading which could please an infant; and he used to condemn me for putting Newbery's books into their hands as too trifling to engage their attention. "Babies do not want (said he) to hear other babies; they like to be told of giants and castles, and of somewhat which can stretch and stimulate their little minds." When in answer I would urge the numerous editions and quick sale of "Tommy Prudent" or "Goody Two Shoes": "Remember always (said he) that the parents *buy* the books, and that the children never read them." Mrs. Barbauld however had his best praise, and deserved it; no man was more struck than Mr. Johnson with voluntary descent from possible splendour to painful duty.

At eight years old he went to school, for his health would not permit him to be sent sooner; and at the age of ten years his mind was disturbed by scruples of infidelity, which preyed upon his spirits, and made him very uneasy; the more so, as he revealed his uneasiness to no one, being naturally (as he said) "of a sullen temper and reserved disposition." He searched, however, diligently but fruitlessly, for evidences of the truth of revelation;

and at length recollecting a book he had once seen in his father's shop, intitled, " De Veritate Religionis, &c." he began to think himself highly culpable for neglecting such a means of information, and took himself severely to task for this sin, adding many acts of voluntary, and to others unknown, penance. The first opportunity which offered (of course) he seized the book with avidity; but on examination, not finding himself scholar enough to peruse its contents, set his heart at rest; and, not thinking to inquire whether there were any English books written on the subject, followed his usual amusements, and considered his conscience as lightened of a crime. He redoubled his diligence to learn the language that contained the information he most wished for; but from the pain which guilt had given him, he now began to deduce the soul's immortality, which was the point that belief first stopped at; and from that moment resolving to be a Christian, became one of the most zealous and pious ones our nation ever produced. When he had told me this odd anecdote of his childhood; "I cannot imagine (said he), what makes me talk of myself to you so, for I really never mentioned this foolish story to any body except Dr. Taylor, not even to my *dear dear* Bathurst, whom I loved better than ever I loved any human creature; but poor Bathurst is dead! ! ! " — Here a long pause and a few tears ensued.

(MRS. PIOZZI)

On Indulging Children

One day when my son was going to school, and dear Dr. Johnson followed as far as the garden gate, praying for his salvation, in a voice which those who listened attentively, could hear plain enough, he said to me suddenly, " Make your boy tell you his dreams: the first corruption that entered into my heart was communicated in a dream." " What was it, Sir? " said I. " *Do* not ask me," replied he, with much violence, and walked away in apparent agitation. I never durst make any further enquiries. He retained a strong aversion for the memory of Hunter, one of his schoolmasters, who, he said once was a brutal fellow: " so brutal (added he), that no man who had been educated by him ever sent his son to the same school." I have however heard him acknowledge his scholarship to be very great. His next master he despised, as knowing less than himself, I found; but the name of that gentleman has slipped my memory. Mr. Johnson was himself exceedingly disposed to the general indulgence of children, and was even scrupulously and ceremoniously attentive not to offend them: he had strongly persuaded himself of the difficulty people always find to erase early impressions either of kindness or resentment, and said, " he should never have so loved his mother when a man, had she not given him coffee she could ill afford, to gratify his appetite when a boy." " If you had had children Sir," said I, " would you have taught them anything? " " I hope (replied he), that I should have willingly lived on bread and water to obtain instruction for them; but I would not have set their future friendship to hazard for the sake of thrusting into their heads knowledge of things for which they might not perhaps have either taste or necessity. You teach your daughters the diameters of the planets, and wonder when you have done that they do not delight in your company. No science can be communicated by mortal creatures without attention from the scholar; no attention can be obtained from children without the infliction of pain, and pain is never remembered without resentment."

(MRS. PIOZZI)

Parental Authority

Of parental authority, indeed, few people thought with a lower degree of estimation. I one day mentioned the resignation of Cyrus to his father's will, as related by Xenophon, when, after all his conquests, he requested the consent of Cambyses to his marriage with a neighbouring princess; and I added Rollin's applause and recommendation of the example. "Do you not perceive then (says Johnson), that Xenophon on this occasion commends like a pedant, and Père Rollin applauds like a slave? If Cyrus by his conquests had not purchased emancipation, he had conquered to little purpose indeed. Can you bear to see the folly of a fellow who has in his care the lives of thousands, when he begs his papa permission to be married, and confesses his inability to decide in a matter which concerns no man's happiness but his own?" — Mr. Johnson caught me another time reprimanding the daughter of my housekeeper for having sat down unpermitted in her mother's presence. "Why, she gets her living, does she not (said he), without her mother's help? Let the wench alone," continued he. And when we were again out of the women's sight who were concerned in the dispute: "Poor people's children, dear Lady (said he) never respect them: I did not respect my own mother, though I loved her: and one day, when in anger she called me a puppy, I asked her if she knew what they called a puppy's mother."

(MRS. PIOZZI)

Boys and Girls

I was relating once to him, how Dr. Collier observed, that the love one bore to children was from the anticipation one's mind made while one contemplated them: " We hope (says he) that they will some time make wise men, or amiable women; and we suffer 'em to take up our affection beforehand. One cannot love *lumps of flesh,* and little infants are nothing more." " On the contrary (says Johnson), one can scarcely help wishing, while one fondles a baby, that it may never live to become a man; for it is *so* probable that when he becomes a man, he should be sure to end in a scoundrel." Girls were less displeasing to him; for as their temptations were fewer (he said), their virtue in this life, and happiness in the next, were less improbable; and he loved (he said) to see a knot of little misses dearly.

(MRS. PIOZZI)

Johnson's Account of his Childhood . . . his Nurse

Sept. 7, 1709, I was born at Lichfield. My mother had a very difficult and dangerous labour, and was assisted by George Hector, a man-midwife of great reputation. I was born almost dead, and could not cry for some time. When he had me in his arms, he said, " Here is a brave boy."

In a few weeks an inflammation was discovered on my buttock, which was at first, I think, taken for a burn; but soon appeared to be a natural disorder. It swelled, broke, and healed.

My Father, being that year Sheriff of Lichfield, and to ride the circuit of the County next day, which was a ceremony then performed with great pomp; he was asked by my mother, " Whom he would invite to the Riding? " and answered, " All the town now." He feasted the citizens with uncommon magnificence, and was the last but one that maintained the splendour of the Riding.

I was, by my father's persuasion, put to one Marclew, commonly called Bellison, the servant, or wife of a servant of my father, to be nursed in George Lane, where I used to call when I was a bigger boy, and eat fruit in the garden, which was full of trees. Here it was discovered that my eyes were bad; and an issue was cut in my left arm; of which I took no great notice, as I think my mother has told me, having my little hand in a custard.

It is observable, that, having been told of this operation, I always imagined that I remembered it, but I laid the scene in the wrong house. Such confusions of memory I suspect to be common.

My mother visited me every day, and used to go different ways, that her assiduity might not expose her to ridicule; and often left her fan or glove behind her, that she might have a pretence to come back unexpected; but she never discovered any token of neglect. Dr. Swinfen told me, that the scrofulous sores which afflicted me proceeded from the bad humours of the nurse, whose son had the same distemper, and was likewise shortsighted, but both in a less degree. My mother thought my diseases derived from her family.

In ten weeks I was taken home, a poor, diseased infant, almost blind.

I remember my aunt Nath. Ford told me, when I was about . . . years old, that she would not have picked such a poor creature up in the street.

In . . . 67, when I was at Lichfield, I went to look for my nurse's house; and, inquiring somewhat obscurely, was told "this is the house in which you were nursed." I saw my nurse's son, to whose milk I succeeded, reading a large Bible, which my nurse had bought, as I was then told, some time before her death.

Dr. Swinfen used to say, that he never knew any child reared with so much difficulty.

. . . his Parents

In the second year I knew [? know] not what happened to me. I believe it was then that my mother carried me to Trysul, to consult Dr. Atwood, an oculist of Worcester. My father and Mrs. Harriots, I think, never had much kindness for each other. She was my mother's relation; and he had none so high to whom he could send any of his family. He saw her seldom himself, and willingly disgusted her, by sending his horses from home on Sunday; which she considered, and with reason, as a breach of duty. My father had much vanity, which his adversity hindered from being fully exerted. I remember, that, mentioning her legacy in the humility of distress, he called her *our good Cousin Harriots.* My mother had no value for his relations; those indeed whom we knew of were much lower than hers. This contempt began, I know not on which side, very early: but, as my father was little at home, it had not much effect.

My father and mother had not much happiness from each other. They seldom conversed; for my father could not bear to talk of his affairs; and my mother, being unacquainted with books, cared not to talk of any thing else. Had my mother been more literate, they had been better companions. She might have sometimes introduced her unwelcome topick with more success, if she could have diversified her conversation. Of business she had no distinct conception; and therefore her discourse was composed only of complaint, fear, and suspicion. Neither of them ever tried to calculate the profits of trade, or the expenses of living. My mother concluded that we were poor, because we lost by some of our trades; but the truth was, that my father, having in the early part of his life contracted debts, never had trade sufficient to enable him to pay them, and maintain his family; he got something, but not enough.

It was not till about 1768, that I thought to calculate the returns of my father's trade, and by that estimate his probable profits. This, I believe, my parents never did.

. . . touched by Queen Anne

This year, in Lent −12, I was taken to London, to be touched for the evil by Queen Anne. My mother was at Nicholson's, the famous bookseller, in Little Britain. I always retained some memory of this journey, though I was then but thirty months old. I remembered a little dark room behind the kitchen, where the jack-weight fell through a hole in the floor, into which I once slipped my leg. [I seem to remember, that I played with a string and a bell, which my cousin Isaac Johnson gave me; and that there was a cat with a white collar, and a dog, called Chops, that leaped over a stick: but I know not whether I remember the thing, or the talk of it.]

I remember a boy crying at the palace when I went to be touched. Being asked " on which side of the shop was the counter? " I answered, " on the left from the entrance," many years after, and spoke, not by guess, but by memory. We went in the stage-coach, and returned in the

waggon, as my mother said, because my cough was violent. The hope of saving a few shillings was no slight
motive; for she, not having been accustomed to money,
was afraid of such expenses as now seem very small. She
sewed two guineas in her petticoat, lest she should be
robbed.

We were troublesome to the passengers; but to suffer
such inconveniences in the stage-coach was common in
these days to persons in much higher rank. [I was
sick; one woman fondled me, the other was disgusted.]
She bought me a small silver cup and spoon, marked
SAM. I. lest if they had been marked S. I. which was her
name, they should, upon her death, have been taken from
me. She bought me a speckled linen frock, which I knew
afterwards by the name of my London frock. The cup
was one of the last pieces of plate which dear Tetty sold
in our distress. I have now the spoon. She bought at the
same time two tea spoons, and till my manhood she had
no more.

My father considered tea as very expensive, and discouraged my mother from keeping company with the
neighbours, and from paying visits or receiving them.
She lived to say, many years after, that, if the time were
to pass again, she would not comply with such unsocial
injunctions.

I suppose that in this year I was first informed of a
future state. I remember, that being in bed with my
mother one morning, I was told by her of the two places
to which the inhabitants of this world were received after
death; one a fine place filled with happiness, called
Heaven; the other a *sad* place, called Hell. That this account much affected my imagination, I do not remember.
When I was risen, my mother bade me repeat what she
had told me to Thomas Jackson. When I told this after-

wards to my mother, she seemed to wonder that she should begin such talk so late as that the first time could be remembered.

. . . first Impressions of School

The progress of examination was this. When we learned *Propria quæ Maribus,* we were examined in the Accidence; particularly we formed Verbs, that is, went through the same person in all the Moods and Tenses. This was very difficult to me; and I was once very anxious about the next day, when this exercise was to be performed, in which I had failed till I was discouraged. My mother encouraged me, and I proceeded better. When I told her of my good escape, " We often," said she, dear mother! " come off best, when we are most afraid." She told me, that, once when she asked me about forming verbs, I said, " I did not form them in an ugly shape." " You could not," said she, " speak plain; and I was proud that I had a boy who was forming verbs." These little memorials sooth my mind. Of the parts of Corderius or Æsop, which we learned to repeat, I have not the least recollection, except of a passage in one of the Morals, where it is said of some man, that, when he hated another, he made him rich; this I repeated emphatically in my mother's hearing, who could never conceive that riches could bring any evil. She remarked it, as I expected.

The whole week before we broke up, and the part of the week in which we broke up, were spent wholly, I know not why, in examination; and were therefore easy to both us and the master. The two nights before the vacation were free from exercise.

This was the course of the school, which I remember

with pleasure; for I was indulged and caressed by my master, and, I think, really excelled the rest.

I was with Hawkins but two years, and perhaps four months. The time, till I had computed it, appeared much longer by the multitude of novelties which it supplied, and of incidents, then in my thoughts important, it produced. Perhaps it is not possible that any other period can make the same impression on the memory.

. . . Birmingham and Uncle Harrison

In the Spring of 1719, our class consisting of eleven, the number was always fixed in my memory, but one of the names I have forgotten, was removed to the upper school, and put under Holbrook, a peevish and ill-tempered man. We were removed sooner than had been the custom; for the head-master, intent upon his boarders, left the town-boys long in the lower school. Our removal was caused by a reproof from the Town-clerk; and Hawkins complained that he had lost half his profit. At this removal I cried. The rest were indifferent. My exercise in Garretson was somewhere about the Gerunds. Our places in Æsop and Helvicus I have totally forgotten.

. . . This Whitsuntide, I and my brother were sent to pass some time at Birmingham; I believe, a fortnight. Why such boys were sent to trouble other houses, I cannot tell. My mother had some opinion that much improvement was to be had by changing the mode of life. My uncle Harrison was a widower; and his house was kept by Sally Ford, a young woman of such sweetness of temper, that I used to say she had no fault. We lived most at uncle Ford's, being much caressed by my aunt, a good-natured, coarse woman, easy of converse, but will-

ing to find something to censure in the absent. My uncle
Harrison did not much like us, nor did we like him. He
was a very mean and vulgar man, drunk every night, but
drunk with little drink, very peevish, very proud, very
ostentatious, but, luckily, not rich. At my aunt Ford's I
eat so much of a boiled leg of mutton, that she used to
talk of it. My mother, who had lived in a narrow sphere,
and was then affected by little things, told me seriously
that it would hardly ever be forgotten. Her mind, I think,
was afterwards much enlarged, or greater evils wore out
the care of less.

I staid after the vacation was over some days; and remember, when I wrote home, that I desired the horses to
come on Thursday of the first school week; and then, and
not till then, they should be welcome to go. I was much
pleased with a rattle to my whip, and wrote of it to my
mother.

When my father came to fetch us home, he told the
ostler, that he had twelve miles home, and two boys under his care. This offended me. He had then a watch,
which he returned when he was to pay for it.

(JOHNSON'S ANNALS)

A Schoolfellow's Recollections

There dwelt at Lichfield a gentleman of the name of Butt,
the father of the reverend Mr. Butt, now a King's Chaplain, to whose house on holidays and in school-vacations
Johnson was ever welcome. The children in the family,
perhaps offended with the rudeness of his behaviour,
would frequently call him the great boy, which the father once overhearing, said, " you call him the great boy,

but take my word for it, he will one day prove a great man."

A more particular character of him while a schoolboy, and of his behaviour at school, I find in a paper now before me, written by a person yet living, and of which the following is a copy:

"Johnson and I were, in early life, school-fellows at Lichfield, and for many years in the same class. As his uncommon abilities for learning far exceeded us, we endeavoured by every boyish piece of flattery to gain his assistance, and three of us, by turns, used to call on him in a morning, on one of whose backs, supported by the other two, he rode triumphantly to school. He never associated with us in any of our diversions, except in the winter when the ice was firm, to be drawn along by a boy barefooted. His ambition to excel was great, though his application to books, as far as it appeared, was very trifling. I could not oblige him more than by sauntering away every vacation, that occurred, in the fields, during which time he was more engaged in talking to himself than his companion. Verses or themes he would dictate to his favourites, but he would never be at the trouble of writing them. His dislike to business was so great, that he would procrastinate his exercises to the last hour. I have known him after a long vacation, in which we were rather severely tasked, return to school an hour earlier in the morning, and begin one of his exercises, in which he purposely left some faults, in order to gain time to finish the rest.

"I never knew him corrected at school, unless it was for talking and diverting other boys from their business, by which, perhaps, he might hope to keep his ascendancy. He was uncommonly inquisitive, and his memory so tena-

cious, that whatever he read or heard he never forgot. I
remember rehearsing to him eighteen verses, which after
a little pause he repeated verbatim, except one epithet,
which improved the line."

(SIR JOHN HAWKINS)

Young Johnson in Lichfield Society

It is true I dwell on classic ground. Within the walls
which my father's family inhabits, in this very dining-
room, the munificent Mr. Walmesley, with the taste, the
learning and the liberality of Maecenas, administered to
rising genius the kind nutriment of attention and praise.
Often to his hospitable board were the school-boys David
Garrick and Samuel Johnson, summoned. The parents of
the former were of Mr. Walmesley's acquaintance; but
those of the latter did not move in his sphere.

It was rumoured that my mother's father, Mr. Hunter,
had a boy of marked ability upon his forms. The huge,
over-grown, mis-shapen, and probably dirty stripling was
brought before the most able scholar and the finest gentleman in Lichfield or its environs, who, perceiving far
more ability than even rumour had promised, placed him
at his table, not merely to gratify a transient curiosity, but
to assure him of a constant welcome.

Two or three evenings every week Mr. Walmesley
called the stupendous stripling and his livelier companion
David Garrick, who was a few years younger, to his own
plentiful board. There, in the hours of convivial gaiety,
did he delight to wave every restraint of superiority
formed by rank, affluence, polished manners and the
dignity of advanced life; and there, " as man to man, as
friend to friend," he drew forth the different powers of

each expanding spirit, by the vivid interchange of sentiment and opinion, and by the cheering influence of generous applause.

Another circumstance combined to heighten the merit
of this patronage. Mr. Walmesley was a zealous Whig.
My grandfather, then master of the free school, perceiving Johnson's abilities, had, to his own honour, taken as
much pains with him as with the young gentlemen whose
parents paid an high price for their pupilage; but my
grandfather was a Jacobite, and Sam. Johnson had im-
bibed his master's absurd zeal for the forfeit rights of the
house of Stuart; and this, though his father had very loyal
principles; but the anxiety attendant on penurious circumstances, probably left old Johnson little leisure or inclination to talk on political subjects.

His son, I am told, even at that early period of life,
maintained his opinions, on every subject, with the same
sturdy, dogmatical and arrogant fierceness with which he
now overbears all opposition to them in company.

At present we can well conceive the probability of his
dogmatism being patiently supported by attending ad-
mirers, awed by the literary eminence on which he stands.
But how great must have been Mr. Walmesley's love of
genius; how great his generous respect for its dependent
situation, that could so far restrain a naturally impetuous
temper, as to induce him to suffer insolent sallies from the
son of an indigent bookseller, and on a subject which, so
handled by people of his own rank, he would have dashed
back in their faces with no small degree of asperity! . . .

(ANNA SEWARD)

Molly Aston

You ask who the Molly Aston was, whom those letters
[Johnson's letters to Mrs. Thrale] mention with such passionate tenderness? Mr. Walmsley, my father's prede-
cessor in this house, was, as you have heard, Johnson's
Mecænas, and this lady, his wife's sister, a daughter of
Sir Thomas Aston, a wit, a beauty, and a toast. Johnson
was always fancying himself in love with some princess
or other. His wife's daughter, Lucy Porter, so often mentioned in those letters, was his first love, when he was a
school-boy, under my grandfather, a clergyman, vicar of
St. Mary's, and master of the free-school, which, by his
scholastic ability, was high in fame, and thronged with
pupils, from some of the first gentlemens' families in this
and the adjoining counties. To the free-school the boys
of the city had a right to come, but every body knows
how superficial, in general, is unpaid instruction. However, my grandfather, aware of Johnson's genius, took the
highest pains with him, though his parents were poor,
and mean in their situation, keeping market stalls, as battledore booksellers. Johnson has not had the gratitude
once to mention his generous master, in any of his writings; but all this is foreign to your inquiries, who Miss
Molly Aston was, and at what period his flame for her
commenced? It was during those school-days, when the
reputation of Johnson's talents, and rapid progress in the
classics, induced the noble-minded Walmsley to endure,
at his elegant table, the low-born squalid youth — here
that he suffered him and Garrick, to "imp their eagle
wings," a delighted spectator and auditor of their efforts.
It was here, that Miss Molly Aston was frequently a
visitor in the family of her brother-in-law, and prob-

ably amused herself with the uncouth adorations of the
learned, though dirty stripling, whose mean appearance
was overlooked, because of the genius and knowledge
that blazed through him; though with " umbered flames,"
from constitutional melancholy and spleen. Lucy Porter,
whose visit to Lichfield had been but for a few weeks, was
then gone back to her parents at Birmingham, and the
brighter Molly Aston became the Laura of our Petrarch.

(ANNA SEWARD)

Molly and Betty

Mr. Johnson had however an avowed and scarcely lim-
ited partiality for all who bore the name or boasted the
alliance of an Aston or a Hervey; and when Mr. Thrale
once asked him which had been the happiest period of
his past life? he replied, " it was that year in which he
spent one whole evening with M——y As——n. That indeed (said he) was not happiness, it was rapture; but
the thoughts of it sweetened the whole year." I must add,
that the evening alluded to was not passed *tête-à-tête*, but
in a select company, of which the present Lord Killmorey
was one. " Molly (says Dr. Johnson) was a beauty and a
scholar, and a wit and a whig; and she talked all in praise
of liberty: and so I made this epigram upon her — She
was the loveliest creature I ever saw! ! !

> " *Liber ut esse velim, suasisti pulchra Maria,*
> *Ut maneam liber — pulchra Maria, vale!* "

"Will it do this way in English, Sir (said I)?

> " Persuasions to freedom fall oddly from you;
> If freedom we seek — fair Maria, adieu! "

" It will do well enough (replied he); but it is translated
by a lady, and the ladies never loved M——y As——n." I
asked him what his wife thought of this attachment?
" She was jealous to be sure (said he), and teized me
sometimes when I would let her; and one day, as a for-
tune-telling gipsey passed us when we were walking out
in company with two or three friends in the country, she
made the wench look at my hand, but soon repented her
curiosity; for (says the gipsey) Your heart is divided, Sir,
between a Betty and a Molly: Betty loves you best, but
you take most delight in Molly's company: when I turned
about to laugh, I saw my wife was crying. Pretty charmer!
she had no reason! "

(MRS. PIOZZI)

Johnson on Gilbert Walmsley

Of Gilbert Walmsley, thus presented to my mind, let me
indulge myself in the remembrance. I knew him very
early; he was one of the first friends that literature procured me, and I hope that at least my gratitude made me
worthy of his notice.

He was of an advanced age, and I was only yet a boy;
yet he never received my notions with contempt. He was
a Whig, with all the virulence and malevolence of his
party; yet difference of opinion did not keep us apart. I
honoured him, and he endured me.

He had mingled with the gay world without exemption
from its vices or its follies, but had never neglected the
cultivation of his mind; his belief of revelation was un-
shaken; his learning preserved his principles; he grew
first regular, and then pious.

His studies had been so various, that I am not able to

name a man of equal knowledge. His acquaintance with books was great; and what he did not immediately know he could at least tell where to find. Such was his amplitude of learning, and such his copiousness of communication, that it may be doubted whether a day now passes in which I have not some advantage from his friendship.

At this man's table I enjoyed many cheerful and instructive hours, with companions such as are not often found; with one who has lengthened, and one who has gladdened life; with Dr. James, whose skill in physic will be long remembered; and with David Garrick, whom I hoped to have gratified with this character of our common friend: but what are the hopes of man! I am disappointed by that stroke of death, which has eclipsed the gaiety of nations, and impoverished the public stock of harmless pleasure.

(THE LIVES OF THE POETS)

Elizabeth Aston of Stowe Hill

You request the conversation that passed between Johnson and myself in company, on the subject of Mrs. Elizabeth Aston of Stowe Hill, then living, with whom he always past so much time when he was in Lichfield, and for whom he professed so great a friendship.

"I have often heard my mother say, Doctor, that Mrs. Elizabeth Aston was, in her youth, a very beautiful woman; and that, with all the censoriousness and spiteful spleen of a very bad temper, she had great powers of pleasing; that she was lively, insinuating, and intelligent.

"I knew her not till the vivacity of her youth had long been extinguished, and I confess I looked in vain for the traces of former ability. I wish to have *your* opinion, Sir, of what she was, *you* who knew her so well in her *best* days."

" My dear, when thy mother told thee Aston was handsome, thy mother told thee truth: She was very handsome. When thy mother told thee that Aston loved to abuse her neighbours, she told thee truth; but when thy mother told thee that Aston had any marked ability in that same abusive business, that wit gave it zest, or imagination colour, thy mother did not tell thee truth. No, no, Madam, Aston's understanding was not of any strength, either native or acquired."

" But, Sir, I have heard you say, that her sister's husband, Mr. Walmsley, was a man of bright parts, and extensive knowledge; that he was also a man of strong passions, and, though benevolent in a thousand instances, yet irascible in as many. It is well known that Mr. Walmsley was considerably governed by this lady; as witness Mr. Hinton's constant visits, and presence at his table, in despite of its master's avowed aversion. Could it be that, without some marked intellectual powers, she could obtain absolute dominion over such a man? "

" Madam, I have said, and truly, that Walmsley had bright and extensive powers of mind; that they had been cultivated by familiarity with the best authors, and by connections with the learned and polite. It is a fact, that Aston obtained nearly absolute dominion over his will; it is no less a fact, that his disposition was irritable and violent. But Walmsley was a man; and there is no man who can resist the repeated attacks of a furious woman. Walmsley had no alternative but to submit, or turn her out of doors."

(ANNA SEWARD)

Sir Thomas Aston

Dr. Johnson's friendship for Mrs. Elizabeth Aston com-
menced at the palace in Lichfield, the residence of Mr.
Walmesley: with Mrs. Gastrel he became acquainted in
London, at the house of her brother-in-law, Mr. Hervey.
During the Doctor's annual visits to his daughter-in-law,
Lucy Porter, he spent much of his time at Stow Hill,
where Mrs. Gastrel and Mrs. Elizabeth Aston resided.
They were the daughters of Sir Thomas Aston, of Aston
Hall in Cheshire, of whom it is said, that being applied
to for some account of his family, to illustrate the history
of Cheshire, he replied, that " the title and estate had descended from father to son for thirty generations, and that
he believed they were neither much richer nor much
poorer than they were at first."

Dr. Johnson used to say of Dr. Hunter, master of the
free grammar school, Lichfield, that he never taught a
boy in his life — he whipped and they learned. Hunter
was a pompous man, and never entered the school without his gown and cassock, and his wig full dressed. He
had a remarkably stern look, and Dr. Johnson said, he
could tremble at the sight of Miss Seward, she was so like
her grandfather.

(THE REV. MR. PARKER)

Johnson at Oxford

Having gone through the rudiments of classic literature,
he returned to his father's house, and was probably intended for the trade of a bookseller. He has been heard
to say that he could bind a book. At the end of two years,

being then about nineteen, he went to assist the studies
of a young gentleman, of the name of Corbet, to the university of Oxford; and on the 31st of October, 1728, both
were entered of Pembroke college; Corbet as a gentle-
man-commoner, and Johnson as a commoner. The college tutor, Mr. Jordan, was a man of no genius; and Johnson, it seems, showed an early contempt of mean abilities,
in one or two instances behaving with insolence to that
gentleman. Of his general conduct at the university there
are no particulars that merit attention, except the translation of Pope's Messiah, which was a college exercise im-
posed upon him as a task by Mr. Jordan. Corbet left the
university in about two years, and Johnson's salary ceased.
He was, by consequence, straitened in his circumstances;
but he still remained at college. Mr. Jordan, the tutor,
went off to a living; and was succeeded by Dr. Adams,
who afterwards became head of the college, and was esteemed through life for his learning, his talents, and his
amiable character. Johnson grew more regular in his attendance. Ethics, theology, and classic literature, were
his favourite studies. He discovered, notwithstanding,
early symptoms of that wandering disposition of mind,
which adhered to him to the end of his life. His reading
was by fits and starts, undirected to any particular science. General philology, agreeably to his cousin Ford's
advice, was the object of his ambition. He received, at
that time, an early impression of piety, and a taste for the
best authors, ancient and modern. It may, notwithstanding, be questioned whether, except his bible, he ever read
a book entirely through. Late in life, if any man praised
a book in his presence, he was sure to ask, "Did you read
it through?" If the answer was in the affirmative, he did
not seem willing to believe it. He continued at the university, till the want of pecuniary supplies obliged him

to quit the place. He obtained, however, the assistance
of a friend, and, returning in a short time, was able to
complete a residence of three years. The history of his
exploits at Oxford, he used to say, was best known to Dr.
Taylor and Dr. Adams. Wonders are told of his memory,
and, indeed, all who knew him late in life can witness, that
he retained that faculty in the greatest vigour.

(ARTHUR MURPHY)

Life at Pembroke College

[When Johnson was at Pembroke College] the want of
that assistance, which scholars in general derive from
their parents, relations, and friends, soon became visible
in his garb and appearance, which, though in some degree concealed by a scholar's gown, and that we know is
never deemed the less honourable for being old, was so
apparent as to excite pity in some that saw and noticed
him. He had scarce any change of raiment, and, in a
short time after Corbet left him, but one pair of shoes,
and those so old, that his feet were seen through them: a
gentleman of his college, the father of an eminent clergyman now living, directed a servitor one morning to place
a new pair at the door of Johnson's chamber, who, seeing
them upon his first going out, so far forgot himself and
the spirit that must have actuated his unknown benefactor, that, with all the indignation of an insulted man, he
threw them away.

The course of his studies was far from regular: he read
by fits and starts, and, in the intervals, digested his reading by meditation, to which he was ever prone. Neither
did he regard the hours of study, farther than the disci-
pline of the college compelled him. It was the practice in

his time, for a servitor, by order of the Master, to go round
to the rooms of the young men, and knocking at the door,
to enquire if they were within, and, if no answer was returned, to report them absent. Johnson could not endure
this intrusion, and would frequently be silent, when the
utterance of a word would have insured him from censure; and, farther to be revenged for being disturbed
when he was profitably employed as perhaps he could be,
would join with others of the young men in the college in
hunting, as they called it, the servitor, who was thus diligent in his duty; and this they did with the noise of pots
and candlesticks, singing to the tune of Chevy-chace, the
words in that old ballad,

"To drive the deer with hound and horn," &c.,

not seldom to the endangering the life and limbs of the
unfortunate victim.

(SIR JOHN HAWKINS)

Oxford in Retrospect

Oxford, June 13, 1782

Who do you think is my principal Cicerone at Oxford?
Only Dr. Johnson! and we do so gallant it about! You
cannot imagine with what delight he showed me every
part of his own College (Pembroke) nor how rejoiced
Henderson looked, to make one in the party. Dr. Adams,
the Master of Pembroke, had contrived a very pretty
piece of gallantry. We spent the day and evening at his
house. After dinner Johnson begged to conduct me to see
the College, he would let no one show it me but himself
— "This was my room; this Shenstone's." Then after

pointing out all the rooms of the poets who had been of his college, "In short," said he, "we were a nest of singing-birds" — "Here we walked, there we played at cricket." He ran over with pleasure the history of the juvenile days he passed there. When we came into the common room, we spied a fine large print of Johnson, framed and hung up that very morning, with this motto: "*And is not Johnson ours, himself a host.*" Under which stared you in the face, "From *Miss More's Sensibility.*" This little incident amused us; — but alas! Johnson looks very ill indeed — spiritless and wan. However, he made an effort to be cheerful, and I exerted myself much to make him so.

(HANNAH MORE)

His Melancholia

His own conjecture was, that he derived it from his father . . . Under this persuasion, he at the age of about twenty, drew up a state of his case for the opinion of an eminent physician in Staffordshire, and from him received an answer, "that from the symptoms therein described, he could think nothing better of his disorder, than that it had a tendency to insanity; and without great care might possibly terminate in the deprivation of his rational faculties." The dread of so great a calamity was an inducement with him to abstain from wine at certain periods of his life, when his fears in this respect were greatest; but it was not without some reluctance that he did it, for he has often been heard to declare, that wine was to him so great a cordial, that it required all his resolution to resist the temptations to ebriety.

(SIR JOHN HAWKINS)

Schoolmastering and Marriage

From the university, Johnson returned to Lichfield. His father died soon after, December, 1731; and the whole receipt out of his effects, as appeared by a memorandum in the son's handwriting, dated 15th of June, 1732, was no more than twenty pounds. In this exigence, determined that poverty should neither depress his spirits nor warp his integrity, he became undermaster of a grammar school at Market Bosworth, in Leicestershire. That resource, however, did not last long. Disgusted by the pride of Sir Wolstan Dixie, the patron of that little seminary, he left the place in discontent, and ever after spoke of it with abhorrence. In 1733, he went on a visit to Mr. Hector, who had been his schoolfellow, and was then a surgeon at Birmingham, lodging at the house of Warren, a bookseller. At that place Johnson translated a Voyage to Abyssinia, written by Jerome Lobo, a Portuguese missionary. This was the first literary work from the pen of Dr. Johnson. His friend, Hector, was occasionally his amanuensis.

His next expedient was to offer his assistance to Cave, the original projector of the Gentleman's Magazine. For this purpose he sent his proposals in a letter, offering on reasonable terms, occasionally to fill some pages with poems and inscriptions, never printed before; with fugitive pieces that deserved to be revived, and critical remarks on authors, ancient and modern. Cave agreed to retain him as a correspondent and contributor to the magazine. What the conditions were cannot now be known; but, certainly, they were not sufficient to hinder Johnson from casting his eyes about him in quest of other employment. Accordingly, in 1735, he made overtures to the reverend Mr. Budworth, master of a grammar school at Brerewood, in Staffordshire, to become his assistant. This proposition did not succeed. Mr. Budworth apprehended, that the involuntary motions, to which Johnson's nerves were subject, might make him an object of ridicule with his scholars, and, by consequence, lessen their respect for their master. Another mode of advancing himself presented itself about this time. Mrs. Porter, the widow of a mercer in Birmingham, admired his talents. It is said that she had about eight hundred pounds; and that sum, to a person in Johnson's circumstances, was an affluent fortune. A marriage took place; and, to turn his wife's money to the best advantage, he projected the scheme of an academy for education. Gilbert Walmsley, at that time, registrar of the ecclesiastical court of the bishop of Lichfield, was distinguished by his erudition, and the politeness of his manners. He was the friend of Johnson, and, by his weight and influence, endeavoured to promote his interest. The celebrated Garrick, whose father, captain Garrick, lived at Lichfield, was placed in the new seminary of education by that gentleman's advice. Garrick was then about eighteen years old. An accession of seven or eight pupils was the most that could be obtained, though notice was given by a public advertisement, that at Edial, near Lichfield, in Staffordshire, young gentlemen are boarded and taught the Latin and Greek languages, by Samuel Johnson.

The undertaking proved abortive. Johnson, having now abandoned all hopes of promoting his fortune in the country, determined to become an adventurer in the world at large. His young pupil, Garrick, had formed the same resolution; and, accordingly, in March, 1737, they arrived in London together.

(ARTHUR MURPHY)

Mrs. Porter

I have often heard my mother say she perfectly remembered his wife. He has recorded of her that beauty which
existed only in his imagination. She had a very red face,
and very indifferent features; and her manners in advanced life, for her children were all grown up when
Johnson first saw her, had an unbecoming excess of girlish
levity, and disgusting affectation. The rustic prettiness,
and artless manners of her daughter, the present Mrs.
Lucy Porter, had won Johnson's youthful heart, when she
was upon a visit at my grandfather's in Johnson's school-
days. Disgusted by his unsightly form, she had a personal
aversion to him, nor could the beautiful verses he addressed to her, teach her to endure him. The nymph, at
length, returned to her parents at Birmingham, and was
soon forgotten. Business taking Johnson to Birmingham,
on the death of his own father, and calling upon his coy
mistress there, he found her father dying. He passed all
his leisure hours at Mr. Porter's, attending his sick-bed,
and, in a few months after his death, asked Mrs. Johnson's consent to marry the old widow. After expressing
her surprise at a request so extraordinary — " no, Sam, my
willing consent you will never have to so preposterous a
union. You are not twenty-five, and she is turned fifty.
If she had any prudence, this request had never been
made to me. Where are your means of subsistence? Porter has died poor, in consequence of his wife's expensive
habits. You have great talents, but, as yet, have turned
them into no profitable channel." — " Mother, I have not
deceived Mrs. Porter: I have told her the worst of me;
that I am of mean extraction; that I have no money; and
that I have had an uncle hanged. She replied, that she

valued no one more or less for his descent; that she had
no more money than myself; and that, though she had
not had a relation hanged, she had fifty who deserved
hanging."

(ANNA SEWARD)

Matrimonial Reminiscences

Though thus uncommonly ready both to give and take
offence, Mr. Johnson had many rigid maxims concerning
the necessity of continued softness and compliance of
disposition: and when I once mentioned Shenstone's idea,
that some little quarrel among lovers, relations, and
friends was useful, and contributed to their general happiness upon the whole, by making the soul feel her elastic
force, and return to the beloved object with renewed
delight: — "Why, what a pernicious maxim is this now
(cries Johnson), *all* quarrels ought to be avoided studi-
ously, particularly conjugal ones, as no one can possibly
tell where they may end; besides that lasting dislike is
often the consequence of occasional disgust, and that the
cup of life is surely bitter enough, without squeezing in
the hateful rind of resentment."

I asked him upon this, if he ever disputed with his
wife? (I had heard that he loved her passionately.) "Perpetually (said he): my wife had a particular reverence
for cleanliness, and desired the praise of neatness in her
dress and furniture, as many ladies do, till they become
troublesome to their best friends, slaves to their own
besoms, and only sigh for the hour of sweeping their hus-
bands out of the house as dirt and useless lumber; a clean
floor is *so* comfortable, she would say sometimes, by way
of twitting; till at last I told her, that I thought we had

had talk enough about the *floor,* we would now have a touch at the *ceiling.*"

On another occasion I have heard him blame her for a fault many people have, of setting the miseries of their neighbours half unintentionally half wantonly before their eyes, shewing them the bad side of their profession, situation, &c. He said, " she would lament the dependence of pupillage to a young heir, &c., and once told a waterman who rowed her along the Thames in a wherry, that he was no happier than a galley-slave, one being chained to the oar by authority, the other by want. I had however (said he, laughing), the wit to get her daughter on my side always before we began the dispute. She read comedy better than any body he ever heard (he said); in tragedy she mouthed too much."

Garrick told Mr. Thrale however, she was a little painted puppet, of no value at all, and quite disguised with affectation, full of odd airs of rural elegance; and he made out some comical scenes, by mimicking her in a dialogue he pretended to have overheard: I do not know whether he meant such stuff to be believed or no, it was so comical; nor did I indeed ever see him represent her ridiculously, though my husband did. The intelligence I gained of her from old Levett, was only perpetual illness and perpetual opium. The picture I found of her at Litchfield was very pretty, and her daughter Mrs. Lucy Porter said it was like. Mr. Johnson has told me, that her hair was eminently beautiful, quite *blonde* like that of a baby; but that she fretted about the colour, and was always desirous to dye it black, which he very judiciously hindered her from doing. His account of their wedding we used to think ludicrous enough: — " I was riding to church (says Johnson), and she following on another single horse; she hung back, however, and I turned about to see whether she could get her steed along, or what was the matter. I had however soon occasion to see it was only coquetry, and *that I despised,* so quickening my pace a little she mended hers; but I believe there was a tear or two —— pretty dear creature! "

Johnson loved his dinner exceedingly, and has often said in my hearing, perhaps for my edification, "that wherever the dinner is ill got there is poverty, or there is avarice, or there is stupidity; in short, the family is somehow grossly wrong; for (continued he) a man seldom thinks with more earnestness of any thing than he does of his dinner; and if he cannot get that well dressed, he should be suspected of inaccuracy in other things." One day when he was speaking upon the subject, I asked him, if he ever huffed his wife about his dinner? "So often (replied he), that at last she called to me, and said, ' Nay, hold Mr. Johnson, and do not make a farce of thanking God for a dinner which in a few minutes you will protest not eatable.' "

(MRS. PIOZZI)

Chapter II

IN LONDON
1737–1752

A Loan of Five Pounds

They (Johnson and Garrick) had been but a short time in London before the stock of money that each set out with was nearly exhausted; and, though they had not, like the prodigal son, " wasted their substance in riotous living," they began, like him, " to be in want." In this extremity, Garrick suggested the thought of obtaining credit from a tradesman, whom he had a slight knowledge of, Mr. Wilcox, a bookseller, in the Strand: to him they applied, and representing themselves to him, as they really were, two young men, friends, and travellers from the same place, and just arrived with a view to settle here, he was so moved with their artless tale, that, in their joint note, he advanced them all that their modesty would permit them to ask (five pounds), which was, soon after, punctually repaid.

(SIR JOHN HAWKINS)

Edward Cave and Richard Savage

Johnson looked around him for employment. Having, while he remained in the country, corresponded with Cave, under a feigned name, he now thought it time to make himself known to a man, whom he considered as a patron of literature. Cave had announced, by public advertisement, a prize of fifty pounds for the best poem on life, death, judgment, heaven, and hell; and this circumstance diffused an idea of his liberality. Johnson became connected with him in business, and in a close and intimate acquaintance. Of Cave's character it is unnecessary to say any thing in this place, as Johnson was afterwards the biographer of his first and most useful patron. To be engaged in the translation of some important work was still the object which Johnson had in view. For this purpose, he proposed to give the history of the council of Trent, with copious notes, then lately added to a French edition. Twelve sheets of this work were printed, for which Johnson received forty-nine pounds, as appears by his receipt, in the possession of Mr. Nichols, the compiler of that entertaining and useful work, the Gentleman's Magazine. Johnson's translation was never completed; a like design was offered to the public, under the patronage of Dr. Zachary Pearce; and, by that contention, both attempts were frustrated. Johnson had been commended by Pope, for the translation of the Messiah into Latin verse; but he knew no approach to so eminent a man. With one, however, who was connected with Pope, he became acquainted at St. John's gate; and that person was no other than the well-known Richard Savage, whose life was afterwards written by Johnson with great elegance, and a depth of moral reflection. Savage was a man of considerable talents. His address, his various accomplishments, and, above all, the peculiarity of his misfortunes, recommended him to Johnson's notice. They became united in the closest intimacy. Both had great parts, and they were equally under the pressure of want. Sympathy joined them in a league of friendship. Johnson has been

often heard to relate, that he and Savage walked round
Grosvenor square till four in the morning; in the course
of their conversation reforming the world, dethroning
princes, establishing new forms of government, and giving laws to the several states of Europe, till, fatigued at
length with their legislative office, they began to feel the
want of refreshment, but could not muster up more than
fourpence-halfpenny. Savage, it is true, had many vices;
but vice could never strike its roots in a mind like Johnson's, seasoned early with religion, and the principles of
moral rectitude.

(ARTHUR MURPHY)

Phlegmatic Temper of Edward Cave

Cave's temper was phlegmatic . . . His discernment was
also slow; and as he had already at his command some
writers of prose and verse, who, in the language of booksellers are called good hands, he was the backwarder in
making advances, or courting an intimacy with Johnson.
Upon the first approach of a stranger, his practice was to
continue sitting, a posture in which he was ever to be
found, and, for a few minutes, to continue silent: if at any
time he was inclined to begin the discourse, it was generally by putting a leaf of the Magazine, then in the press,
into the hand of his visitor, and asking his opinion of it.
I remember that, calling in on him once, he gave me to
read the beautiful poem of Collins, written for Shakespeare's Cymbeline, "To fair Fidele's grassy tomb,"
which, though adapted to a particular circumstance in
the play, Cave was for inserting in his Magazine, without
any reference to the subject: I told him it would lose of
its beauty if it were so published: this he could not see;

nor could he be convinced of the propriety of the name Fidele: he thought Pastora a better, and so printed it.

(SIR JOHN HAWKINS)

Johnson Sees Mr. Browne

Cave was so incompetent a judge of Johnson's abilities, that, meaning at one time to dazzle him with the splendour of some of those luminaries in literature who favoured him with their correspondence, he told him that, if he would, in the evening, be at a certain alehouse in the neighbourhood of Clerkenwell, he might have a chance of seeing Mr. Browne and another or two of the persons mentioned in the preceding note: Johnson accepted the invitation; and being introduced by Cave, dressed in a loose horseman's coat, and such a great bushy uncombed wig as he constantly wore, to the sight of Mr. Browne, whom he found sitting at the upper end of a long table, in a cloud of tobacco-smoke, had his curiosity gratified.

(SIR JOHN HAWKINS)

Garrick Plays to Edward Cave

Cave had no great relish for mirth, but he could bear it; and having been told by Johnson, that his friend had talents for the theatre, and was come to London with a view to the profession of an actor, expressed a wish to see him in some comic character: Garrick readily complied; and, as Cave himself told me, with a little preparation of the room over the great arch of St. John's Gate, and, with the assistance of a few journeymen printers, who were called

together for the purpose of reading the other parts, rep-
resented, with all the graces of comic humour, the principal character in Fielding's farce of the Mock-Doctor.

(SIR JOHN HAWKINS)

"London"

In the year 1738 Savage was reduced to the last distress.
Mr. Pope, in a letter to him, expressed his concern for
"the miserable withdrawing of his pension after the
death of the queen," and gave him hopes that, "in a short
time, he should find himself supplied with a competence,
without any dependance on those little creatures, whom
we are pleased to call the great." The scheme proposed
to him was, that he should retire to Swansea in Wales, and
receive an allowance of fifty pounds a year, to be raised
by subscription: Pope was to pay twenty pounds. This
plan, though finally established, took more than a year
before it was carried into execution. In the mean time,
the intended retreat of Savage called to Johnson's mind
the third satire of Juvenal, in which that poet takes leave
of a friend, who was withdrawing himself from all the
vices of Rome. Struck with this idea, he wrote that well-
known poem called London. The first lines manifestly
point to Savage.

> " Though grief and fondness in my breast rebel,
>   When injur'd Thales bids the town farewell;
>   Yet still my calmer thoughts his choice commend;
>   I praise the hermit, but regret the friend:
>   Resolv'd, at length, from vice and London far,
>   To breathe, in distant fields, a purer air:
>   And, fix'd on Cambria's solitary shore,
>   Give to St. David one true Briton more."

Johnson, at that time, lodged at Greenwich. He there fixes the scene, and takes leave of his friend; who, he says in his life, parted from him with tears in his eyes. The poem, when finished, was offered to Cave. It happened, however, that the late Mr. Dodsley was the purchaser, at the price of ten guineas. It was published in 1738; and Pope, we are told, said, " The author, whoever he is, will not be long concealed "; alluding to the passage in Terence, " Ubi, ubi, est, diu celari non potest." Notwithstanding that prediction, it does not appear that, besides the copy-money, any advantage accrued to the author of a poem, written with the elegance and energy of Pope. Johnson, in August, 1739, went, with all the fame of his poetry, to offer himself a candidate for the mastership of the school at Appleby, in Leicestershire.

(ARTHUR MURPHY)

Since Hope but Soothes . . .

" Since worth," he cries, " in these degenerate days
   Wants even the cheap reward of empty praise;
   In those curs'd walls, devote to vice and gain,
   Since unrewarded science toils in vain;
   Since hope but soothes to double my distress,
   And ev'ry moment leaves my little less;
   While yet my steady steps no staff sustains,
   And life still vig'rous revels in my veins;
   Grant me, kind heaven, to find some happier place,
   Where honesty and skill are no disgrace. . . .
   Others with softer smiles, and subtler art,
   Can sap the principles, or taint the heart;
   . . . Well may they rise, while I, whose rustick tongue
   Ne'er knew to puzzle right, or varnish wrong,

Spurn'd as a beggar, dreaded as a spy,
Live unregarded, unlamented die.
. . . How, when competitors like these contend,
Can surly virtue hope to fix a friend? "

("LONDON ")

To His Wife

DEAREST TETTY,

After hearing that you are in so much danger, as I ap-
prehend from a hurt on a tendon, I shall be very uneasy
till I know that you are recovered, and beg that you will
omit nothing that can contribute to it, nor deny yourself
any thing that may make confinement less melancholy.
You have already suffered more than I can bear to reflect
upon, and I hope more than either of us shall suffer again.
One part at least I have often flattered myself we shall
avoid for the future, our troubles will surely never separate us more. If M does not easily succeed in his en-
deavours, let him not [scruple] to call in another Surgeon
to consult with him, Y[ou may] have two or three visits
from Ranby or Shipton, who is [thought] to be the best,
for a guinea, which you need not fear to part with on so
pressing an occasion, for I can send you twenty pouns
more on Monday, which I have received this night; I beg
therefore that you will more regard my happiness, than to
expose yourself to any hazards. I still promise myself
many happy years from your tenderness and affection,
which I sometimes hope our misfortunes have not yet deprived me of. David wrote to me this day on the affair of
Irene, who is at last become a kind of Favourite among
the Players, Mr. Fletewood promises to give a promise in
writing that it shall be the first next season, if it cannot
be introduced now, and Chetwood the Prompter is de-

sirous of bargaining for the copy, and offers fifty Guineas
for the right of printing after it shall be played. I hope it
will at length reward me for my perplexities.

Of the time which I have spent from thee, and of my
dear Lucy and other affairs, my heart will be at ease on
Monday to give Thee a particular account, especially if
a Letter should inform me that thy leg is better, for I
hope you do not think so unkindly of me as to imagine
that I can be at rest while I believe my dear Tetty in pain.

Be assured, my dear Girl, that I have seen nobody in
these rambles upon which I have been forced, that has
not contributed to confirm my esteem and affection for
thee though that esteem and affection only contributed to
encrease my unhappiness when I reflected that the most
amiable woman in the world was exposed by my means
to miseries which I could not relieve.

I am

My charming Love

Yours

SAM: JOHNSON

Jan. 31*st*. 1739–40

Lucy always sends her Duty and my Mother her
Service.

*To Mrs. Johnson at Mrs. Crow's in Castle Street near
Cavendish Square, London.*

Johnson's Parliamentary Debates

(1)

As the debates on that occasion (February 1741) were
warmer than had ever then been known, the drawing
them up required, in Cave's opinion, the pen of a more
nervous writer than he who had hitherto conducted them.

. . . Cave therefore, dismissing Guthrie, committed the
care of it to Johnson.

. . . Cave, who had no idea of the powers of eloquence
over the human mind, became sensible of its effect in the
profits it brought him, and manifested his good fortune
by buying an old coach and a pair of older horses.

. . . Johnson had his reward, over and above the pecuniary recompense vouchsafed him by Cave, in the general applause of his labours, which the increased demand
for the Magazine implied; but he disapproved the deceit
he was compelled to practice, and was not easy till he
had disclosed the deception.

(SIR JOHN HAWKINS)

(2)

The debates penned by Johnson were not only more me-
thodical and better connected than those of Guthrie, but
in all the ornaments of stile superior: they were written
at those seasons when he was able to raise his imagination to such a pitch of fervour as bordered upon enthusiasm, which, that he might the better do, his practice
was to shut himself up in a room assigned him at St. John's
gate, to which he would not suffer any one to approach,
except the compositor or Cave's boy for matter, which,
as fast as he composed it, he tumbled out at the door.

(SIR JOHN HAWKINS)

(3)

That Johnson was the author of the debates, during that
period, was not generally known; but the secret transpired several years afterwards, and was avowed, by himself, on the following occasion. Mr. Wedderburne, now
lord Loughborough, Dr. Johnson, Dr. Francis, the trans-
lator of Horace, the present writer, and others, dined with

the late Mr. Foote. An important debate, towards the end
of Sir Robert Walpole's administration, being mentioned,
Dr. Francis observed, " that Mr. Pitt's speech, on that occasion, was the best he had ever read." He added, " that
he had employed eight years of his life in the study of
Demosthenes, and finished a translation of that celebrated
orator, with all the decorations of style and language
within the reach of his capacity; but he had met with
nothing equal to the speech above mentioned." Many of
the company remembered the debate, and some passages
were cited, with the approbation and applause of all
present. During the ardour of conversation, Johnson remained silent. As soon as the warmth of praise subsided,
he opened with these words: " That speech I wrote in a
garret in Exeter street." The company was struck with
astonishment. After staring at each other in silent amaze,
Dr. Francis asked, " how that speech could be written by
him? " " Sir," said Johnson, " I wrote it in Exeter street.
I never had been in the gallery of the house of commons
but once. Cave had interest with the door-keepers. He,
and the persons employed under him, gained admittance;
they brought away the subject of discussion, the names
of the speakers, the side they took, and the order in which
they rose, together with notes of the arguments advanced
in the course of the debate. The whole was afterwards
communicated to me, and I composed the speeches in the
form which they now have in the parliamentary debates."
To this discovery, Dr. Francis made answer: " Then, sir,
you have exceeded Demosthenes himself; for to say, that
you have exceeded Francis's Demosthenes, would be saying nothing." The rest of the company bestowed lavish
encomiums on Johnson: one, in particular, praised his im-
partiality; observing, that he dealt out reason and eloquence, with an equal hand to both parties. " That is not

quite true," said Johnson; " I saved appearances tolerably
well; but I took care that the WHIG DOGS should not have
the best of it." The sale of the magazine was greatly increased by the parliamentary debates, which were continued by Johnson till the month of March, 1742–3.

(ARTHUR MURPHY)

Osborne, the Bookseller

(1)

In 1743–4, Osborne, the bookseller, who kept a shop in
Gray's inn, purchased the earl of Oxford's library, at the
price of thirteen thousand pounds. He projected a catalogue in five octavo volumes, at five shillings each. Johnson was employed in that painful drudgery. He was,
likewise, to collect all such small tracts as were, in any
degree, worth preserving, in order to reprint and publish
the whole in a collection, called The Harleian Miscellany.
The catalogue was completed; and the miscellany, in
1749, was published in eight quarto volumes. In this
business Johnson was a day-labourer for immediate subsistence, not unlike Gustavus Vasa, working in the mines
of Dalecarlia. What Wilcox, a bookseller of eminence in
the Strand, said to Johnson, on his first arrival in town,
was now almost confirmed. He lent our author five guineas, and then asked him, " How do you mean to earn your
livelihood in this town? " " By my literary labours," was
the answer. Wilcox, staring at him, shook his head: " By
your literary labours! You had better buy a porter's knot."
Johnson used to tell this anecdote to Mr. Nichols: but he
said, " Wilcox was one of my best friends, and he meant
well." In fact, Johnson, while employed in Gray's inn,
may be said to have carried a porter's knot. He paused

occasionally to peruse the book that came to his hand. Osborne thought that such curiosity tended to nothing but delay, and objected to it with all the pride and insolence of a man who knew that he paid daily wages. In the dispute that of course ensued, Osborne, with that roughness which was natural to him, enforced his argument by giving the lie. Johnson seized a folio, and knocked the bookseller down.

(ARTHUR MURPHY)

(2)

I made one day very minute enquiries about the tale of his knocking down the famous Tom Osborne with his own Dictionary in the man's own house. " And how was that affair, in earnest? do tell me, Mr. Johnson? " " There is nothing to tell, dearest lady, but that he was insolent and I beat him, and that he was a blockhead and told of it, which I should never have done; so the blows have been multiplying, and the wonder thickening for all these years, as Thomas was never a favourite with the Public. I have beat many a fellow, but the rest had the wit to hold their tongues."

(MRS. PIOZZI)

An Athletic Constitution

He had possessed an athletic constitution, as he said the man who dipped people in the sea at Brighthelmstone acknowledged; for seeing Mr. Johnson swim in the year 1766, " Why Sir (says the dipper), you must have been a stout-hearted gentleman forty years ago."

Mr. Thrale and he used to laugh about that story very often: but Garrick told a better, for he said that in their

young days, when some strolling players came to Litchfield, our friend had fixed his place upon the stage and
got himself a chair accordingly; which leaving for a few
minutes, he found a man in it at his return, who refused
to give it back at the first entreaty: Mr. Johnson however,
who did not think it worth his while to make a second,
took chair and man and all together, and threw them all
at once into the pit. I asked the Doctor if this was a fact?
"Garrick has not *spoiled* it in the telling (said he), it is
very *near* true to be sure."

Mr. Beauclerc too related one day, how on some occasion he ordered two large mastiffs into his parlour, to
shew a friend who was conversant in canine beauty and
excellence, how the dogs quarrelled, and fastening on
each other, alarmed all the company except Johnson, who
seizing one in one hand by the cuff of the neck, the other
in the other hand, said gravely, "Come, gentlemen!
where's your difficulty? put one dog out at the door, and
I will shew this fierce gentleman the way out of the window": which, lifting up the mastiff and the sash, he contrived to do very expeditiously, and much to the satisfac-
tion of the affrighted company. We inquired as to the
truth of this curious recital. "The dogs have been somewhat magnified, I believe Sir (was the reply): they were,
as I remember, two stout young pointers: but the story
has gained but little."

(MRS. PIOZZI)

On Hunting and Other Recreations

He certainly rode on Mr. Thrale's old hunter with a good
firmness, and though he would follow the hounds fifty
miles on end sometimes, would never own himself either

tired or amused. "I have now learned (said he), by hunting, to perceive, that it is no diversion at all, nor ever takes a man out of himself for a moment: the dogs have less sagacity than I could have prevailed on myself to suppose; and the gentlemen often call to me not to ride over them. It is very strange, and very melancholy, that the paucity of human pleasures should persuade us ever to call hunting one of them." — He was however proud to be amongst the sportsmen; and I think no praise ever went so close to his heart, as when Mr. Hamilton called out one day upon Brighthelmstone Downs, "Why Johnson rides as well, for ought I see, as the most illiterate fellow in England."

. . . Mr. Johnson indeed always measured other people's notions of every thing by his own, and nothing could persuade him to believe, that the books which he disliked were agreeable to thousands, or that air and exercise which he despised were beneficial to the health of other mortals. When poor Smart, so well known for his wit and misfortunes, was first obliged to be put in private lodgings, a common friend of both lamented in tender terms the necessity which had torn so pleasing a companion from their acquaintance — " A madman must be confined, Sir," (replies Dr. Johnson:) "but," says the other, "I am now apprehensive for his general health, he will lose the benefit of exercise." "Exercise! (returns the Doctor) I never heard that he used any: he might, for aught I know, walk *to* the alehouse; but I believe he was always *carried* home again."

. . . Nor was Mr. Johnson more merciful with regard to the amusements people are contented to call such: "You hunt in the morning (says he), and crowd to the public rooms at night, and call it *diversion;* when your heart knows it is perishing with poverty of pleasures, and

your wits get blunted for want of some other mind to
sharpen them upon. There is in this world no real delight
(excepting those of sensuality), but exchange of ideas in
conversation; and whoever has once experienced the full
flow of London talk, when he retires to country friendships and rural sports, must either be contented to turn
baby again and play with the rattle, or he will pine away
like a great fish in a little pond, and die for want of his
usual food."

(MRS. PIOZZI)

Johnson and William Collins

(1)

He (Collins) now (about 1744) came to London a literary adventurer, with many projects in his head, and very
little money in his pocket. He designed many works; but
his great fault was irresolution, or the frequent calls of
immediate necessity broke his schemes, and suffered him
to pursue no settled purpose. A man doubtful of his dinner, or trembling at a creditor, is not much disposed to
abstracted meditation, or remote inquiries. He published
proposals for a History of the Revival of Learning; and I
have heard him speak with great kindness of Leo the
Tenth, and with keen resentment of his tasteless successor. But probably not a page of his history was ever written. He planned several tragedies, but he only planned
them. He wrote now and then odes and other poems, and
did something, however little.

About this time I fell into his company. His appearance was decent and manly; his knowledge considerable,
his views extensive, his conversation elegant, and his disposition cheerful. By degrees I gained his confidence;
and one day was admitted to him when he was immured

by a bailiff that was prowling in the street. On this occasion recourse was had to the booksellers, who, on the
credit of a translation of Aristotle's *Poetics*, which he engaged to write with a large commentary, advanced as
much money as enabled him to escape into the country.
He showed me the guineas safe in his hand. Soon afterwards his uncle, Mr. Martin, a lieutenant-colonel, left
him about two thousand pounds; a sum which Collins
could scarcely think exhaustible, and which he did not
live to exhaust. The guineas were then repaid, and the
translation neglected.

But man is not born for happiness. Collins, who, while
he *studied to live*, felt no evil but poverty, no sooner *lived
to study* than his life was assailed by more dreadful calamities: disease and insanity.

. . . After his return from France, the writer of this
character paid him a visit at Islington, where he was waiting for his sister, whom he had directed to meet him:
there was then nothing of disorder discernible in his mind
by any but himself; but he had withdrawn from study,
and travelled with no other book than an English Testament, such as children carry to the school: when his
friend took it into his hand, out of curiosity to see what
companion a man of letters had chosen, " I have but one
book," said Collins, " but that is the best."

Such was the fate of Collins, with whom I once delighted to converse, and whom I yet remember with tenderness.

(THE LIVES OF THE POETS)

(2)

But how little can we venture to exult in any intellectual
powers or literary attainments, when we consider the condition of poor Collins. I knew him a few years ago full

of hopes and full of projects, versed in many languages, high in fancy, and strong in retention. This busy and forcible mind is now under the government of those who lately would not have been able to comprehend the least and most narrow of its designs. What do you hear of him? are there hopes of his recovery? or is he to pass the remainder of his life in misery and degradation? perhaps with complete consciousness of his calamity.

(LETTERS)

Johnson and Psalmanaazar

He was very well acquainted with Psalmanaazar, the pretended Formosan, and said, he had never seen the close of the life of any one that he wished so much his own to resemble, as that of him, for its purity and devotion. He told many anecdotes of him; and said he was supposed by his accent to have been a Gascon. He said, that Psalmanaazar spoke English with the city accent, and coarsely enough. He for some years spent his evenings at a publick house near Old-Street, where many persons went to talk with him; Johnson was asked whether he ever contradicted Psalmanaazar; — " I should as soon," said he, " have thought of contradicting a bishop "; so high did he hold his character in the latter part of his life. When he was asked whether he had ever mentioned Formosa before him, he said, he was afraid to mention even China.

(SIR JOHN HAWKINS)

Richardson and Fielding

And when he talked of authors, his praise went spontaneously to such passages as are sure in his own phrase to leave something behind them useful on common occasions, or observant of common manners. For example, it was not the two *last,* but the two *first,* volumes of " Clarissa " that he prized; " For give me a sick bed, and a dying lady (said he), and I'll be pathetic myself: but Richardson had picked the kernel of life (he said), while Fielding was contented with the husk."

. . . We were talking of Richardson who wrote Clarissa: " You think I love flattery (says Dr. Johnson), and so I do; but a little too much always disgusts me: that fellow Richardson, on the contrary, could not be contented to sail quietly down the stream of reputation, without longing to taste the froth from every stroke of the oar."

. . . His attention to veracity was without equal or example: and when I mentioned Clarissa as a perfect character; " On the contrary (said he), you may observe there is always something which she prefers to truth. Fielding's Amelia was the most pleasing heroine of all the romances (he said); but that vile broken nose never cured, ruined the sale of perhaps the only book, which being printed off betimes one morning, a new edition was called for before night."

(MRS. PIOZZI)

Chesterfield and Johnson

In 1744, he published the life of Savage; and then projected a new edition of Shakespeare. As a prelude to this design, he published, in 1745, Miscellaneous Observations on the Tragedy of Macbeth, with remarks on Sir Thomas Hanmer's edition; to which were prefixed, Proposals for a new Edition of Shakespeare, with a speci-

men. Of this pamphlet, Warburton, in the preface to
Shakespeare, has given his opinion: "As to all those
things, which have been published under the title of essays, remarks, observations, &c. on Shakespeare, if you
except some critical notes on Macbeth, given as a speci-
men of a projected edition, and written, as appears, by a
man of parts and genius, the rest are absolutely below a
serious notice." But the attention of the public was not
excited; there was no friend to promote a subscription;
and the project died to revive at a future day. A new undertaking, however, was soon after proposed; namely, an
English dictionary upon an enlarged plan. Several of the
most opulent booksellers had meditated a work of this
kind; and the agreement was soon adjusted between the
parties. Emboldened by this connexion, Johnson thought
of a better habitation than he had hitherto known. He
had lodged with his wife in courts and alleys about the
Strand; but now, for the purpose of carrying on his ardu-
ous undertaking, and to be nearer his printer and friend,
Mr. Strahan, he ventured to take a house in Gough square,
Fleet street. He was told, that the earl of Chesterfield
was a friend to his undertaking; and, in consequence of
that intelligence, he published, in 1747, the Plan of a Dictionary of the English Language, addressed to the right
honourable Philip Dormer, earl of Chesterfield, one of his
majesty's principal secretaries of state. Mr. Whitehead,
afterwards poet laureate, undertook to convey the manu-
script to his lordship: the consequence was an invitation
from lord Chesterfield to the author. A stronger contrast
of characters could not be brought together; the nobleman, celebrated for his wit, and all the graces of polite
behaviour; the author, conscious of his own merit, tower-
ing in idea above all competition, versed in scholastic
logic, but a stranger to the arts of polite conversation, un-

couth, vehement, and vociferous. The coalition was too
unnatural. Johnson expected a Mæcenas, and was disappointed. No patronage, no assistance followed.

(ARTHUR MURPHY)

The Scholar's Life

Yet hope not life from pain and danger free,
Nor think the doom of man revers'd for thee:
Deign on the passing world to turn thine eyes,
And pause awhile from letters to be wise;
There mark what ills the scholar's life assail,
Toil, envy, want, the patron, and the jail.
See nations slowly wise, and meanly just,
To buried merit raise the tardy bust.

(THE VANITY OF HUMAN WISHES)

A Passion of Tears

When Dr. Johnson read his own satire, in which the life
of a scholar is painted, with the various obstructions
thrown in his way to fortune and to fame, he burst into
a passion of tears one day: the family and Mr. Scott only
were present, who, in a jocose way, clapped him on the
back, and said, "What's all this, my dear Sir? Why you,
and I, and *Hercules,* you know, were all troubled with
melancholy." As there are many gentlemen of the same
name, I should say, perhaps, that it was a Mr. Scott who
married Miss Robinson, and that I think I have heard Mr.
Thrale call him George Lewis, or George Augustus, I
have forgot which. He was a very large man, however,
and made out the triumvirate with Johnson and Hercules

comically enough. The Doctor was so delighted at his
odd sally, that he suddenly embraced him, and the subject was immediately changed.

(MRS. PIOZZI)

Green-Room Finery

In the course of the year 1747, Garrick, in conjunction
with Lacy, became patentee of Drury lane playhouse.
For the opening of the theatre, at the usual time, Johnson
wrote, for his friend, the well-known prologue, which, to
say no more of it, may, at least, be placed on a level with
Pope's to the tragedy of Cato. The playhouse being now
under Garrick's direction, Johnson thought the opportunity fair to think of his tragedy of Irene, which was his
whole stock on his first arrival in town, in the year 1737.
That play was, accordingly, put into rehearsal in January,
1749. As a precursor to prepare the way, and to awaken
the public attention, The Vanity of Human Wishes, a
poem in imitation of the tenth satire of Juvenal, by the
author of London, was published in the same month. In
the Gentleman's Magazine, for February, 1749, we find
that the tragedy of Irene was acted at Drury lane, on
Monday, February the 6th, and, from that time, without
interruption, to Monday, February the 20th, being in all
thirteen nights. Since that time, it has not been exhibited
on any stage. Irene may be added to some other plays in
our language, which have lost their place in the theatre,
but continue to please in the closet. During the repre-
sentation of this piece, Johnson attended every night behind the scenes. Conceiving that his character, as an author, required some ornament for his person, he chose,
upon that occasion, to decorate himself with a handsome

waistcoat, and a gold-laced hat. The late Mr. Topham Beauclerc, who had a great deal of that humour, which pleases the more for seeming undesigned, used to give a pleasant description of this green-room finery, as related by the author himself; " But," said Johnson, with great gravity, " I soon laid aside my gold-laced hat, lest it should make me proud." The amount of the three benefit nights for the tragedy of Irene, it is to be feared, was not very considerable, as the profit, that stimulating motive, never invited the author to another dramatic attempt. Some years afterwards, when the present writer was intimate with Garrick, and knew Johnson to be in distress, he asked the manager, why he did not produce another tragedy for his Lichfield friend? Garrick's answer was remarkable: " When Johnson writes tragedy, ' declamation roars, and passion sleeps ': when Shakespeare wrote, he dipped his pen in his own heart."

We are now arrived at the brightest period, he had hitherto known.

His fame was widely diffused; and he had made his agreement with the booksellers for his English dictionary at the sum of fifteen hundred guineas; a part of which was to be, from time to time, advanced, in proportion to the progress of the work. This was a certain fund for his support, without being obliged to write fugitive pieces for the petty supplies of the day. Accordingly we find that, in 1749, he established a club, consisting of ten in number, at Horseman's, in Ivy lane, on every Tuesday evening. This is the first scene of social life to which Johnson can be traced, out of his own house.

(ARTHUR MURPHY)

The Throne of Human Felicity

The great delight of his life was conversation and mental intercourse. That he might be able to indulge himself in this, he had, in the winter of 1749, formed a club that met weekly at the King's Head, a famous beef-steak house, in Ivy Lane near St. Paul's, every Tuesday evening. Thither he constantly resorted, and, with a disposition to please and be pleased, would pass those hours in a free and unrestrained interchange of sentiments, which otherwise had been spent at home in painful reflection.

. . . In contradiction to those, who, having a wife and children, prefer domestic enjoyments to those which a tavern affords, I have heard him assert, that a tavern-chair was the throne of human felicity. — " As soon," said he, " as I enter the door of a tavern, I experience an oblivion of care, and a freedom from solicitude: when I am seated, I find the master courteous, and the servants obsequious to my call; anxious to know and ready to supply my wants: wine there exhilarates my spirits, and prompts me to free conversation and an interchange of discourse with those whom I most love: I dogmatise and am contradicted, and in this conflict of opinions and sentiments I find delight."

. . . In these disputations [at the Ivy Lane Club] I had opportunities of observing what others have taken occasion to remark, viz. not only that in conversation Johnson made it a rule to talk his best, but that on many subjects he was not uniform in his opinions, contending as often for victory as for truth: at one time *good*, at another *evil* was predominant in the moral constitution of the world. Upon one occasion, he would deplore the non-observance of Good-Friday, and on another deny, that among us of the present age there is any decline of public worship. He would sometimes contradict self-evident propositions, such as, that the luxury of this country has increased with its riches and that the practice of card-playing is more general than heretofore. At this versatility of temper, none, however, took offence; as Alexander and Cæsar were born for conquest, so was Johnson for the office of a symposiarch, to preside in all conversations; and I never yet saw the man who would venture to contest his right.

Let it not, however, be imagined, that the members of this our club met together, with the temper of gladiators, or that there was wanting among us a disposition to yield to each other in all diversities of opinion: and indeed, disputation was not, as in many associations of this kind, the purpose of our meeting: nor were our conversations, like those of the Rota club, restrained to particular topics. On the contrary, it may be said, that with our gravest discourses was intermingled

" Mirth, that after no repenting draws,"
MILTON (Sonnet to Cyriac Skinner)

for not only in Johnson's melancholy there were lucid intervals, but he was a great contributor to the mirth of conversation, by the many witty sayings he uttered, and the many excellent stories which his memory had treasured up, and he would on occasion relate; so that those are greatly mistaken who infer, either from the general tendency of his writings, or that appearance of hebetude which marked his countenance when living, and is discernible in the pictures and prints of him, that he could only reason and discuss, dictate and controul.

In the talent of humour there hardly ever was his equal, except perhaps among the old comedians, such as Tarle-

ton, and a few others mentioned by Cibber. By means of
this he was enabled to give to any relation that required
it, the graces and aids of expression, and to discriminate
with the nicest exactness the characters of those whom it
concerned.

(SIR JOHN HAWKINS)

A Party at the Devil Tavern

One evening at the club, Johnson proposed to us the cele-
brating the birth of Mrs. Lenox's first literary child, as he
called her book, by a whole night spent in festivity. Upon
his mentioning it to me, I told him I had never sat up a
whole night in my life; but he continuing to press me,
and saying, that I should find great delight in it, I, as did
all the rest of our company, consented. The place appointed was the Devil tavern, and there, about the hour
of eight, Mrs. Lenox and her husband, and a lady of her
acquaintance, now living, as also the [Ivy Lane] club,
and friends to the number of near twenty, assembled.
Our supper was elegant, and Johnson had directed that
a magnificent hot apple-pye should make a part of it, and
this he would have stuck with bay-leaves, because, forsooth, Mrs. Lenox was an authoress, and had written
verses; and further, he had prepared for her a crown of
laurel, with which, but not till he had invoked the muses
by some ceremonies of his own invention, he encircled
her brows. The night passed, as must be imagined, in
pleasant conversation, and harmless mirth, intermingled
at different periods with the refreshments of coffee and
tea. About five, Johnson's face shone with meridian splendour, though his drink had been only lemonade; but the
far greater part of us had deserted the colours of Bacchus,

and were with difficulty rallied to partake of a second refreshment of coffee, which was scarcely ended when the
day began to dawn. This phenomenon began to put us
in mind of our reckoning; but the waiters were all so overcome with sleep, that it was two hours before we could
get a bill, and it was not till near eight that the creaking
of the street-door gave the signal for our departure.

My mirth had been considerably abated by a severe fit
of the tooth-ach, which had troubled me the greater part
of the night, and which Bathurst endeavoured to alleviate
by all the topical remedies and palliatives he could think
of; and I well remember, at the instant of my going out
of the tavern-door, the sensation of shame that affected
me, occasioned not by reflection on any thing evil that
had passed in the course of the night's entertainment, but
on the resemblance it bore to a debauch. However, a few
turns in the Temple, and a breakfast at a neighbouring
coffee-house enabled me to overcome it.

(SIR JOHN HAWKINS)

To His Step-Daughter

Goff Square, July 12, 1749

DEAR MISS,

I am extremely obliged to you for your letter, which I
would have answered last post, but that illness prevented
me. I have been often out of order of late, and have very
much neglected my affairs. You have acted very prudently with regard to Levett's affair, which will, I think,
not at all embarrass me, for you may promise him, that
the mortgage shall be taken up at Michaelmas, or, at
least, some time between that and Christmas; and if he
requires to have it done sooner, I will endeavour it. I

make no doubt, by that time, of either doing it myself, or persuading some of my friends to do it for me.

Please to acquaint him with it, and let me know if he be satisfied. When he once called on me, his name was mistaken, and therefore I did not see him; but, finding the mistake, wrote to him the same day, but never heard more of him, though I entreated him to let me know where to wait on him. You frighted me, you little gipsy, with your black wafer, for I had forgot you were in mourning, and was afraid your letter had brought me ill news of my mother, whose death is one of the few calamities on which I think with terror. I long to know how she does, and how you all do. Your poor mamma is come home, but very weak; yet I hope she will grow better, else she shall go into the country. She is now up-stairs, and knows not of my writing.

I am, dear Miss,

Your most humble servant,

SAM: JOHNSON

The Rambler

Having invoked the special protection of heaven, and by that act of piety fortified his mind, he began the great work of the Rambler. The first number was published on Tuesday, March the 20th, 1750; and from that time was continued regularly every Tuesday and Saturday, for the space of two years, when it finally closed on Saturday, March 14, 1752. As it began with motives of piety, so it appears that the same religious spirit glowed, with unabated ardour, to the last. His conclusion is: " The essays professedly serious, if I have been able to execute my own intentions, will be found exactly conformable to the precepts of christianity, without any accommodation to

the licentiousness and levity of the present age. I, therefore, look back on this part of my work with pleasure,
which no man shall diminish or augment. I shall never
envy the honours which wit and learning obtain in any
other cause, if I can be numbered among the writers who
have given ardour to virtue, and confidence to truth."
The whole number of essays amounted to two hundred
and eight. Addison's, in the Spectator, are more in number, but not half in point of quantity: Addison was not
bound to publish on stated days; he could watch the ebb
and flow of his genius, and send his paper to the press,
when his own taste was satisfied. Johnson's case was very
different. He wrote singly and alone. In the whole progress of the work he did not receive more than ten essays.
This was a scanty contribution. For the rest, the author
has described his situation: "He that condemns himself
to compose on a stated day, will often bring to his task
an attention dissipated, a memory embarrassed, an imagination overwhelmed, a mind distracted with anxieties,
a body languishing with disease: he will labour on a barren topick, till it is too late to change it; or, in the ardour
of invention, diffuse his thoughts into wild exuberance,
which the pressing hour of publication cannot suffer judgment to examine or reduce." Of this excellent production,
the number sold on each day did not amount to five hundred: of course, the bookseller, who paid the author four
guineas a week, did not carry on a successful trade. His
generosity and perseverance deserve to be commended;
and happily, when the collection appeared in volumes,
were amply rewarded. Johnson lived to see his labours
flourish in a tenth edition. His posterity, as an ingenious
French writer has said, on a similar occasion, began in
his life-time.

(ARTHUR MURPHY)

The Death of His Wife

In March, 1752, he felt a severe stroke of affliction in the death of his wife. The last number of the Rambler, as already mentioned, was on the 14th of that month. The loss of Mrs. Johnson was then approaching, and, probably, was the cause that put an end to those admirable periodical essays. It appears that she died on the 28th of March, in a memorandum, at the foot of the Prayers and Meditations, that is called her Dying Day.

(ARTHUR MURPHY)

Farewell to the Rambler

Time, which puts an end to all human pleasures and sorrows, has likewise concluded the labours of the RAMBLER. Having supported for two years the anxious employment of a periodical writer, and multiplied my essays to four volumes, I have now determined to desist.

The reasons of this resolution it is of little importance to declare, since justification is unnecessary when no objection is made. I am far from supposing, that the cessation of my performances will raise any inquiry, for I have never been much a favourite of the publick, nor can boast that, in the progress of my undertaking, I have been animated by the rewards of the liberal, the caresses of the great, or the praises of the eminent.

But I have no design to gratify pride by submission, or malice by lamentation; nor think it reasonable to complain of neglect from those whose regard I never solicited. If I have not been distinguished by the distributors of literary honours, I have seldom descended to the arts by which favour is obtained. I have seen the meteors of fashion rise and fall, without any attempt to add a moment to their duration. I have never complied with temporary curiosity, nor enabled my readers to discuss the topick of the day; I have rarely exemplified my assertions by living characters; in my papers, no man could look for censures of his enemies, or praises of himself; and they only were expected to peruse them, whose passions left them leisure for abstracted truth, and whom virtue could please by its naked dignity.

(THE RAMBLER)

A Prayer on His Wife's Death

April 25, 1752

Grant me the assistance and comfort of thy Holy Spirit, that I may remember with thankfulness the blessings so long enjoyed by me in the society of my departed wife; make me so to think on her precepts and example, that I may imitate whatever was in her life acceptable in thy sight, and avoid all by which she offended Thee. Forgive me, O merciful Lord, all my sins, and enable me to begin and perfect that reformation which I promised her, and to persevere in that resolution, which she implored Thee to continue, in the purposes which I recorded in thy sight, when she lay dead before me, in obedience to thy laws, and faith in thy word.

(PRAYERS AND MEDITATIONS)

Chapter III

IN LONDON
1753–1762

Prayers for His Wife

arch 28, 1753. I kept this day as the anniversary of my Tetty's death, with prayer and tears in the morning. In the evening I prayed for her conditionally, if it were lawful.

April 23, 1753. I know not whether I do not too much indulge the vain longings of affection; but I hope they intenerate my heart, and that when I die like my Tetty, this affection will be acknowledged in a happy interview, and that in the mean time I am incited by it to piety. I will, however, not deviate too much from common and received methods of devotion.

(PRAYERS AND MEDITATIONS)

Anna Williams

(1)

Mrs. Johnson left a daughter, Lucy Porter, by her first husband. She had contracted a friendship with Mrs. Anne Williams, the daughter of Zachary Williams, a physician of eminence in South Wales, who had devoted more than thirty years of a long life to the study of the longitude, and was thought to have made great advances towards that important discovery.

. . . Dr. Williams, after all his labour and expense, died in a short time after, a melancholy instance of unrewarded merit. His daughter possessed uncommon talents, and, though blind, had an alacrity of mind that made her conversation agreeable, and even desirable. To relieve and appease melancholy reflexions, Johnson took her home to his house in Gough Square.

(ARTHUR MURPHY)

(2)

Mrs. Anna Williams I remember as long as I can remember any one. . . . I see her now, a pale shrunken old lady, dressed in scarlet made in the handsome French fashion of the time, with a lace cap, with two stiffened projecting wings on the temples, and a black lace hood over it; her grey or powdered hair appearing. Her temper has been recorded as marked with the Welsh fire, and this might be excited by some of the meaner inmates of the upper floors; but her gentle kindness to me I never shall forget, or think consistent with a bad temper.

. . . What the economy of Dr. Johnson's house might be under his wife's administration, I cannot tell; but under Miss Williams' management, and, indeed, afterwards, when he was even more at the mercy of those around him, it always exceeded my expectation, as far as the condition of the apartment into which I was admitted could enable me to judge. It was not, indeed, his study: amongst his books he probably might bring Magliabecchi to recollection; but I saw him only in a decent drawing-room of a house not inferior to others in the same local situation, and with stout old-fashioned mahogany chairs and tables.

(LAETITIA HAWKINS)

(3)

As poor Miss Williams, whose history is so connected
with that of Johnson, has not had common justice done
her by his biographers, it may be proper to mention, that
so far from being a constant source of disquiet and vexation to him, although she had been totally blind for the
last thirty years of her life, her mind was so well cultivated, and her conversation so agreeable, that she very
much enlivened and diverted his solitary hours; and,
though there may have happened some slight disagree-
ments between her and Mrs. Desmoulins, which, at the
moment, disquieted him, the friendship of Miss Williams
contributed very much to his comfort and happiness. For,
having been the intimate friend of his wife, who had invited her to his house, she continued to reside with him,
and in her he had always a conversable companion; who,
whether at his dinners or at his tea-table, entertained his
friends with her sensible conversation. Being extremely
clean and neat in her person and habits, she never gave
the least disgust by her manner of eating; and when she
made tea for Johnson and his friends, conducted it with
so much delicacy, by gently touching the outside of the
cup, to feel, by the heat, the tea as it ascended within,
that it was rather matter of admiration than of dislike to
every attentive observer.

(BISHOP PERCY)

(4)

Nor has any one, I believe, described his extraordinary
gestures or anticks with his hands and feet, particularly
when passing over the threshold of a Door, or rather before he would venture to pass through *any* doorway. On

entering Sir Joshua's house with poor Mrs. Williams, a
blind lady who lived with him, he would quit her hand,
or else whirl her about on the steps as he whirled and
twisted about to perform his gesticulations; and as soon
as he had finish'd, he would give a sudden spring, and
make such an extensive stride over the threshold, as if
he was trying for a wager how far he could stride, Mrs.
Williams standing groping about outside the door, unless
the servant or the mistress of the House more commonly
took hold of her hand to conduct her in, leaving Dr. Johnson to perform at the Parlour Door much the same exercise over again.

(MISS REYNOLDS)

A Housemaid's Mistake

His best dress was, at that time, so very mean, that one
afternoon as he was following some ladies up stairs, on
a visit to a lady of fashion, the Housemaid, not knowing
him, suddenly seized him by the shoulder, and exclaimed,
"Where are you going?" striving at the same time to
drag him back; but a gentleman who was a few steps
behind prevented her from doing or saying more, and
Mr. Johnson growled all the way up stairs, as well he
might. He seemed much chagrined and apparently disposed to revenge the insult of the maid upon the mistress.
Unluckily, whilst in this humour, a lady of high rank happening to call on Miss Cotterel, he was much offended
with her for not introducing him to her Ladyship, at least
not in the manner he liked, and still more for her seeming to shew more attention to this Lady than to him.
After sitting some time silent, meditating how to *down*
Miss C., he address'd himself to Mr. Reynolds, who sat

next him, and, after a few introductory words, with a loud
voice said, "I wonder which of us two could get most
money by his trade in one week, were we to work hard at
it from morning till night." I don't remember the answer;
but I know that the lady, rising soon after, went away
without knowing what trade they were of. She might
probably suspect Mr. Johnson to be a poor author by his
dress, and because neither a Porter, a Chairman, or a
blacksmith, Trades much more suitable to his apparent
abilities, were quite so suitable to the place she saw him
in. This incident Dr. Johnson used to mention with great
glee — how he had *downed* Miss C., though at the same
time he professed a great friendship and esteem for that
lady.

(MISS REYNOLDS)

A Three-legged Chair

In the latter part of his life, indeed, his circumstances
were very different from what they were in the beginning.
Before he had the Pension, he literally drest like a Beggar;
and from what I have been told, literally lived as such;
at least respecting common conveniences in his apart-
ments, wanting even a chair to sit on, particularly in
his study, where a gentleman who frequently visited him
whilst writing his *Idlers* always found him at his Desk,
sitting on one with three legs; and on rising from it, he
remark'd that Mr. Johnson never forgot its defect, but
would either hold it in his hand or place it with great
composure against some support, taking no notice of its
imperfection to his visitor.

(MISS REYNOLDS)

At Work on the Dictionary

(1. *To William Strahan*)

DEAREST SIR,

The message which you sent me by Mr. Stuart I do not consider as at all your own, but if you were contented to be the deliverer of it to me, you must favour me so far as to return my answer, which I have written down to spare you the unpleasing office of doing it in your own words. You advise me to write, I know with very kind intentions, nor do I intend to treat your counsel with any disregard when I declare that in the present state of the matter " I shall *not* write " — otherwise than the words following: —

" That my resolution has long been, and is *not* now altered, and is now *less* likely to be altered, that I shall *not* see the Gentlemen Partners till the first volume is in the press, which they may forward or retard by dispensing or not dispensing with the last message."

Be pleased to lay this my determination before them this morning, for I shall think of taking my measures accordingly to-morrow evening, only this that I mean no harm, but that my citadel shall not be taken by storm while I can defend it, and that if a blockade is intended, the country is under the command of my batteries, I shall think of laying it under contribution to-morrow Evening.

I am, Sir,
Your most obliged, most obedient,
and most humble servant,
SAM: JOHNSON *

---

* The meaning of this letter is that unless Johnson received something on account from the booksellers who were

(*2. To William Strahan*)

DEAR SIR,

I must desire you to add to your other civilities this
one, to go to Mr. Millar and represent to him the manner of going on, and inform him that I know not how to
manage. I pay three and twenty shillings a week to my
assistants, in each instance having much assistance from
them, but they tell me they shall be able to pull better
in method, as indeed I intend they shall. The point is to
get two Guineas.

Sir,
Your humble servant,
SAM: JOHNSON

(*3. To William Strahan*)

SIR,

I have often suspected that it is as you say, and have
told Mr. Dodsley of it. It proceeds from the haste of the
amanuensis to get to the end of his day's work. I have
desired the passages to be clipped close, and then perhaps for two or three leaves it is done. But since poor
Stuart's time I could never get that part of the work into
regularity, and perhaps never shall. I will try to take
some more care, but can promise nothing; when I am
told there is a sheet or two I order it away. You will find
it sometimes close; when I make up any myself, which
never happens but when I have nobody with me, I generally clip it close, but one cannot always be on the watch.

I am, Sir,
Your most, &c.,
SAM: JOHNSON

---

financing the Dictionary, he would strike work until they
yielded. William Strahan was the printer of the Dictionary.

Johnson and Chesterfield

(1)

In the course of the winter, preceding this grand publication, the late earl of Chesterfield gave two essays in the periodical paper, called The World, dated November 28, and December 5, 1754, to prepare the public for so important a work. The original plan, addressed to his lordship in the year 1747, is there mentioned, in terms of the highest praise; and this was understood, at the time, to be a courtly way of soliciting a dedication of the Dictionary to himself. Johnson treated this civility with disdain. He said to Garrick and others: " I have sailed a long and painful voyage round the world of the English language; and does he now send out two cockboats to tow me into harbour? " He had said, in the last number of the Rambler, "that, having laboured to maintain the dignity of virtue, I will not now degrade it by the meanness of dedication."

(ARTHUR MURPHY)

(2)

Further to appease Johnson Lord Chesterfield sent two persons, the one a specious but empty man, Sir Thomas Robinson, more distinguished by the tallness of his person than for any estimable qualities; the other an eminent painter now living. These were instructed to apologize for his lordship's treatment of him, and to make him tenders of his future friendship and patronage. Sir Thomas, whose talent was flattery, was profuse in his commendations of Johnson and his writings, and declared that were his circumstances other than they were, himself would settle five hundred pounds a year on him. "And who are you," asked Johnson, "that talk thus liberally?" "I am," said the other, "Sir Thomas Robinson, a Yorkshire baronet," "Sir," replied Johnson, "if the first peer of the realm were to make me such an offer, I would shew him the way down stairs."

[This person, who is now at rest in Westminster-abbey, was, when living, distinguished by the name of long Sir Thomas Robinson. He was a man of the world or rather of the town, and a great pest to persons of high rank or in office. He was very troublesome to the earl of Burlington, and when in his visits to him he was told that his lordship was gone out, would desire to be admitted to look at the clock, or to play with a monkey that was kept in the hall, in hopes of being sent for in to the earl. This he had so frequently done, that all in the house were tired of him. At length it was concerted among the servants that he should receive a summary answer to his usual questions, and accordingly at his next coming, the porter as soon as he had opened the gate and without waiting for what he had to say, dismissed him with these words, "Sir, his lordship is gone out, the clock stands, and the monkey is dead." *Note by Hawkins.*]

(SIR JOHN HAWKINS)

The Dictionary Concluded

It is the fate of those who toil at the lower employments of life, to be rather driven by the fear of evil, than attracted by the prospect of good; to be exposed to censure, without hope of praise; to be disgraced by miscarriage, or punished for neglect, where success would have been without applause, and diligence without reward.

Among these unhappy mortals is the writer of dictionaries; whom mankind have considered, not as the pupil, but the slave of science, the pioneer of literature, doomed only to remove rubbish and clear obstructions from the paths through which Learning and Genius press forward to conquest and glory, without bestowing a smile on the humble drudge that facilitates their progress. Every other author may aspire to praise; the lexicographer can only hope to escape reproach, and even this negative recompence has been yet granted to very few.

. . . In this work, when it shall be found that much is omitted, let it not be forgotten that much likewise is performed; and though no book was ever spared out of tenderness to the author, and the world is little solicitous to know whence proceed the faults of that which it condemns; yet it may gratify curiosity to inform it, that the English Dictionary was written with little assistance of the learned, and without any patronage of the great; not in the soft obscurities of retirement, or under the shelter of academick bowers, but amidst inconvenience and distraction, in sickness and in sorrow. It may repress the triumph of malignant criticism to observe, that if our language is not here fully displayed, I have only failed in an attempt which no human powers have hitherto completed. If the lexicons of ancient tongues, now immutably fixed, and comprized in a few volumes, be yet, after the toil of successive ages, inadequate and delusive; if the aggregated knowledge, and co-operating diligence of the Italian academicians, did not secure them from the censure of Beni; if the embodied criticks of France, when fifty years had been spent upon their work, were obliged to change its economy, and give their second edition another form, I may surely be contented without the praise of perfection, which, if I could obtain, in this gloom of

solitude, what would it avail me? I have protracted my
work till most of those whom I wished to please have sunk
into the grave, and success and miscarriage are empty
sounds: I therefore dismiss it with frigid tranquillity, having little to fear or hope from censure or from praise.

(PREFACE TO THE DICTIONARY)

Miss Hill Boothby

The friend of this lady, Miss B—thby, succeeded her in
the management of Mr. F—tzh—b—t's family, and in the
esteem of Dr. Johnson; though he told me she pushed
her piety to bigotry, her devotion to enthusiasm; that she
somewhat disqualified herself for the duties of *this* life,
by her perpetual aspirations after the *next:* such was however the purity of her mind, he said, and such the graces
of her manner, that Lord Lyttelton and he used to strive
for her preference with an emulation that occasioned
hourly disgust, and ended in lasting animosity. "You
may see (said he to me, when the Poets' Lives were
printed) that dear B—thby is at my heart still. She *would*
delight in that fellow Lyttelton's company though, all
that I could do; and I cannot forgive even his memory
the preference given by a mind like her's." I have heard
Baretti say, that when this lady died, Dr. Johnson was
almost distracted with his grief; and that the friends about
him had much ado to calm the violence of his emotion.

(MRS. PIOZZI)

A Use for Orange Peel

(*To Miss Boothby*)

Dec. 31, [1755]

MY SWEET ANGEL,

I have read your book, I am afraid you will think without any great improvement; whether you can read my notes I know not. You ought not to be offended; I am perhaps as sincere as the writer. In all things that terminate here I shall be much guided by your influence, and should take or leave by your direction; but I cannot receive my religion from any human hand. I desire however to be instructed, and am far from thinking myself perfect.

I beg you to return the book when you have looked into it. I should not have written what is in the margin, had I not had it from you, or had I not intended to shew it you.

It affords me a new conviction, that in these books there is little new, except new forms of expression; which may be sometimes taken, even by the writer, for new doctrines.

I sincerely hope that God, whom you so much desire to serve aright, will bless you, and restore you to health, if he sees it best. Surely no human understanding can pray for any thing temporal otherwise than conditionally. Dear Angel, do not forget me. My heart is full of tenderness.

It has pleased God to permit me to be much better; which I believe will please you.

Give me leave, who have thought much on medicine, to propose to you an easy, and I think a very probable remedy for indigestion and lubricity of the bowels. Dr.

Lawrence has told me your case. Take an ounce of dried orange-peel finely powdered, divide it into scruples, and take one scruple at a time in any manner; the best way is perhaps to drink it in a glass of hot red port, or to eat it first and drink the wine after it. If you mix cinnamon or nutmeg with the powder, it were not worse; but it will be more bulky, and so more troublesome. This is a medicine not disgusting, not costly, easily tried, and if not found useful, easily left off.

Miss Boothby Dying

January 8, 1756

HONOURED MADAM,

I beg of you to endeavour to live. I have returned your *Law,* which however I earnestly entreat you to give me. I am in great trouble; if you can write three words to me, be pleased to do it. I am afraid to say much, and cannot say nothing when my dearest is in danger.

The all-merciful GOD have mercy on you.

I am, Madam,

Your, &c.,

SAM: JOHNSON

Arrested for Debt

(*To Samuel Richardson*)

SIR,

I am obliged to entreat your assistance. I am now under an arrest for five pounds eighteen shillings. Mr. Strahan, from whom I should have received the necessary help in this case, is not at home; and I am afraid of not finding Mr. Millar. If you will be so good as to

send me this sum, I will very gratefully repay you, and
add it to all former obligations.

> I am, Sir,
>> Your most obedient.
>>> and most hunble servant,
>>>> SAM: JOHNSON

Gough Square, March 16, [1756]

Editing Shakespeare

(*To Edmund Hector*)

Oct. 7, 1756

DEAR SIR,

After a long intermission of our correspondence you
took some time ago a very kind method of informing me
that there was no intermission of our friendship, yet I
know not why, after the interchange of a letter or two,
we have fallen again into our former silence. I remember that when we were nearer each other we were more
diligent in our correspondence, perhaps only because we
were both younger, and more ready to employ ourselves
in things not of absolute necessity. In early life every
new action or practice is a kind of experiment, which
when it has been tried, one is naturally less eager to try
again. Friendship is indeed one of those few states of
which it is reasonable to wish the continuance through
life, but the form and exercise of friendship varies, and
we grow to show kindness on important occasions without squandering our ardour in superfluities of empty
civility.

It is not in mere civility that I write now to you but
to inform you that I have undertaken a new Edition of
Shakespeare, and that the profits of it are to arise from

a subscription, I therefore solicit the interest of all my
friends, and believe myself sure of yours without solicita-
tion. The proposals and receipts may be had from my
mother, to whom I beg you to send for as many as you
can dispose of, and to remit to her money which you or
your acquaintances shall collect. Be so kind as to mention my undertaking to any other friends that I may have
in your part of the kingdom, the activity of a few solicitors
may produce great advantages to me.

I have been thinking every month of coming down into
the country, but every month has brought its hinderances.
From that kind of melancholy indisposition which I had
when we lived together at Birmingham, I have never
been free, but have always had it operating against my
health and my life with more or less violence. I hope
however to see all my friends, all that are remaining, in
no very long time, and particularly you whom I always
think on with great tenderness.

I am, Sir,

Your most affectionate servant,

SAM: JOHNSON

To Mr. Hector, in Birmingham

Dr. Taylor of Ashbourne

" And who will be my biographer (said he), do you
think? " " Goldsmith, no doubt," replied I, " and he will
do it the best among us." " The dog would write it best
to be sure," replied he; " but his particular malice towards
me, and general disregard for truth, would make the book
useless to all, and injurious to my character." " Oh! as to
that," said I, " we should all fasten upon him, and force
him to do you justice; but the worst is, the Doctor does

not *know* your life; nor can I tell indeed who does, except Dr. Taylor of Ashbourne." "Why Taylor," said he, " is better acquainted with my *heart* than any man or woman now alive; and the history of my Oxford exploits lies all between him and Adams; but Dr. James knows my very early days better than he."

(MRS. PIOZZI)

The Quarrels of Dr. Taylor

It is in your power to be very useful as a neighbour, a magistrate, and a Clergyman, and he that is useful, must conduct his life very imprudently not to be beloved. If Mousley makes advances, I would wish you not to reject them. You once esteemed him, and the quarrel between you arose from misinformation and ought to be forgotten.

When you come to town let us contrive to see one another more frequently, at least once a week. We have both lived long enough to bury many friends, and have therefore learned to set a value on those who are left. Neither of us now can find many whom he has known so long as we have known each other. Do not let us lose our intimacy at a time when we ought rather to think of encreasing it. We both stand almost single in the world, I have no brother, and with your sister you have little correspondence. But if you will take my advice, you will make some overtures of reconciliation to her. If you have been to blame, you know it is your duty first to seek a renewal of kindness. If she has been faulty, you have an opportunity to exercise the virtue of forgiveness. You must consider that of her faults and follies no very great part is her own. Much has been the consequence of her education, and part may he imputed to the neglect with which you have sometime treated her. Had you endeavoured to gain her kindness and her confidence, you would have had more influence over her. I hope that before I shall see you, she will have had a visit or a letter from you. The longer you delay the more you will sometime repent. When I am musing alone, I feel a pang for every moment that any human being has by my peevishness or obstinacy spent in uneasiness. I know not how I have fallen upon this, I had no thought of it, when I began the letter, [yet] am glad that I have written it.

                    I am, dearest Sir,
                              Your most affectionate
                                        SAM: JOHNSON
Nov. 18, 1756
To the Rev. Dr. Taylor, at Market Bosworth, Leicester-
shire

The Death of Johnson's Mother

(*To Mrs. Johnson*)

HONOURED MADAM,

The account which Miss gives me of your health pierces my heart. God comfort and preserve you and save you, for the sake of Jesus Christ.

I would have Miss read to you from time to time the Passion of our Saviour, and sometimes the sentences in the Communion Service, beginning " *Come unto me, all ye that travail and are heavy laden, and I will give you rest.*"

I have just now read a physical book, which inclines me to think that a strong infusion of the bark would do you good. Do, dear mother, try it.

Pray, send me your blessing, and forgive all that I have done amiss to you. And whatever you would have done, and what debts you would have paid first, or anything else that you would direct, let Miss put it down; I shall endeavour to obey you.

I have got twelve guineas to send you, but unhappily am at a loss how to send it to-night. If I cannot send it to-night, it will come by the next post.

Pray, do not omit any thing mentioned in this letter: God bless you for ever and ever.

I am your dutiful son,

Sam: Johnson

Jan. 13, 1758
To Mrs. Johnson in Lichfield

(*To Miss Porter*)

My Dear Miss,

I think myself obliged to you beyond all expression of gratitude for your care of my dear mother. God grant it may not be without success. Tell Kitty that I shall never forget her tenderness for her mistress. Whatever you can do, continue to do. My heart is very full.

I hope you received twelve guineas on Monday. I found a way of sending them by means of the postmaster, after I had written my letter, and hope they came safe. I will send you more in a few days. God bless you all.

I am, my dear,

Your most obliged

and most humble servant,

Sam: Johnson

Jan. 16, 1759
Over the leaf is a letter to my mother.
To Miss Porter, at Mrs. Johnson's, in Lichfield

(To Mrs. Johnson)

DEAR HONOURED MOTHER,

Your weakness afflicts me beyond what I am willing to communicate to you. I do not think you unfit to face death, but I know not how to bear the thought of losing you. Endeavour to do all you [can] for yourself. Eat as much as you can.

I pray often for you; do you pray for me. I have nothing to add to my last letter.

I am, dear, dear mother,
Your dutiful son,
SAM: JOHNSON

Jan. 16, 1759

(To Mrs. Johnson)

DEAR HONOURED MOTHER,

I fear you are too ill for long letters; therefore I will only tell you, you have from me all the regard that can possibly subsist in the heart. I pray God to bless you for evermore, for Jesus Christ's sake. Amen.

Let Miss write to me every post, however short.

I am, dear mother,
Your dutiful son,
SAM: JOHNSON

Jan. 18, 1759
To Mrs. Johnson, in Lichfield

(To Miss Porter)

DEAR MISS,

I will, if it be possible, come down to you. God grant I may yet [find] my dear mother breathing and sensible.

Do not tell her lest I disappoint her. If I miss to write
next post, I am on the road.

> I am, my dearest Miss,
>> Your most humble servant,
>>> SAM: JOHNSON

Jan. 20, 1759
To Miss Porter, at Mrs. Johnson's, in Lichfield

(*To Mrs. Johnson*)

DEAR HONOURED MOTHER,

Neither your condition nor your character make it fit
for me to say much. You have been the best mother, and
I believe the best woman in the world. I thank you for
your indulgence to me, and beg forgiveness of all that
I have done ill, and all that I have omitted to do well.
God grant you his Holy Spirit, and receive you to ever-
lasting happiness, for Jesus Christ's sake. Amen. Lord
Jesus receive your spirit. Amen.

> I am, dear, dear mother,
>> Your dutiful son,
>>> SAM: JOHNSON

Jan. 20, 1759

(*To William Strahan*)

SIR,

When I was with you last night I told you of a story *
which I was preparing for the press. The title will be

> " The Choice of Life
>> or
> The History of . . . . . Prince of Abissinia."

---

* *Rasselas*, which was written during this week to pay
for his mother's funeral and settle her debts.

It will make about two volumes like little Pompadour, that is about one middling volume. The bargain which I made with Mr. Johnson was seventy five pounds (or guineas) a volume, and twenty-five pounds for the second edition. I will sell this either at that price or for sixty, the first edition of which he shall himself fix the number, and the property then to revert to me, or for forty pounds, and I share the profit, that is retain half the copy. I shall have occasion for thirty pounds on Monday night when I shall deliver the book which I must entreat you upon such delivery to procure me. I would have it offered to Mr. Johnson, but have no doubt of selling it, on some of the terms mentioned.

I will not print my name, but expect it to be known.

I am, dear Sir,

Your most humble servant,

SAM: JOHNSON

Jan. 20, 1759

Get me the money if you can.

(To Miss Porter)

You will conceive my sorrow for the loss of my mother, of the best mother. If she were to live again, surely I should behave better to her. But she is happy, and what is past is nothing to her; and for me, since I cannot repair my faults to her, I hope repentance will efface them. I return you and all those that have been good to her my sincerest thanks, and pray God to repay you all with infinite advantage. Write to me, and comfort me, dear child. I shall be glad likewise, if Kitty * will write to me. I shall send a bill of twenty pounds in a few days, which I thought to have brought to my mother; but God suf-

---

* Catherine Chambers, Mrs. Johnson's maidservant.

fered it not. I have not power or composure to say much more. God bless you and bless us all.

> I am, dear Miss,
> > Your affectionate humble servant,
> > > SAM: JOHNSON

Jan. 23, 1759
To Miss Porter in Lichfield

Correspondence with Lucy Porter after Mrs. Johnson's Death

(To Miss Porter. The beginning is torn and lost.)

. . . .

You will forgive me if I am not yet so composed as to give any directions about any thing. But you are wiser and better than I, and I shall be pleased with all that you shall do. It is not of any use for me now to come down; nor can I bear the place. If you want any directions, Mr. Howard will advise you. The twenty pounds I could not get a bill for to-night, but will send it on Saturday.

> I am, my dear,
> > Your affectionate servant,
> > > SAM: JOHNSON

Jan. 25, 1759

(To Miss Porter)

DEAR MISS,

I have no reason to forbear writing, but that it makes my heart heavy, and I had nothing particular to say which might not be delayed to the next post; but had no thoughts of ceasing to correspond with my dear Lucy, the only person now left in the world with whom I think myself connected. There needed not my dear mother's desire, for every heart must lean to somebody, and I have nobody but you; in whom I put all my little affairs with too much confidence to desire you to keep receipts, as you prudently proposed.

If you and Kitty will keep the house, I think I shall like it best. Kitty may carry on the trade for herself, keeping her own stock apart, and laying aside any money that she receives for any of the goods which her good mistress has left behind her. I do not see, if this scheme be followed, any need of appraising the books. My mother's debts, dear mother, I suppose I may pay with little difficulty; and the little trade may go silently forward. I fancy Kitty can do nothing better; and I shall not want to put her out of a house, where she has lived so long, and with so much virtue. I am very sorry that she is ill, and earnestly hope that she will soon recover; let her know that I have the highest value for her, and would do any thing for her advantage. Let her think of this proposal. I do not see any likelier method by which she may pass the remaining part of her life in quietness and competence.

You must have what part of the house you please, while you are inclined to stay in it; but I flatter myself with the hope that you and I shall some time pass our days together. I am very solitary and comfortless, but will not invite you to come hither till I can have hope of making you live here so as not to dislike your situation. Pray, my dearest, write to me as often as you can.

I am, dear Madam,
Your affectionate humble servant,
SAM: JOHNSON

Feb. 6, 1759

(*To Miss Porter*)

MY DEAR MISS,

I am very much pleased to find that your opinion concurs with mine. I think all that you propose is right and beg that you would manage every thing your own way, for I do not doubt but I shall like all that you do.

Kitty shall be paid first, and I will send her down money to pay the London debts afterwards, for as I have had no connexion with the trade, it is not worth while to appear in it now. Kitty may close her mistress's account and begin her own. The stock she shall have as you mention. I hope she continues to recover.

I am very much grieved at my Mother's death, and do not love to think nor to write about it. I wish you all kinds of good, and hope sometime to see you.

I am, dear Miss,

Your affectionate servant,

SAM: JOHNSON

London, Feb. 15, 1759

(*To Miss Porter*)

March 1, 1758[9]

DEAR MADAM,

I thought your last letter long in coming; and did not require or expect such an inventory of little things as you have sent me. I could have taken your word for a matter of much greater value. I am glad that Kitty is better; let her be paid first, as my dear, dear mother ordered, and then let me know at once the sum necessary to discharge her other debts, and I will find it you very soon.

I beg, my dear, that you would act for me without the least scruple, for I can repose myself very confidently

upon your prudence, and hope we shall never have reason
to love each other less. I shall take it very kindly if you
make it a rule to write to me once at least every week, for
I am now very desolate, and am loth to be universally
forgotten.

> I am, dear sweet,
> > Your affectionate servant,
> > > SAM: JOHNSON

(To Miss Porter)

March 23, 1759

DEAR MADAM,

I beg your pardon for having so long omitted to write.
One thing or other has put me off. I have this day moved
my things, and you are now to direct to me at Staple Inn,
London. I hope, my dear, you are well, and Kitty mends.
I wish her success in her trade. I am going to publish a
little story book, which I will send you when it is out.
Write to me, my dearest girl, for I am always glad to hear
from you.

> I am, my dear,
> > Your humble servant,
> > > SAM: JOHNSON

(To Miss Porter)

May 10, 1759

DEAR MADAM,

I am almost ashamed to tell you that all your letters
came safe, and that I have been always very well, but hindered, I hardly know how, from writing. I sent, last week,
some of my works, one for you, one for your aunt Hunter,
who was with my poor dear mother when she died, one
for Mr. Howard, and one for Kitty.

I beg you, my dear, to write often to me, and tell me how you like my little book.*

I am, dear love,

Your affectionate humble servant,

SAM: JOHNSON

A Portrait of Lucy Porter

Lichfield, Jan. 30, 1786

After a gradual decline of a few months, we have lost dear Mrs. Porter, the earliest object of Dr. Johnson's love. This was some years before he married her mother. In youth, her fair, clean complexion, bloom, and rustic prettiness, pleased the men. More than once she might have married advantageously; but as to the enamoured affections,

" High Taurus' snow, fann'd by the eastern wind,
    Was not more cold."

Spite of the accustomed petulance of her temper and odd perverseness, since she had no malignance, I regret her as a friendly creature, of intrinsic worth, with whom, from childhood, I had been intimate. She was one of those few beings who, from a sturdy singularity of temper, and some prominent good qualities of head and heart, was enabled, even in her days of scanty maintenance, to make society glad to receive, and pet the grown spoiled child. Affluence was not hers till it came to her in her fortieth year, by the death of her eldest brother. From the age of twenty till that period, she had boarded in Lichfield with Dr. Johnson's mother, who still kept that little bookseller's shop, by which her husband had supplied the scanty means of existence. Meantime, Lucy Porter kept

---

* *Rasselas.*

the best company of our little city, but would make no engagement on market-days, lest Granny, as she called Mrs. Johnson, should catch cold by serving in the shop. There Lucy Porter took her place, standing behind the counter, nor thought it a disgrace to thank a poor person who purchased from her a penny battledore.

With a marked vulgarity of address and language, and but little intellectual cultivation, she had a certain shrewdness of understanding, and piquant humour, with the most perfect truth and integrity. By these good traits in her character, were the most respectable inhabitants of this place induced to bear, with kind smiles, her mulish obstinacy, and perverse contradictions. Johnson himself, often her guest, set the example, and extended to her that compliant indulgence which he shewed not to any other person. I have heard her scold him like a school-boy, for soiling her floor with his shoes, for she was clean as a Dutchwoman in her house, and exactly neat in her person. Dress too she loved in her odd way; but we will not assert that the Graces were her handmaids. Friendly, cordial, and cheerful to those she loved, she was more esteemed, more amusing, and more regretted, than many a polished character, over whose smooth, but insipid surface, the attention of those who have *mind* passes listless and uninterested.

(ANNA SEWARD)

The Idler

The proposal for a new edition of Shakespeare, which had formerly miscarried, was resumed in the year 1756. The booksellers readily agreed to his terms: and subscription-tickets were issued out. For undertaking this work, money, he confessed, was the inciting motive. His friends

exerted themselves to promote his interest; and, in the
mean time, he engaged in a new periodical production,
called The Idler. The first number appeared on Saturday,
April 15, 1758; and the last April 5, 1760. The profits of
this work, and the subscriptions for the new edition of
Shakespeare, were the means by which he supported himself for four or five years.

. . . Johnson now found it necessary to retrench his expenses. He gave up his house in Gough square. Mrs. Williams went into lodgings. He retired to Gray's inn, and
soon removed to chambers in the Inner Temple lane,
where he lived in poverty, total idleness, and the pride of
literature: "Magni stat nominis umbra."

(ARTHUR MURPHY)

Applications for Counsel and Advice

(1)

Johnson was now become so well known, and had by the
Rambler, and other of his writings, given such evidences,
not only of great abilities, and of his skill in human life
and manners, but of a sociable and benevolent disposition, that many became desirous of his acquaintance, and
to this they were farther tempted by the character he had
acquired of delighting in conversation, and being free and
communicative in discourse. He had removed, about the
beginning of the year 1760, to chambers two doors down
the Inner-Temple Lane; and I have been told by his
neighbour at the corner, that during the time he dwelt
there, more enquiries were made at his shop for Mr. Johnson, than for all the inhabitants put together of both the
Inner and Middle Temple.

(SIR JOHN HAWKINS)

(2)

The strangest applications in the world were certainly
made from time to time towards Mr. Johnson, who by that
means had an inexhaustible fund of anecdote, and could,
if he pleased, tell the most astonishing stories of human
folly and human weakness that ever were confided to any
man not a confessor by profession.

One day when he was in a humour to record some of
them, he told us the following tale: " A person (said he)
had for these last five weeks often called at my door, but
would not leave his name, or other message; but that he
wished to speak with me. At last we met, and he told me
that he was oppressed by scruples of conscience: I blamed
him gently for not applying, as the rules of our church direct, to his parish priest or other discreet clergyman;
when, after some compliments on his part, he told me,
that he was clerk to a very eminent trader, at whose ware-
houses much business consisted in packing goods in order
to go abroad: that he was often tempted to take paper and
packthread enough for his own use, and that he had indeed done so so often, that he could recollect no time when
he ever had bought any for himself. — But probably (said
I), your master was wholly indifferent with regard to such
trivial emoluments; you had better ask for it at once, and
so take your trifles with consent. — Oh, Sir! replies the visitor, my master bid me have as much as I pleased, and was
half angry when I talked to him about it. — Then pray Sir
(said I), teize me no more about such airy nothings; —
and was going on to be very angry, when I recollected
that the fellow might be mad perhaps; so I asked him,
When he left the counting-house of an evening? — At
seven o'clock, Sir. — And when do you go to bed, Sir? —
At twelve o'clock. — Then (replied I) I have at least

learned thus much by my new acquaintance; — that five hours of the four-and-twenty unemployed are enough for a man to go mad in; so I would advise you Sir, to study algebra, if you are not an adept already in it: your head would get less *muddy,* and you will leave off tormenting your neighbours about paper and packthread, while we all live together in a world that is bursting with sin and sorrow. — It is perhaps needless to add, that this visitor came no more."

Mr. Johnson had indeed a real abhorrence of a person that had ever before him treated a little thing like a great one: and he quoted this scrupulous gentleman with his packthread very often, in ridicule of a friend who, looking out on Streatham Common from our windows one day, lamented the enormous wickedness of the times, because some bird-catchers were busy there one fine Sunday morning. "While half the Christian world is permitted (said he) to dance and sing, and celebrate Sunday as a day of festivity, how comes your puritanical spirit so offended with frivolous and empty deviations from exactness. Whoever loads life with unnecessary scruples, Sir (continued he), provokes the attention of others on his conduct, and incurs the censure of singularity without reaping the reward of superior virtue."

I must not, among the anecdotes of Dr. Johnson's life, omit to relate a thing that happened to him one day, which he told me of himself. As he was walking along the Strand a gentleman stepped out of some neighbouring tavern, with his napkin in his hand and no hat, and stopping him as civilly as he could — I beg your pardon, Sir; but you are Dr. Johnson, I believe. "Yes, Sir." "We have a wager depending on your reply: Pray, Sir, is it irrèparable or irrepàirable that one should say?" "The *last* I think, Sir (answered Dr. Johnson), for the adjective

ought to follow the verb; but you had better consult my
Dictionary than me, for that was the result of more
thought than you will now give me time for." " No, no,"
replied the gentleman gaily, " the book I have no certainty
at all of; but here is the *author,* to whom I referred: Is he
not, Sir? " to a friend with him. " I have won my twenty
guineas quite fairly, and am much obliged to you, Sir "; so
shaking Mr. Johnson kindly by the hand, he went back to
finish his dinner or dessert.

Another strange thing he told me once which there was
no danger of forgetting: how a young gentleman called on
him one morning, and told him that his father having, just
before his death, dropped suddenly into the enjoyment of
an ample fortune, he, the son, was willing to qualify himself for genteel society by adding some literature to his
other endowments, and wished to be put in an easy way of
obtaining it. Johnson recommended the university: " for
you read Latin, Sir, with *facility.*" " I read it a little to be
sure, Sir." " But do you read it *with facility,* I say? "
" Upon my word, Sir, I do not very well know, but I rather
believe not." Mr. Johnson now began to recommend other
branches of science, when he found languages at such an
immeasurable distance, and advising him to study natural
history, there arose some talk about animals, and their di-
visions into oviparous and viviparous; " And the cat here,
Sir," said the youth who wished for instruction, " pray in
which class is she? " Our Doctor's patience and desire of
doing good began now to give way to the natural roughness of his temper. " You would do well (said he) to look
for some person to be always about you, Sir, who is capable of explaining such matters, and not come to us (there
were some literary friends present as I recollect) to know
whether the cat lays eggs or not: get a discreet man to

keep you company, there are many who would be glad of your table and fifty pounds a year."

(MRS. PIOZZI)

An Offer of a Living

About this time he had, from a friend who highly esteemed him, the offer of a living, of which he might have rendered himself capable by entering into holy orders: it was a rectory, in a pleasant country, and of such a yearly value as might have tempted one in better circumstances than himself to accept it; but he had scruples about the duties of the ministerial function, that he could not, after deliberation, overcome. " I have not," said he, " the requisites for the office, and I cannot, in my conscience, shear that flock which I am unable to feed." — Upon conversing with him on that inability which was his reason for declining the offer, it was found to be a suspicion of his patience to undergo the fatigue of catechising and instructing a great number of poor ignorant persons, who, in religious matters, had, perhaps, every thing to learn.

(SIR JOHN HAWKINS)

Robert Levett

Johnson had, early in his life, been a dabbler in physic, and laboured under some secret bodily infirmities that gave him occasion once to say to me, that he knew not what it was to be totally free from pain. He now drew into a closer intimacy with him a man, with whom he had been acquainted from the year 1746, one of the lowest

practitioners in the art of healing that ever sought a livelihood by it: him he consulted in all that related to his
health, and made so necessary to him as hardly to be able
to live without him.

    . . . The account of Levett in the Gentleman's Maga-
zine is anonymous; I nevertheless give it verbatim, and
mean hereafter to insert a letter of Johnson's to Dr. Lawrence, notifying his death, and stanzas of his writing on
that occasion.

" Mr. Levett, though an Englishman by birth, became
early in life a waiter at a coffee-house in Paris. The sur-
geons who frequented it, finding him of an inquisitive
turn, and attentive to their conversation, made a purse for
him, and gave him some instructions in their art. They
afterwards furnished him with the means of other knowledge, by procuring him free admission to such lectures in
pharmacy and anatomy as were read by the ablest profes-
sors of that period. Hence his introduction to a business,
which afforded him a continual, though slender maintenance. Where the middle part of his life was spent, is un-
certain. He resided, however, above twenty years under
the roof of Johnson, who never wished him to be regarded
as an inferior, or treated him like a dependent. He breakfasted with the doctor every morning, and perhaps was
seen no more by him till mid-night. Much of the day was
employed in attendance on his patients, who were chiefly
of the lowest rank of tradesmen. The remainder of his
hours he dedicated to Hunter's lectures, and to as many
different opportunities of improvement, as he could meet
with on the same gratuitous conditions. ' All his medical
knowledge,' said Johnson, ' and it is not inconsiderable,
was obtained through the ear. Though he buys books, he
seldom looks into them, or discovers any power by which
he can be supposed to judge of an author's merit.'

" Before he became a constant inmate of the Doctor's
house, he married, when he was near sixty, a woman of
the town, who had persuaded him (notwithstanding their
place of congress was a small coal-shed in Fetter-lane)
that she was nearly related to a man of fortune, but was
injuriously kept by him out of large possessions. It is almost needless to add, that both parties were disappointed
in their views. If Levett took her for an heiress, who in
time might be rich, she regarded him as a physician
already in considerable practice. — Compared with the
marvels of this transaction, as Johnson himself declared
when relating them, the tales in the Arabian Nights' Entertainments seem familiar occurrences. Never was infant
more completely duped than our hero. He had not been
married four months, before a writ was taken out against
him, for debts incurred by his wife. — He was secreted,
and his friend then procured him a protection from a foreign minister. In a short time afterwards, she ran away
from him, and was tried, providentially, in his opinion, for
picking pockets at the Old Bailey. Her husband was, with
difficulty, prevented from attending the court, in the hope
she would be hanged. She pleaded her own cause, and
was acquitted; a separation between this ill-starred cou-
ple took place; and Dr. Johnson then took Levett home,
where he continued till his death, which happened suddenly, without pain, Jan. 17, 1782. His vanity in supposing that a young woman of family and fortune should be
enamoured of him, Dr. Johnson thought, deserved some
check. — As no relations of his were known to Johnson, he
advertised for them. In the course of a few weeks an heir
at law appeared, and ascertained his title to what effects
the deceased had left behind.

" Levett's character was rendered valuable by repeated
proof of honesty, tenderness, and gratitude to his benefac-

tor, as well as by an unwearied diligence in his profession. — His single failing was, an occasional departure from sobriety. Johnson would observe, he was, perhaps, the only man who ever became intoxicated through motives of prudence. He reflected, that if he refused the gin or brandy offered him by some of his patients, he could have been no gainer by their cure, as they might have had nothing else to bestow on him. This habit of taking a fee, in whatever shape it was exhibited, could not be put off by advice or admonition of any kind. He would swallow what he did not like, nay, what he knew would injure him, rather than go home with an idea, that his skill had been exerted without recompense. 'Had (said Johnson) all his patients maliciously combined to reward him with meat and strong liquors instead of money, he would either have burst, like the dragon in the Apocrypha, through repletion, or been scorched up, like Portia, by swallowing fire.' But let not from hence an imputation of rapaciousness be fixed upon him. Though he took all that was offered him, he demanded nothing from the poor, nor was known in any instance to have enforced the payment of even what was strictly his due.

"His person was middle-sized and thin; his visage swarthy, adust and corrugated. His conversation, except on professional subjects, barren. When in deshabille, he might have been mistaken for an alchemist, whose complexion had been hurt by the fumes of the crucible, and whose clothes had suffered from the sparks of the furnace.

"Such was Levett, whose whimsical frailty, if weighed against his good and useful qualities, was

> 'A floating atom, dust that falls unheeded
> Into the adverse scale, nor shakes the balance.'
>> *Irene,* Act i. sc. 3.''

To this character I here add as a supplement to it, a dictum of Johnson respecting Levett, viz. that his external appearance and behaviour were such, that he disgusted the rich, and terrified the poor.

. . . The sincere and lasting friendship that subsisted between Johnson and Levett, may serve to shew, that although a similarity of dispositions and qualities has a tendency to beget affection, or something very nearly resembling it, it may be contracted and subsist where this inducement is wanting; for hardly were ever two men less like each other, in this respect, than were they. Levett had not an understanding capable of comprehending the talents of Johnson: the mind of Johnson was therefore, as to him, a blank; and Johnson, had the eye of his mind been more penetrating than it was, could not discern, what did not exist, any particulars in Levett's character that at all resembled his own. He had no learning, and consequently was an unfit companion for a learned man; and though it may be said, that having lived for some years abroad, he must have seen and remarked many things that would have afforded entertainment in the relation, this advantage was counter-balanced by an utter inability for continued conversation, taciturnity being one of the most obvious features in his character: the consideration of all which particulars almost impels me to say, that Levett admired Johnson because others admired him, and that Johnson in pity loved Levett, because few others could find any thing in him to love.

And here I cannot forbear remarking, that, almost throughout his life, poverty and distressed circumstances seemed to be the strongest of all recommendations to his favour. When asked by one of his most intimate friends, how he could bear to be surrounded by such necessitous and undeserving people as he had about him, his answer

was, " If I did not assist them no one else would, and they
must be lost for want."

(SIR JOHN HAWKINS)

A Retrospect

" Praise is to an old man an empty sound. I have neither
mother to be delighted with the reputation of her son, nor
wife to partake the honours of her husband. I have out-
lived my friends and rivals. Nothing is now of much importance; for I cannot extend my interest beyond myself.
. . . Riches would now be useless, and high employment
would be pain. My retrospect of life recalls to my view
many opportunities of good neglected, much time squan-
dered upon trifles, and more lost in idleness and vacancy.
I leave many great designs unattempted, and many great
attempts unfinished. My mind is burdened with no heavy
crime, and therefore I compose myself to tranquillity; endeavour to abstract my thoughts from hopes and cares
which, though reason knows them to be vain, still try to
keep their old possession of the heart; expect, with serene
humility, that hour which nature cannot long delay, and
hope to possess in a better state that happiness which here
I could not find, and that virtue which here I have not
attained."

(RASSELAS)

Chapter IV

AFTER THE PENSION
1762–1781

Offer and Acceptance of a Pension

In the month of May, 1762, his majesty, to reward literary merit, signified his pleasure to grant to Johnson a pension of three hundred pounds a year. The earl of Bute was minister. Lord Loughborough, who, perhaps, was originally a mover in the business, had authority to mention it. He was well acquainted with Johnson; but, having heard much of his independent spirit, and of the downfall of Osborne, the bookseller, he did not know but his benevolence might be rewarded with a folio on his head. He desired the author of these memoirs to undertake the task. The writer thought the opportunity of doing so much good the most happy incident in his life. He went, without delay, to the chambers, in the Inner Temple lane, which, in fact, were the abode of wretchedness. By slow and studied approaches the message was disclosed. Johnson made a long pause: he asked if it was seriously intended: he fell into a profound meditation, and his own definition of a pensioner occurred to him. He was told, " that he, at least, did not come within the definition." He desired to meet next day, and dine at the Mitre tavern. At that meeting he gave up all his scruples. On the following day, lord Loughborough conducted him to the earl of Bute. The conversation that passed, was, in the evening, related to this writer, by Dr. Johnson. He expressed his sense of his majesty's bounty, and thought himself the more highly honoured, as the favour was not bestowed on him for having dipped his pen in faction. " No, sir," said lord Bute, " it is not offered to you for having dipped your pen in faction, nor with a design that you ever should." Sir John Hawkins will have it, that, after this interview, Johnson was often pressed to wait on lord Bute, but with a sullen spirit refused to comply. However that be, Johnson was never heard to utter a disrespectful word of that nobleman. The writer of this essay remembers a circumstance, which may throw some light on this subject. The late Dr. Rose, of Chiswick, whom Johnson loved and respected, contended for the pre-eminence of the Scotch writers; and Ferguson's book on Civil Society, then on the eve of publication, he said, would give the laurel to North Britain. " Alas! what can he do upon that subject? " said Johnson: " Aristotle, Polybius, Grotius, Puffendorf, and Burlamaqui, have reaped in that field before him." " He will treat it," said Dr. Rose, " in a new manner." " A new manner! Buckinger had no hands, and he wrote his name with his toes, at Charing Cross, for half a crown a piece; that was a new manner of writing! " Dr. Rose replied: " If that will not satisfy you, I will name a writer, whom you must allow to be the best in the kingdom." " Who is that? " " The earl of Bute, when he wrote an order for your pension." " There, sir," said Johnson, " you have me in the toil: to lord Bute I must allow whatever praise you claim for him." Ingratitude was no part of Johnson's character.

(ARTHUR MURPHY)

Easy Circumstances

Johnson was now at ease in his circumstances: he wanted his usual motive to impel him to the exertion of his talents, necessity, and he sunk into indolence. Whoever called in on him at about mid-day, found him and Levett at breakfast, Johnson in deshabille, as just risen from bed, and Levett filling out tea for himself and his patron alternately, no conversation passing between them. All that visited him at these hours were welcome. A night's rest, and breakfast, seldom failed to refresh and fit him for discourse, and whoever withdrew went too soon. His invitations to dinners abroad were numerous, and he seldom balked them. At evening parties, where were no cards, he very often made one; and from these, when once engaged, most unwillingly retired.

In the relaxation of mind, which almost any one might have foreseen would follow the grant of his pension, he made little account of that lapse of time, on which, in many of his papers, he so severely moralizes. And, though he was so exact an observer of the passing minutes, as frequently, after his coming from church, to note in his diary how many the service took up in reading, and the sermon in preaching; he seemed to forget how many years had passed since he had begun to take in subscriptions for his edition of Shakespeare. Such a torpor had seized his faculties, as not all the remonstrances of his friends were able to cure: applied to some minds, they would have burned like caustics, but Johnson felt them not.

(SIR JOHN HAWKINS)

Improved Surroundings

He removed from the Temple into a house in Johnson's
court, Fleet-street, and invited thither his friend Mrs. Williams. An upper room, which had the advantages of a
good light and free air, he fitted up for a study, and furnished with books, chosen with so little regard to editions
or their external appearance, as shewed they were intended for use, and that he disdained the ostentation of
learning. Here he was in a situation and circumstances
that enabled him to enjoy the visits of his friends, and to
receive them in a manner suitable to the rank and condition of many of them. A silver standish, and some useful
plate, which he had been prevailed on to accept as
pledges of kindness from some who most esteemed him,
together with furniture that would not have disgraced a
better dwelling, banished those appearances of squalid in-
digence, which, in his less happy days, disgusted those
who came to see him.

(SIR JOHN HAWKINS)

Dr. Taylor's Unhappy Marriage

(*To the Reverend Dr. Taylor*)

DEAR SIR,

You may be confident that what I can do for you either
by help or counsel in this perplexity shall not be wanting,
and I take it as a proof of friendship that you have recourse to me on this strange revolution of your domestick
life.

I do not wonder that the commotion of your mind made
it difficult for you to give me a particular account, but

while my knowledge is only general, my advice must be general too.

Your first care must be of yourself and your own quiet. Do not let this vexation take possession of your thoughts, or sink too deeply into your heart. To have an unsuitable or unhappy marriage happens every day to multitudes, and you must endeavour to bear it like your fellow sufferers by diversion at one time and reflection at another. The happiness of conjugal life cannot be ascertained or secured either by sense or by virtue, and therefore its miseries may be numbered among those evils which we cannot prevent and must only labour to endure with patience, and palliate with judgement. If your condition is known I should [think] it best to come from the place, that you may not be a gazing-stock to idle people who have nobody but you to talk of. You may live privately in a thousand places till the novelty of the transaction is worn away. I shall be glad to contribute to your peace by any arrangement in my power.

. . . Your ill health proceeds immediately from the perturbation of your mind. Any incident that makes a man the talk and spectacle of the world without any addition to his honour is naturally vexatious, but talk and looks are all the evils which this domestick revolution has brought upon you. I knew that you and your wife lived unquietly together, I find that provocations were greater than I had known, and do not see what you have to regret but that you did not separate in a very short time after you were united.

(LETTERS)

Garrick and the Literary Club

The institution of this society was in the winter of 1763, at which time Mr. Garrick was abroad with his wife, who, for the recovery of her health, was sent to the baths at Padua. Upon his return, he was informed of our association, and trusted that the least intimation of a desire to come among us would procure him a ready admission, but in this he was mistaken. Johnson consulted me upon it, and when I could find no objection to receiving him, exclaimed: — "He will disturb us by his buffoonery"; — and afterwards so managed matters, that he was never formally proposed, nor, by consequence, ever admitted.

Garrick took his reception very patiently, and shewed his resentment of it no otherwise than by enquiring of me from time to time how we went on at the club. He would often stop at my gate, in his way to and from Hampton and ask such questions as these: — "Were you at the club on Monday night?" — "What did you talk of?" — "Was Johnson there?" — "I suppose he said something of Davy — that Davy was a clever fellow in his way, full of convivial pleasantry, but no poet, no writer, ha?" — I was vexed at these enquiries, and told him that this perpetual solicitude about what was said of him was unnecessary, and that he might well be content with that share of the public favour which he enjoyed.

(SIR JOHN HAWKINS)

Garrick's Petrarca

Garrick, giving a thundering stamp on some mark on the carpet — not with passion or displeasure, but merely as if

from singularity — took off Dr. Johnson's voice in a short
dialogue with himself that had passed the preceding
week.

" David! Will you lend me your *Petrarca*? "

" Y-e-s, Sir! "

" David! you sigh? "

" Sir — you shall have it certainly."

" Accordingly," Mr. Garrick continued, " the book, stu-
pendously bound, I sent to him that very evening. But
scarcely had he taken it in his hands, when, as Boswell
tells me, he poured forth a Greek ejaculation and a coup-
let or two from Horace, and then in one of those fits of enthusiasm which always seem to require that he should
spread his arms aloft, he suddenly pounces my poor *Petrarca* over his head upon the floor. And then, standing
for several minutes lost in abstraction, he forgot probably
that he had ever seen it."

(FANNY BURNEY)

Johnson Praises Garrick

When Dr. Johnson and I were talking of Garrick, I observed that he was a very moderate, fair, and pleasing
companion; when we considered what a constant influx
had flowed upon him, both of fortune and fame, to throw
him off of his bias of moral and social self-government.
" Sir," replied Johnson, in his usual emphatical and glow-
ing manner, " you are very right in your remark; Garrick
has undoubtedly the merit of a temperate and unassum-
ing behaviour in society; for more pains have been taken
to spoil that fellow, than if he had been heir apparent to
the empire of India! "

When Garrick was one day mentioning to me Dr. John-

son's illiberal treatment of him, on different occasions; " I
question," said he, " whether, in his calmest and most dis-
passionate moments, he would allow me the high theatrical merit which the public have been so generous as to
attribute to me." I told him, that I would take an early
opportunity to make the trial, and that I would not fail to
inform him of the result of my experiment. As I had
rather an active curiosity to put Johnson's disinterested
generosity fairly to the test, on this apposite subject, I
took an early opportunity of waiting on him, to hear his
verdict on Garrick's pretensions to his great and universal
fame. I found him in very good and social humour; and
I began a conversation which naturally led to the mention
of Garrick. I said something particular on his excellence
as an actor; and I added, " But pray, Dr. Johnson, do you
really think that he deserves that illustrious theatrical
character, and that prodigious fame, which he has acquired? " " Oh Sir," said he, " he deserves every thing
that he has acquired, for having seized the very soul of
Shakspeare; for having embodied it in himself; and for
having expanded its glory over the world." I was not slow
in communicating to Garrick the answer of the Delphic
oracle. The tear started in his eye — " Oh! Stockdale,"
said he, " such a praise from such a man! — *this* atones for
all that has passed."

(THE REV. PERCIVAL STOCKDALE)

Easter Resolutions, 1764

April 21. I read the whole Gospel of St. John. Then sat up
till the 22d.

My Purpose is from this time

To reject or expel sensual images, and idle thoughts.

To provide some useful amusement for leisure time.
To avoid Idleness.
To rise early.
To study a proper portion of every day.
To Worship God diligently.
To read the Scriptures.
To let no week pass without reading some part.
To write down my observations.
I will renew my resolutions made at Tetty's death.

I perceive an insensibility and heaviness upon me. I am less than commonly oppressed with the sense of sin, and less affected with the shame of Idleness. Yet I will not despair. I will pray to God for resolution, and will endeavour to strengthen my faith in Christ by commemorating his death.

I prayed for Tett.

Ap. 22, Easter Day

Having before I went to bed composed the foregoing meditation and the following prayer, I tried to compose myself but slept unquietly. I rose, took tea, and prayed for resolution and perseverance. Thought on Tetty, dear poor Tetty, with my eyes full.

I went to church, came in at the first of the Psalms, and endeavoured to attend the service which I went through without perturbation. After sermon I recommended Tetty in a prayer by herself, and my Father, Mother, Brother, and Bathurst, in another. I did it only once, so far as it might be lawful for me.

I then prayed for resolution and perseverance to amend my Life. I received soon, the communicants were many. At the altar it occurred to me that I ought to form some resolutions. I resolved, in the presence of God, but without a vow, to repel sinful thoughts, to study eight hours

daily, and, I think, to go to church every Sunday, and
read the Scriptures. I gave a shilling, and seeing a poor
girl at the Sacrament in a bedgown, gave her privately a
crown, though I saw Hart's hymns in her hand. I prayed
earnestly for amendment, and repeated my prayer at
home. Dined with Miss W., went to Prayers at church;
went to Davies's, spent the evening not pleasantly.
Avoided wine and tempered a very few glasses with Sher-
bet. Came home, and prayed.

I saw at the Sacrament a man meanly dressed whom
I have always seen there at Easter.

(PRAYERS AND MEDITATIONS)

Easter Resolutions, 1765

Easter Day, Apr. 7, 1765, *about* 3 *in the morning*
I purpose again to partake of the blessed Sacrament, yet
when I consider how vainly I have hitherto resolved at
this annual commemoration of my Saviour's deathe, to
regulate my life by his laws, I am almost afraid to renew
my resolutions. Since the last Easter I have reformed no
evil habits, my time has been unprofitably spent, and
seems as a dream that has left nothing behind. My memory grows confused, and I know not how the days pass
over me.

Good Lord deliver me.

I will call upon God to morrow for repentance and
amendment. O heavenly Father, let not my call be vain,
but grant me to desire what may please thee, and fulfill
those desires for Jesus Christs sake. Amen.

My resolutions, which God perfect, are,

1. to avoid loose thoughts.
2. to rise at eight every morning.

I hope to extend these purposes to other duties, but it is necessary to combat evil habits singly. I purpose to rise at eight because though I shall not yet rise early it will be much earlier than I now rise, for I often lye till two, and will gain me much time, and tend to a conquest over idleness, and give time for other duties. I hope to rise yet earlier.

At church I purpose
before I leave the pew to pray the occasional prayer, and read my resolutions.

To pray for Tetty and the rest
the like after Communion.

at intervals to use the collects of Fourth after Trinity, and First and Fourth after Epiphany and to meditate.

After church, 3 p.m.

This was done, as I purposed, but with some distraction. I came in at the Psalms, and could not well hear. I renewed my resolutions at the altar. God perfect them. When I came home I prayed, and have hope, grant O Lord for the sake of Jesus Christ that my hope may not be in vain.

I invited home with me the man whose pious behaviour I had for several years observed on this day, and found him a kind of Methodist, full of texts, but ill-instructed. I talked to him with temper, and offered him twice wine, which he refused. I suffered him to go without the dinner which I had purposed to give him. I thought this day that there was something irregular and particular in his look and gesture, but having intended to invite him to acquaintance, and having a fit opportunity by finding him near my own seat after I had missed him, I did what I at first designed, and am sorry to have been so much disappointed. Let me not be prejudiced hereafter against the appearance of piety in mean persons, who, with indeterminate notions, and perverse or inelegant conversation perhaps are doing all that they can.

At night I used the occasional prayer with proper collects.

(PRAYERS AND MEDITATIONS)

The Death of Catherine Chambers

Oct. 18, 1767, *Sunday*

Yesterday, *Oct.* 17, at about ten in the morning I took my leave for ever of my dear old friend Catherine Chambers, who came to live with my mother about 1724, and has been but little parted from us since. She buried my Father, my Brother, and my Mother. She is now fifty-eight years old.

I desired all to withdraw, then told her that we were to part for ever, that as Christians we should part with prayer, and that I would, if she was willing say a short prayer beside her. She expressed great desire to hear me, held up her poor hands, as she lay in bed, with great fervour, while I prayed kneeling by her, nearly in the following words:

Almighty and most merciful Father, whose loving-kindness is over all thy works, behold, visit, and relieve this thy Servant, who is grieved with sickness. Grant that the sense of her weakness may add strength to her faith, and seriousness to her Repentance. And grant that by the help of thy Holy Spirit after the pains and labours of this short life, we may all obtain everlasting happiness through Jesus Christ our Lord, for whose sake hear our prayers. Amen. Our Father.

I then kissed her. She told me that to part was the

greatest pain that she had ever felt, and that she hoped we should meet again in a better place. I expressed with swelled eyes and great emotion of tenderness the same hopes. We kissed, and parted. I humbly hope, to meet again, and to part no more.

(PRAYERS AND MEDITATIONS)

First Meeting of Johnson and Mrs. Thrale

It was on the second Thursday of the month of January, 1765, that I first saw Mr. Johnson in a room. Murphy, whose intimacy with Mr. Thrale had been of many years' standing, was one day dining with us at our house in Southwark, and was zealous that we should be acquainted with Johnson, of whose moral and literary character he spoke in the most exalted terms; and so whetted our desire of seeing him soon that we were only disputing *how* he should be invited, *when* he should be invited, and what should be the pretence. At last it was resolved that one Woodhouse, a shoemaker, who had written some verses, and been asked to some tables, should likewise be asked to ours, and made a temptation to Mr. Johnson to meet him: accordingly he came, and Mr. Murphy at four o'clock brought Mr. Johnson to dinner. We liked each other so well that the next Thursday was appointed for the same company to meet, exclusive of the shoemaker, and since then Johnson has remained till this day our constant acquaintance, visitor, companion, and friend.

(MRS. PIOZZI)

Johnson Invites Himself to Ashbourne

(*To the Reverend Dr. Taylor*)

DEAR SIR,

It is so long since I heard from you that I know not well whither to write. With all your building and feasting you might have found an hour in some wet day for the remembrance of your old friend. I should have thought that since you have led a life so festive and gay you would have [invited] me to partake of your hospitality. I do not [know] but I may come, invited or uninvited, and pass a few days with you in August or September, unless you send me a prohibition, or let me know that I shall be insupportably burthensome. Let me know your thoughts on this matter, because I design to go to some place or other and would be [loth] to produce any inconvenience for my own gratification.

Let me know how you go on in the world, and what entertainment may be expected in your new room by,

Dear Sir,

Your most affectionate Servant,

SAM: JOHNSON

Temple, July 15, 1765
To the Reverend Dr. Taylor in Ashbourn, Derbyshire

Johnson Described by Mrs. Thrale

It is usual, I know not why, when a character is given, to begin with a description of the person; that which contained the soul of Mr. Johnson deserves to be particularly described. His stature was remarkably high, and his limbs exceedingly large: his strength was more than common I believe, and his activity had been greater I have heard than such a form gave one reason to expect: his features were strongly marked, and his countenance particularly rugged; though the original complexion had certainly been fair, a circumstance somewhat unusual: his sight was near, and otherwise imperfect; yet his eyes, though of a light-grey colour, were so wild, so piercing, and at times so fierce, that fear was I believe the first emotion in the hearts of all his beholders.

(MRS. PIOZZI)

Johnson and Mrs. Thrale's Mother

(1)

Mr. Thrale's attentions and my own now became so acceptable to him, that he often lamented to us the horrible condition of his mind, which he said was nearly distracted; and though he charged *us* to make him odd solemn promises of secrecy on so strange a subject, yet when we waited on him one morning, and heard him, in the most pathetic terms, beg the prayers of Dr. Delap, who had left him as we came in, I felt excessively affected with grief, and well remember my husband involuntary lifted up one hand to shut his mouth, from provocation at hearing a man so wildly proclaim what he could at last persuade no one to believe; and what, if true, would have been so very unfit to reveal.

Mr. Thrale went away soon after, leaving me with him, and bidding me prevail on him to quit his close habitation in the court and come with us to Streatham, where I undertook the care of his health, and had the honour and happiness of contributing to its restoration. This task, though distressing enough sometimes, would have been less so had not my mother and he disliked one another extremely, and teized me often with perverse opposition, petty contentions, and mutual complaints. Her superfluous attention to such accounts of the foreign politics as are transmitted to us by the daily prints, and her willingness to talk on subjects he could not endure, began the aversion; and when, by the peculiarity of his style, she found out that he teized her by writing in the newspapers concerning battles and plots which had no existence, only to feed her with new accounts of the division of Poland perhaps, or the disputes between the states of Russia and Turkey, she was exceedingly angry to be sure, and scarcely I think forgave the offence till the domestic distresses of the year 1772 reconciled them to and taught them the true value of each other; excellent as *they both* were, far beyond the excellence of any other man and woman I ever yet saw. As her conduct too extorted his truest esteem, her cruel illness excited all his tenderness; nor was the sight of beauty, scarce to be subdued by disease, and wit, flashing through the apprehension of evil, a scene which Dr. Johnson could see without sensibility. He acknowledged himself improved by her piety, and astonished at her fortitude, and hung over her bed with the affection of a parent, and the reverence of a son.

(MRS. PIOZZI)

(2)

Johnson spoke as he wrote. He would take up a topic, and utter upon it a number of the *Rambler*. On a question, one day, at Miss Porter's, concerning the authority of a newspaper for some fact, he related, that a lady of his acquaintance implicitly believed every thing she read in the papers; and that, by way of curing her credulity, he fabricated a story of a battle between the Russians and Turks, then at war; and "that it might," he said, "bear internal evidence of its futility, I laid the scene in an island at the conflux of the Boristhenes and the Danube; rivers which run at the distance of a hundred leagues from each other. The lady, however, believed the story, and never forgave the deception; the consequence of which was, that I lost an agreeable companion, and she was deprived of an innocent amusement."

(BROOKE BOOTHBY)

Sitting Up with Johnson

Mr. Johnson loved late hours extremely, or more properly hated early ones. Nothing was more terrifying to him than the idea of retiring to bed, which he never would call going to rest, or suffer another to call so. "I lie down (said he) that my acquaintance may sleep; but I lie down to endure oppressive misery, and soon rise again to pass the night in anxiety and pain." By this pathetic manner, which no one ever possessed in so eminent a degree, he used to shock me from quitting his company, till I hurt my own health not a little by sitting up with him when I was myself far from well: nor was it an easy matter to oblige him even by compliance, for he always maintained that no one forbore their own gratifications for the sake of pleasing another, and if one *did* sit up it was probably to amuse one's self. Some right however he certainly had to say so, as he made his company exceedingly entertaining when he had once forced one, by his vehement lamentations and piercing reproofs, not to quit the room, but to sit quietly and make tea for him, as I often did in London till four o'clock in the morning. At Streatham indeed I

managed better, having always some friend who was kind
enough to engage him in talk, and favour my retreat.

(MRS. PIOZZI)

Needless Scrupulosity

When the company were retired, we happened to be
talking of Dr. Barnard, the Provost of Eton, who died
about that time; and after a long and just eulogium on
his wit, his learning, and his goodness of heart: " He was
the only man too (says Mr. Johnson quite seriously) that
did justice to my good breeding; and you may observe
that I am well-bred to a degree of needless scrupulosity.
No man, (continued he, not observing the amazement of
his hearers) no man is so cautious not to interrupt another; no man thinks it so necessary to appear attentive
when others are speaking; no man so steadily refuses
preference to himself, or so willingly bestows it on another, as I do; no body holds so strongly as I do the necessity of ceremony, and the ill effects which follow the
breach of it: yet people think me rude; but Barnard did
me justice."

. . . No one was indeed so attentive not to offend in
all such sort of things as Dr. Johnson; nor so careful to
maintain the ceremonies of life: and though he told Mr.
Thrale once that he never sought to please till past thirty
years old, considering the matter as hopeless, he had been
always studious not to make enemies, by apparent preference of himself. It happened very comically, that the
moment this curious conversation past, of which I was a
silent auditress, was in the coach, in some distant province, either Shropshire or Derbyshire I believe; and as
soon as it was over, Mr. Johnson took out of his pocket a

little book and read, while a gentleman of no small distinction for his birth and elegance suddenly rode up to the carriage, and paying us all his proper compliments, was desirous not to neglect Dr. Johnson; but observing that he did not see him, tapt him gently on the shoulder — " 'Tis Mr. Ch—lm—ley," says my husband; — " Well, Sir! and what if it is Mr. Ch—lm—ley! " says the other sternly, just lifting his eyes a moment from his book, and returning to it again with renewed avidity.

He had sometimes fits of reading very violent; and when he was in earnest about getting through some particular pages, for I have heard him say he never read but one book, which he did not consider as obligatory, through in his whole life (and Lady Mary Wortley's Letters was the book); he would be quite lost to company, and withdraw all his attention to what he was reading, without the smallest knowledge or care about the noise made round him. His deafness made such conduct less odd and less difficult to him than it would have been to another man; but his advising others to take the same method, and pull a little book out when they were not entertained with what was going forward in society, seemed more likely to advance the growth of science than of polished manners, for which he always pretended extreme veneration.

(MRS. PIOZZI)

Outward Customs

Mr. Johnson was indeed unjustly supposed to be a lover of singularity. Few people had a more settled reverence for the world than he, or was less captivated by new modes of behaviour introduced, or innovations on the long-received customs of common life. He hated the way of leaving a company without taking notice to the lady of the house that he was going; and did not much like any of the contrivances by which ease has been lately introduced into society instead of ceremony, which had more of his approbation. Cards, dress, and dancing, however, all found their advocates in Dr. Johnson who inculcated, upon principle, the cultivation of those arts, which many a moralist thinks himself bound to reject, and many a Christian holds unfit to be practised. "No person (said he one day) goes undressed till he thinks himself of consequence enough to forbear carrying the badge of his rank upon his back." And in answer to the arguments urged by Puritans, Quakers, &c. against showy decorations of the human figure, I once heard him exclaim, "Oh, let us not be found when our Master calls us, ripping the lace off our waistcoats, but the spirit of contention from our souls and tongues! Let us all conform in outward customs, which are of no consequence, to the manners of those whom we live among, and despise such paltry distinctions. Alas, Sir (continued he), a man who cannot get to heaven in a green coat, will not find his way thither the sooner in a grey one."

(MRS. PIOZZI)

Johnson and Lady Visitors

It is very certain that he piqued himself much upon his knowledge of the rules of true politeness, and particularly on his most punctilious observances of them towards the ladies. A remarkable instance of this was his never suffering any lady to walk from his house to her carriage, through Bolt Court, unattended by himself to hand her into it (at least I have reason to suppose it to be his general custom, from his constant performance of it to those with whom he was the most intimately acquainted); and if any obstacle prevented it from driving off, there he would stand by the door of it, and gather a mob around him. Indeed they would begin to gather the moment he appear'd handing the lady down the steps into Fleet Street.

(MISS REYNOLDS)

Francis Barber

(1)

The uses for which Francis Barber was intended to serve his master were not very apparent, for Diogenes himself never wanted a servant less than he seemed to do: the great bushy wig, which throughout his life he affected to wear, by that closeness of texture which it had contracted and been suffered to retain, was ever nearly as impenetrable by a comb as a quickset hedge; and little of the dust that had once settled on his outer garments was ever known to have been disturbed by the brush.

(SIR JOHN HAWKINS)

(2)

He told us however in the course of the same chat, how his negro Francis had been eminent for his success among the girls. Seeing us all laugh, " I must have you know, ladies (said he), that Frank has carried the empire of Cupid further than most men. When I was in Lincolnshire so many years ago, he attended me thither; and when we returned home together, I found that a female haymaker had followed him to London for love." Francis

was indeed no small favourite with his master, who retained however a prodigious influence over his most violent passions.

On the birthday of our eldest daughter, and that of our
friend Dr. Johnson, the 17th and 18th of September, we
every year made up a little dance and supper, to divert
our servants and their friends, putting the summerhouse
into their hands for the two evenings, to fill with acquaintance and merriment. Francis and his white wife
were invited of course. She was eminently pretty, and he
was jealous, as my maids told me. On the first of these
days' amusements (I know not what year) Frank took
offence at some attentions paid his Desdemona, and
walked away next morning to London in wrath. His master and I driving the same road an hour after, overtook
him. "What is the matter, child (says Dr. Johnson), that
you leave Streatham? *Art sick?* " He is jealous (whispered I). "Are you jealous of your wife, you stupid
blockhead (cries out his master in another tone)? " The
fellow hesitated; and, *To be sure Sir, I don't quite approve
Sir,* was the stammering reply. "Why, what do they *do*
to her, man? do the footmen kiss her? " No Sir, no! — Kiss
my *wife Sir! — I hope not Sir.* "Why, what *do* they do to
her, my lad? " "Why nothing Sir, I'm sure Sir." "Why
then go back directly and dance you dog, do; and let's
hear no more of such empty lamentations."

(MRS. PIOZZI)

Love of Travel

His desire to go abroad, particularly to see Italy, was very
great; and he had a longing wish to leave some Latin
verses at the Grand Chartreux. He loved indeed the very

act of travelling, and I cannot tell how far one might have taken him in a carriage before he would have wished for refreshment. He was therefore in some respects an admirable companion on the road, as he piqued himself upon feeling no inconvenience, and on despising no accommodations. On the other hand however, he expected no one else to feel any, and felt exceedingly inflamed with anger if any one complained of the rain, the sun, or the dust. " How (said he), do other people bear them? " As for general uneasiness, or complaints of long confinement in a carriage, he considered all lamentations on their account as proofs of an empty head, and a tongue desirous to talk without materials of conversation. "A mill that goes without grist (said he), is as good a companion as such creatures."

(MRS. PIOZZI)

Ashbourne

We went to the Church, where Dr. Taylor has a magnificent seat; indeed, everything around him is both elegant and splendid. He has very fine pictures which he does not understand the beauties of, a glorious Harpsichord which he sends for a young man out of the town to play upon, a waterfall murmuring at the foot of his garden, deer in his paddock, pheasants in his menagerie, the finest coach horses in the County, the largest horned cattle, I believe, in England, particularly a Bull of an enormous size, his table liberally spread, his wines all excellent in their kinds, his companions, indeed, are as they must be — such as the Country affords.

(MRS. THRALE)

Johnson at Stowe Hill, Lichfield

(1. *To Mrs. Thrale*)

Lichfield, July 7, 1770

DEAR MADAM,

I thought I should have heard something to-day about
Streatham; but there is no letter; and I need some consolation, for Rheumatism is come again, though in a less
degree than formerly. I reckon to go next week to Ashbourne, and will try to bring you the dimensions of the
great bull. The skies and the ground are all so wet, that
I have been very little abroad; and Mrs. Aston is from
home, so that I have no motive to walk. When she is at
home, she lives on the top of Stow Hill, and I commonly
climb up to see her once a day. There is nothing there
now but the empty nest.

(LETTERS)

(2)

A large party had one day been invited to meet the
Doctor at Stow-Hill: the dinner waited far beyond the
usual hour, and the company were about to sit down,
when Johnson appeared at the great gate; he stood for
some time in deep contemplation, and at length began
to climb it, and, having succeeded in clearing it, advanced
with hasty strides towards the house. On his arrival Mrs.
Gastrel asked him, " if he had forgotten that there was a
small gate for foot passengers by the side of the carriage
entrance." " No, my dear lady, by no means," replied the
Doctor; " but I had a mind to try whether I could climb
a gate now as I used to do when I was a lad."

(THE REV. MR. PARKER)

Mrs. Cobb

(1. *To Mrs. Thrale*)

Lichfield, July, [1770]

DEAR MADAM,

Do not say that I never write to you, and do not think that I expected to find any friends here that could make me wish to prolong my stay. For your strawberries, however, I have no care. Mrs. Cobb has strawberries, and will give me as long as they last; and she has cherries too. Of the strawberries at Streatham I consign my part to Miss and Harry. I hope Susy grows, and Lucy begins to walk. Though this rainy weather confines us all in the house, I have neither frolicked nor fretted.

In the tumult, whatever it was, at your house, I hope my countrywomen either had no part, or behaved well. I told Mr. Heartwell, about three days ago, how well Warren was liked in her place.

I have passed one day at Birmingham with my old friend Hector — there's a name — and his sister, an old love. My mistress is grown much older than my friend.

> — O, quid habes illius, illius
> Quæ spirabat amores,
> Quæ me surpuerat mihi.

Time will impair the body, and uses us well if it spares the mind.

I am, &c.,

SAM: JOHNSON

(2)

You would be sorry to hear that poor Moll Cobb, as
Dr. Johnson used to call her, is gone to her long home.
If you saw the ridiculous puffing, hyperbolic character
of her in the public papers, it would make you stare and
smile at the credence due to newspaper portraits. Those,
however, who draw them in colour so false and glaring,
are very reprehensible. This was the disgrace of a pen
capable of far better things than such a tribute of gross
and mean flattery to the vanity of the surviving relation.
Its author well knew the uniform contempt with which
Johnson spoke both of the head and heart of this person-
age, well as he liked the convenience of her chaise, " the
taste of her sweetmeats and strawberries," and the idol-
atry of her homage. Nauseous therefore, was the public
and solemn mention of Johnson's mention of Mrs. Cobb,
of whose declaration respecting her, in a room full of company here, the panegyrist had so often heard: — " How
should," exclaimed Johnson, " how should Moll Cobb be
a wit! Cobb has read nothing. Cobb knows nothing; and
where nothing has been put in the brain, nothing can
come out of it to any purpose of rational entertainment."
Somebody replied — " Then why is Dr. Johnson so often
her visitor? " " Oh! I love Cobb — I love Moll Cobb for
her impudence." The despot was right in his premises,
but his conclusion was erroneous. Little as had been put
into Mrs. Cobb's brain, much of shrewd, biting and hu-
morous satire was native in the soil, and has often amused
very superior minds to her own. Of that superiority, however, she had no consciousness: her ignorance and self
sufficience concealed it effectually. She was a very selfish
character, nor knew the warmth of friendship, nor the
luxury of bestowing. Thus has her monumental wall been

daubed by very untempered mortar indeed. Yet, to her we may apply what Henry V says of Falstaff:

> We could have better spared a better man;
> O! we should have a heavy miss of thee,
> If we were much in love with vanity.

Adio!

(ANNA SEWARD)

Dr. Taylor's Great Bull

(*To Mrs. Thrale*)

I have seen the great bull; and very great he is. I have seen likewise his heir apparent, who promises to inherit all the bulk and all the virtues of his sire. I have seen the man who offered an hundred guineas for the young bull, while he was yet little better than a calf. Matlock, I am afraid, I shall not see, but I purpose to see Dovedale; and after all this seeing, I hope to see you.

I am, &c.,
SAM: JOHNSON

July 23, 1770.

Lichfield and Ashbourne, 1771

(*To Mrs. Thrale*)

Thursday, June 20, 1771

DEAR MADAM,

This night, at nine o'clock, Sam. Johnson and Francis Barber Esquires, set out in the Lichfield stage; Francis is indeed rather upon it. What adventures we may meet with who can tell?

I shall write when I come to Lichfield, and hope to hear

in return, that you are safe, and Mrs. Salusbury better, and all the rest as well as I left them.

I am, &c.,
SAM: JOHNSON

(*To Mrs. Thrale*)
Ashbourne, July 3, 1771

DEAR MADAM,

Last Saturday I came to Ashbourne; the dangers or the pleasures of the journey I have at present no disposition to recount; else might I paint the beauties of my native plains; might I tell of "the smiles of nature, and the charms of art: " else might I relate how I crossed the Staffordshire canal, one of the great efforts of human labour, and human contrivance; which, from the bridge on which I viewed it, passed away on either side, and loses itself in distant regions, uniting waters that nature had divided, and dividing lands which nature had united. I might tell how these reflections fermented in my mind till the chaise stopped at Ashbourne, at Ashbourne in the Peak. Let not the barren name of the Peak terrify you; I have never wanted strawberries and cream. The great bull has no disease but age. I hope in time to be like the great bull; and hope you will be like him too a hundred years hence.

I am, &c.,
SAM: JOHNSON

(*To Mrs. Thrale*)
Ashbourne, July 10, 1771

DEAREST MADAM,

I am obliged to my friend Harry, for his remembrance; but think it a little hard that I hear nothing from Miss.

There has been a man here to-day to take a farm. After some talk he went to see the bull, and said that he had seen a bigger.

(*To Mrs. Thrale*)
Ashbourne, July 17, 1771

MADAM,

At Lichfield I found little to please me. One more of my few school-fellows is dead; upon which I might make a new reflection, and say, *Mors omnibus communis.* Miss Porter was rather better than last year; but I think Miss Aston grows rather worse. I took a walk in quest of juvenile images, but caught a cloud instead of Juno.

I longed for Taylor's chaise; but I think Lucy did not long for it, though she was not sorry to see it. Lucy is a philosopher; and considers me as one of the external and accidental things that are to be taken and left without emotion. If I could learn of Lucy would it be better? Will you teach me?

I would not have it thought that I forget Mrs. Salusbury; but nothing that I can say will be of use; and what comfort she can have, your duty will not fail to give her.

What is the matter that Queeney uses me no better? I should think she might have written to me; but she has neither sent a message nor a compliment. I thank Harry for remembering me.

Rheumatism teazes me yet.

I am, &c.,
SAM: JOHNSON

(To Mrs. Thrale)

Lichfield, Sat. Aug. 3, 1771

DEAR MADAM,

If you were well enough to write last Tuesday, you will surely be well enough to read on Monday; and therefore I will now write to you as before.

Having stayed my month with Taylor, I came away on Wednesday, leaving him, I think, in a disposition of mind not very uncommon, at once weary of my stay, and grieved at my departure.

My purpose was to have made haste to you and Streatham; and who would have expected that I should be stopped by Lucy? Hearing me give Francis orders to take us places, she told me that I should not go till after next week. I thought it proper to comply; for I was pleased to find that I could please, and proud of shewing you that I do not come an universal outcast. Lucy is likewise a very peremptory maiden; and if I had gone without permission, I am not very sure that I might have been welcome at another time.

When we meet, we may compare our different uses of this interval. I shall charge you with having lingered away, in expectation and disappointment, two months, which are both physically and morally considered as analogous to the fervid and vigorous part of human life; two months, in which Nature exerts all her powers of benefaction, and graces the liberality of her hand by the elegance of her smile; two months, which, as Doodle says, "you never saw before," and which, as La Bruyere says, "you shall never see again."

But complaints are vain; we will try to do better another time. — To-morrow and to-morrow. — A few designs and a few failures, and the time of designing will be past.

(LETTERS)

Ashbourne in Autumn

(To Mrs. Thrale)

. . . Our bulls and cows are all well; but we yet hate the man that had seen a bigger bull. Our deer have died; but many are left. Our waterfall at the garden makes a great roaring this wet weather.

(To Mrs. Thrale)

Ashbourne, Nov. 7, 1772

DEAR MADAM,

So many days and never a letter! — *Fugere fides, pietasque pudorque.* This is Turkish usage. And I have been hoping and hoping. But you are so glad to have me out of your mind.

I think you were quite right in your advice about the thousand pounds, for the payment could not have been delayed long; and a short delay would have lessened credit, without advancing interest. But in great matters you are hardly ever mistaken.

We have here very rainy weather; but it makes the grass grow, and makes our waterfall roar. I wish Queeney heard it; she would think it very pretty. I go down to it every day, for I have not much to do; and have not been very well; but by physick am grown better. You and all your train may be supposed to keep me company in my walks. I wish I could know how you brew, and how you go on; but you tell me nothing.

(LETTERS)

Thoughts of His Wife

1770, *March* 28, *Wednesday*

This is the day on which in –52, I was deprived of poor dear Tetty. Having left off the practice of thinking on her with some particular combinations, I have recalled her to my mind of late less frequently, but when I recollect the time in which we lived together, my grief for her departure is not abated, and I have less pleasure in any good that befals me, because she does not partake it. On many occasions I think what she would have said or done. When I saw the sea at Brighthelmston, I wished for her to have seen it with me. But with respect to her no rational wish is now left, but that we may meet at last where the mercy of God shall make us happy, and perhaps make us instrumental to the happiness of each other. It is now eighteen years.

(PRAYERS AND MEDITATIONS)

Easter Resolutions, 1772

Easter Eve, Apr. 18, 1772

I am now again preparing by Divine Mercy to commemorate the Death of my gracious Redeemer, and to form, as God shall enable me, resolutions and purposes of a better life.

When I review the last year, I am able to recollect so little done, that shame and sorrow, though perhaps too weakly, come upon me. Yet I have been generally free from local pain, and my strength has seemed gradually to increase. But my sleep has generally been unquiet, and I have not been able to rise early. My mind is unsettled, and my memory confused. I have of late turned my thoughts, with a very useless earnestness, upon past incidents. I have yet got no command over my thoughts; an unpleasing incident is almost certain to hinder my rest. This is the remainder of my last illness. By sleepless or unquiet nights and short days, made short by late rising the time passes away uncounted and unheeded. Life so spent is useless.

I hope to cast my time into some stated method.

To let no hour pass unemployed.

To rise by degrees more early in the morning.

To keep a Journal.

I have, I think, been less guilty of neglecting public worship than formerly. I have commonly on Sunday gone once to church, and if I have missed, have reproached myself.

(PRAYERS AND MEDITATIONS)

On Public Worship

Good Friday, April 9, 1773

On this day I went twice to Church and Boswel was with me. I had forborn to attend Divine Service for some time in the winter, having a cough which would have interrupted both my own attention and that of others, and when the cough grew less troublesome I did not regain the habit of going to church, though I did not wholly omit it. I found the service not burthensome nor tedious, though I could not hear the lessons. I hope in time to take pleasure in public Worship.

(PRAYERS AND MEDITATIONS)

Rereading His Resolutions

July 22, —73

This day I found this book with the resolutions, some of which I had forgotten, but remembered my design of reading the Pentateuch and Gospels, though I have not perused it.

Of the time past since these resolutions were made I can give no very laudable account. Between Easter and Whitsuntide, having always considered that time as propitious to study, I attempted to learn the low Dutch Language, my application was very slight, and my memory very fallacious, though whether more than in my earlier years, I am not very certain. My progress was interrupted by a fever, which, by the imprudent use of a small print, left an inflammation in my useful eye, which was not removed but by two copious bleedings, and the daily use of catharticks for a long time. The effect yet remains.

My memory has been for a long time very much confused. Names, and Persons, and Events, slide away strangely from me. But I grow easier.

The other day looking over old papers, I perceived a resolution to rise early always occurring. I think I was ashamed, or grieved, to find how long and how often I had resolved, what yet except for about one half year I have never done. My Nights are now such as give me no quiet rest, whether I have not lived resolving till the possibility of performance is past, I know not. God help me, I will yet try.

(PRAYERS AND MEDITATIONS)

Boswell on Good Friday

Apr. 14, *Good Friday,* 1775

Boswel came in before I was up. We breakfasted, I only drank tea without milk or bread. We went to Church, saw Dr. Wetherel in the pew, and by his desire took him home with us. He did not go very soon, and Boswel staid. Dilly and Millar called. Boswel and I went to Church, but came very late. We then took tea, by Boswel's desire, and I eat one bun, I think, that I might not seem to fast ostentatiously. Boswel sat with me till night; we had some serious talk. When he went I gave Francis some directions for preparation to communicate. Thus has passed hitherto this awful day.

(PRAYERS AND MEDITATIONS)

Easter Resolutions, 1776

1776, *Apr.* 7, *Easter Day*

The time is again at which, since the death of my poor dear Tetty, on whom God have mercy, I have annually commemorated the mystery of Redemption, and annually purposed to amend my life. My reigning sin, to which perhaps many others are appendant, is waste of time, and general sluggishness, to which I was always inclined, and in part of my life have been almost compelled by morbid melancholy and disturbance of mind. Melancholy has had in me its paroxisms and remissions, but I have not improved the intervals, nor sufficiently resisted my natural inclination, or sickly habits. I will resolve henceforth to rise at eight in the morning, so far as resolution is proper,

and will pray that God will strengthen me. I have begun
this morning.

Though for the past week I have had an anxious design
of communicating to-day, I performed no particular act
of devotion, till on Friday I went to Church. My design
was to pass part of the day in exercises of piety, but Mr.
Boswel interrupted me; of him, however, I could have rid
myself, but poor Thrale, orbus et exspes,* came for comfort and sat till seven when we all went to Church.

In the morning I had at Church some radiations of
comfort.

I fasted though less rigorously than at other times. I by
negligence poured milk into the tea, and, in the afternoon
drank one dish of coffee with Thrale; yet at night, after a
fit of drowsiness I felt myself very much disordered by
emptiness, and called for tea with peevish and impatient
eagerness. My distress was very great.

Yesterday I do not recollect that to go to Church came
into my thoughts, but I sat in my chamber, preparing for
preparation; interrupted, I know not how. I was near
two hours at dinner.

I go now with hope

To rise in the morning at eight.

To use my remaining time with diligence.

To study more accurately the Christian Religion.

. . . p.m. In the pew I read my prayer and commended my friends, and those that θ † this year. At the
Altar I was generally attentive, some thoughts of vanity
came into my mind while others were communicating,
but I found when I considered them, that they did not
tend to irreverence of God. At the altar I renewed my

* He had just lost a son.
† θ signifies " died."

resolutions. When I received, some tender images struck
me. I was so mollified by the concluding address to our
Saviour that I could not utter it. The Communicants
were mostly women. At intervals I read collects, and recollected, as I could, my prayer. Since my return I have
said it. 2 p.m.

May 21

These resolutions I have not practised nor recollected.
O God grant me to begin now for Jesus Christ's Sake.
Amen.

(PRAYERS AND MEDITATIONS)

Praying Aloud

Indeed, he seemed to struggle almost incessantly with
some mental evil, and often, by the expression of his
countenance and the motion of his lips, appeared to be
offering up some ejaculation to Heaven to remove it. But
in Lent, or near the approach of any great festival, he
would generally retire from the company to a corner of
the room, but most commonly behind a window-curtain,
to pray, and with such energy, and in so loud a whisper,
that every word was heard distinctly, particularly the
Lord's Prayer and the Apostles' Creed, with which he constantly concluded his devotions. Sometimes some words
would emphatically escape him in his usual tone of voice.

(MISS REYNOLDS)

"Oh! Dear Good Man!"

Dr. Johnson had a most sincere and tender regard for
Mrs. Thr–le, and no wonder; she would with much appar-

ent affection overlook his foibles. One Day at her own
Table, before a large company, he spoke so very roughly
to her, that every person present was surprised how she
could bear it so placidly; and on the Ladies withdrawing,
one of them express'd great astonishment how Dr. Johnson could speak in such harsh terms to her! But to this
she said no more than " Oh! Dear good man! " This short
reply appeared so strong a proof of her *generous virtues*
that the Lady took the first opportunity of communicating it to him, repeating her own animadversion that had
occasion'd it. *He seem'd much delighted* with this intelligence, and sometime after, as he was lying back in his
Chair, seeming to be half asleep, but more evidently musing on this pleasing incident, he repeated in a loud whisper, " *Oh! Dear good man!* " This was a common habit of
his, when anything very flattering, or very extraordinary
ingross'd his thoughts, and I rather wonder that none of
his Biographers have taken any notice of it, or of his praying in the same manner; at least I do not know that they
have.

(MISS REYNOLDS)

A Child's Grave

It was about this time when a lady was traveling with
him in a post-chaise near a village Churchyard, in which
she had seen a very stricking object of maternal affection,
a little verdent flowery monument, raised by the Widow'd
Mother over the grave of her only child, and had heard
some melancholy circumstances concerning them, and as
she was relating them to Dr. Johnson, she heard him make
heavy sighs, indeed sobs, and turning round she saw his
Dear Face bathed in tears.

(MISS REYNOLDS)

In Twickenham Meadows

One Sunday morning, as I was walking with him in Twick-enham meadows, he began his antics both with his feet and hands, with the latter as if he was holding the reins of a horse like a jockey on full speed. But to describe the strange positions of his feet is a difficult task; sometimes he would make the back part of his heels to touch, some-times his toes, as if he was aiming at making the form of a triangle, at least the two sides of one. Though indeed, whether these were his gestures on this particular occa-sion in Twickenham meadows I do not recollect, it is so long since; but I well remember that they were so extraor-dinary that men, women, and children gathered round him, laughing. At last we sat down on some logs of wood by the river side, and they nearly dispersed; when he pulled out of his pocket Grotius *De Veritate Religionis,* over which he seesawed at such a violent rate as to excite the curiosity of some people at a distance to come and see what was the matter with him.

(MISS REYNOLDS)

Feats of Activity

Dr. Johnson was very ambitious of excelling in common acquirements, as well as the uncommon, and particularly in feats of activity. One day, as he was walking in Gunis-bury Park (or Paddock) with some gentlemen and ladies, who were admiring the extraordinary size of some of the trees, one of the gentlemen said that, when he was a boy, he made nothing of climbing (swarming, I think, was the phrase) the largest there. "Why, I can swarm it now," replied Dr. Johnson, which excited a hearty laugh — (he was then, I believe, between fifty and sixty); on which he ran to the tree, clung round the trunk, and ascended to the branches, and, I believe, would have gone in amongst them, had he not been very earnestly entreated to descend; and down he came with a triumphant air, seeming *to make nothing of it.*

At another time, at a gentleman's seat in Devonshire, as he and some company were sitting in a saloon, before which was a spacious lawn, it was remarked as a very proper place for running a Race. A young lady present boasted that she could outrun any person; on which Dr. Johnson rose up and said, "Madam, you cannot outrun me"; and, going out on the Lawn, they started. The lady at first had the advantage; but Dr. Johnson happening to have slippers on much too small for his feet, kick'd them off up into the air, and ran a great length without them, leaving the lady far behind him, and, having won the victory, he returned, leading Her by the hand, with looks of high exultation and delight.

It was at this place, when the lady of the House was pressing him to eat something, he rose up with his knife in his hand, and loudly exclaim'd, "I vow to God I cannot eat a bit more," to the great terror, it was said, of all the company.

(MISS REYNOLDS)

A Race with Mr. Payne

Amongst those who were so intimate with Dr. Johnson as to have him occasionally an intimate in their families, it is a well known fact that he would frequently descend from the contemplation of subjects the most profound imaginable to the most childish playfulness. It was no uncommon thing to see him hop, step, and jump; he would often seat himself on the back of his chair, and more than once has been known to propose a race on some grassplat adapted to the purpose. He was very intimate and much attached to Mr. John Payne, once a bookseller in Paternoster Row, and afterwards Chief Accountant of the Bank. Mr. Payne was of a very diminutive appearance, and once when they were together on a visit with a friend at some distance from town, Johnson in a gaiety of humour proposed to run a race with Mr. Payne — the proposal was accepted; but, before they had proceeded more than half of the intended distance, Johnson caught his little adversary up in his arms, and without any ceremony placed him upon the arm of a tree which was near, and then continued running as if he had met with a hard match. He afterwards returned with much exultation to release his friend from the no very pleasant situation in which he had left him.

(EUROPEAN MAGAZINE, 1798)

A Roll Downhill

In early youth I knew Bennet Langton, *of that ilk,* as the Scotch say. With great personal claims to the respect of the public, he is known to that public chiefly as a friend of Johnson. He was a very tall, meagre, long-visaged man, much resembling, according to Richard Paget, a stork standing on one leg, near the shore, in Raphael's cartoon of the miraculous draught of fishes. His manners were in the highest degree polished; his conversation mild, equable, and always pleasing. He had the uncommon faculty of being a good reader. I formed an intimacy with his

son, and went to pay him a visit at Langton. After breakfast we walked to the top of a very steep hill behind the
house. When we arrived at the summit, Mr. Langton said,
" Poor, dear Dr. Johnson, when he came to this spot, turned
to look down the hill, and said he was determined ' to take
a roll down.' When we understood what he meant to do,
we endeavoured to dissuade him; but he was resolute,
saying, he had not had a roll for a long time; and taking
out of his lesser pockets whatever might be in them —
keys, pencil, purse, or pen-knife, and laying himself parallel with the edge of the hill, he actually descended, turning himself over and over till he came to the bottom."

(H. D. BEST)

The Laws of Hospitality

Dr. Johnson, in his tour through North Wales, passed
two days at the seat of Colonel Middleton of Gwynagag.
While he remained there, the gardener caught a hare
amidst some potatoe plants, and brought it to his master,
then engaged in conversation with the Doctor. An order
was given to carry it to the cook. As soon as Johnson
heard this sentence, he begged to have the animal placed
in his arms; which was no sooner done, than approaching
the window then half open, he restored the hare to her
liberty, shouting after her to accelerate her speed. " What
have you done? " cried the Colonel; " why, Doctor, you
have robbed my table of a delicacy, perhaps deprived us
of a dinner." "So much the better, Sir," replied the hu-
mane champion of a condemned hare; " for if your table
is to be supplied at the expense of the laws of hospitality,
I envy not the appetite of him who eats it. This, Sir, is
not a hare *feræ naturæ,* but one which had placed itself

under your protection; and savage indeed must be that man who does not make his hearth an asylum for the confiding stranger."

(EUROPEAN MAGAZINE, 1798)

An Unauthorized Publication

When Davies printed the "Fugitive Pieces" without his knowledge or consent; "How," said I, "would Pope have raved, had he been served so?" "We should never (replied he) have heard the last on't, to be sure; but then Pope was a narrow man: I will however (added he) storm and bluster *myself* a little this time"; — so went to London in all the wrath he could muster up. At his return I asked how the affair had ended: "Why (said he), I was a fierce fellow, and pretended to be very angry, and Thomas was a good-natured fellow, and pretended to be very sorry: so *there* the matter ended: I believe the dog loves me dearly."

(MRS. PIOZZI)

Johnson's Talk

In arguing he did not trouble himself with much circumlocution, but opposed, directly and abruptly, his antagonist. He fought with all sorts [of] weapons; [with] ludicrous comparisons and similes; if all failed, with rudeness and overbearing. He thought it necessary never to be worsted in argument. He had one virtue which I hold one of the most difficult to practise. After the heat of contest was over, if he had been informed that his antagonist resented his rudeness, he was the first to seek after a reconciliation; and of his virtues the most distinguished was his love of truth.

He sometimes, it must be confessed, covered his ignorance by generals rather than appear ignorant. You will wonder to hear a person who loved him so sincerely speak thus freely of his friend, but, you must recollect I am not writing his panegyrick, but as if upon oath, not only to give the truth but the whole truth.

His pride had no meanness in it; there was nothing little or mean about him.

Truth, whether in great or little matters, he held sacred.

From the violation of truth, he said, in great things your character or your interest was affected, in lesser things your pleasure is equally destroyed. I remember, on his relating some incident, I added something to his relation which I supposed might likewise have happened: "It would have been a better story," says he, "if it had been so; but it was not." Our friend Dr. Goldsmith was not so scrupulous; but he said he only indulged himself in white lyes, light as feathers, which he threw up in the air, and on whomever they fell, nobody was hurt. "I wish," says Dr. Johnson, "you would take the trouble of moulting your feathers."

(SIR JOSHUA REYNOLDS)

A Dialogue *

REYNOLDS. Let me alone, I'll bring him out. (*Aside.*) I have been thinking, Dr. Johnson, this morning, on a matter that has puzzled me very much; it is a subject that I dare say has often passed in your thoughts, and though *I* cannot, I dare say *you* have made up your mind upon it.

* A reconstruction by Reynolds of Johnson in the heat of contest.

JOHNSON. Tilly fally! what is all this preparation, what is all this mighty matter?

REY. Why, it is a very weighty matter. The subject I have been thinking upon is predestination and freewill, two things I cannot reconcile together for the life of me; in my opinion, Dr. Johnson, freewill and foreknowledge cannot be reconciled.

JOHNS. Sir, it is not of very great importance what your opinion is upon such a question.

REY. But I meant only, Dr. Johnson, to know your opinion.

JOHNS. No, Sir, you meant no such thing; you meant only to show these gentlemen that you are not the man they took you to be, but that you think of high matters sometimes, and that you may have the credit of having it said that you held an argument with Sam Johnson on predestination and freewill; a subject of that magnitude as to have engaged the attention of the world, to have perplexed the wisdom of man for these two thousand years; a subject on which the fallen angels, who *had yet not lost their original brightness,* found themselves *in wandering mazes lost.* That such a subject could be discussed in the levity of convivial conversation, is a degree of absurdity beyond what is easily conceivable.

REY. It is so, as you say, to be sure; I talked once to our friend Garrick upon this subject, but I remember we could make nothing of it.

JOHNS. O noble pair!

REY. Garrick was a clever fellow, Dr. J.; Garrick, take him altogether, was certainly a very great man.

JOHNS. Garrick, Sir, may be a great man in your opinion, as far as I know, but he was not so in mine; little things are great to little men.

REY. I have heard you say, Dr. Johnson —

JOHNS. Sir, you never heard me say that David Garrick was a great man; you may have heard me say that Garrick was a good repeater — of other men's words — words put into his mouth by other men; this makes but a faint approach towards being a great man.

REY. But take Garrick upon the whole, now, in regard to conversation —

JOHNS. Well, Sir, in regard to conversation, I never discovered in the conversation of David Garrick any intellectual energy, any wide grasp of thought, any extensive comprehension of mind, or that he possessed any of those powers to which *great* could, with any degree of propriety, be applied.

REY. But still —

JOHNS. Hold, Sir, I have not done — there are, to be sure, in the laxity of colloquial speech, various kinds of greatness; a man may be a great tobacconist, a man may be a great painter, he may be likewise a great mimic: now you may be the one, and Garrick the other, and yet neither of you be great men.

REY. But, Dr. Johnson —

JOHNS. Hold, Sir, I have often lamented how dangerous it is to investigate and to discriminate character, to men who have no discriminative powers.

REY. But Garrick, as a companion, I heard you say — no longer ago than last Wednesday, at Mr. Thrale's table —

JOHNS. You tease me, Sir. Whatever you may have heard me say, no longer ago than last Wednesday, at Mr. Thrale's table, I tell you I do not say so now: besides, as I said before, you may not have understood me, you misapprehended me, you may not have heard me.

REY. I am very sure I heard you.

JOHNS. Besides, besides, Sir, besides, — do you not

know, — are you so ignorant as not to know, that it is the highest degree of rudeness to quote a man against himself?

REY. But if you differ from yourself, and give one opinion to-day —

JOHNS. Have done, Sir; the company, you see, are tired, as well as myself.

(SIR JOSHUA REYNOLDS)

Ladylike

(Johnson to Miss Reynolds. Enclosing a letter written by himself to be sent in her name to Sir Joshua Reynolds)

DEAR BROTHER,

I know that complainers are never welcome yet you must allow me to complain of your unkindness, because it lies heavy at my heart and because I am not conscious that I ever deserved it. I have not perhaps been always careful enough to please but you can charge me, and I can charge myself with no offence which a Brother may not forgive.

If you ask me what I suffer from you, I can answer that I suffer too much in the loss of your notice; but to that is added the neglect of the world which is the consequence of yours.

If you ask what will satisfy me, I shall be satisfied with such a degree of attention when I visit you, as may set me above the contempt of your servants, with your calling now and then at my lodgings and with your inviting me from time to time with such parties as I may properly appear in. This is not much for a sister who has at least done you no harm, and this I hope you will promise by

your answer to this letter; for a refusal will give me more
pain than you can desire or intend to inflict.

I am, &c.

DEAR MADAM,

This is my letter, which at least I like better than yours.
But take your choice, and if you like mine alter any thing
that you think not ladylike. I shall call at about one.

(LETTERS)

Johnson in the Western Highlands . . . Dunvegan Castle

(*To Mrs. Thrale*)

Skie, Sept. 21, 1773

DEAREST MADAM,

I am so vexed at the necessity of sending yesterday so
short a letter, that I purpose to get a long letter beforehand by writing something every day, which I may the
more easily do, as a cold makes me now too deaf to take
the usual pleasure in conversation. Lady Macleod is very
good to me, and the place at which we now are, is equal
in strength of situation, in the wildness of the adjacent
country, and in the plenty and elegance of the domestick
entertainment, to a castle in Gothick romance. The sea
with a little island is before us; cascades play within view.
Close to the house is the formidable skeleton of an old
castle probably Danish, and the whole mass of building
stands upon a protuberance of rock, inaccessible till of
late but by a pair of stairs on the sea side, and secure in
ancient times against any enemy that was likely to invade
the kingdom of Skie.

Macleod has offered me an island; if it were not too
far off I should hardly refuse it: my island would be

pleasanter than Brighthelmstone, if you and my master could come to it; but I cannot think it pleasant to live quite alone.

Oblitusque meorum, obliviscendus et illis.

That I should be elated by the dominion of an island to forgetfulness of my friends at Streatham I cannot believe, and I hope never to deserve that they should be willing to forget me.

It has happened that I have been often recognised in my journey where I did not expect it. At Aberdeen I found one of my acquaintance professor of physick; turning aside to dine with a country gentleman, I was owned at table by one who had seen me at a philosophical lecture; at Macdonald's I was claimed by a naturalist, who wanders about the islands to pick up curiosities; and I had once in London attracted the notice of Lady Macleod. I will now go on with my account.

. . . the Vale of Glenmorrison

The Highland girl made tea, and looked and talked not inelegantly; her father was by no means an ignorant or a weak man; there were books in the cottage, among which were some volumes of Prideaux's Connection: this man's conversation we were glad of while we staid. He had been *out*, as they call it, in forty-five, and still retained his old opinions. He was going to America, because his rent was raised beyond what he thought himself able to pay.

At night our beds were made, but we had some difficulty in persuading ourselves to lie down in them, though we had put on our own sheets; at last we ventured, and I slept very soundly in the vale of Glenmorrison, amidst the rocks and mountains. Next morning our landlord liked us so well, that he walked some miles with us for our company, through a country so wild and barren that the proprietor does not, with all his pressure upon his tenants, raise more than four hundred pounds a-year for near one hundred square miles, or sixty thousand acres. He let us know that he had forty head of black cattle, an hundred goats, and an hundred sheep, upon a farm that he remembered let at five pounds a-year, but for which he now paid twenty. He told us some stories of their march into England. At last he left us, and we went forward, winding among mountains, sometimes green and sometimes naked, commonly so steep as not easily to be climbed by the greatest vigour and activity: our way was often crossed by little rivulets, and we were entertained with small streams trickling from the rocks, which after heavy rains must be tremendous torrents.

. . . Boswell Distributes Tobacco

About noon we came to a small glen, so they call a valley, which compared with other places appeared rich and fertile; here our guides desired us to stop, that the horses might graze, for the journey was very laborious, and no more grass would be found. We made no difficulty of compliance, and I sat down to take notes on a green bank, with a small stream running at my feet, in the midst of savage solitude, with mountains before me, and on either hand covered with heath. I looked around me, and wondered that I was not more affected, but the mind is not at all times equally ready to be put in motion; if my mistress and master and Queeney had been there we should have produced some reflections among us, either poetical or philosophical, for though *solitude be the nurse of woe,* conversation is often the parent of remarks and discoveries.

In about an hour we remounted, and pursued our journey. The lake by which we had travelled for some time ended in a river, which we passed by a bridge, and came to another glen, with a collection of huts, called Auknashealds; the huts were generally built of clods of earth, held together by the intertexture of vegetable fibres, of which earth there are great levels in Scotland which they call mosses. Moss in Scotland is bog in Ireland, and moss-trooper is bog-trotter: there was, however, one hut built of loose stones, piled up with great thickness into a strong though not solid wall. From this house we obtained some great pails of milk, and having brought bread with us, were very liberally regaled. The inhabitants, a very coarse tribe, ignorant of any language but Earse, gathered so fast about us, that if we had not had Highlanders with us, they might have caused more alarm than pleasure; they are called the Clan of Macrae.

We had been told that nothing gratified the Highlanders so much as snuff and tobacco, and had accordingly stored ourselves with both at Fort Augustus. Boswell opened his treasure, and gave them each a piece of tobacco roll. We had more bread than we could eat for the present, and were more liberal than provident. Boswell cut it in slices, and gave them an opportunity of tasting wheaten bread for the first time. I then got some halfpence for a shilling, and made up the deficiencies of Boswell's distribution, who had given some money among the children. We then directed that the mistress of the stone house should be asked what we must pay her: she, who perhaps had never before sold any thing but cattle, knew not, I believe, well what to ask, and referred herself to us: we

obliged her to make some demand, and one of the Highlanders settled the account with her at a shilling. One
of the men advised her, with the cunning that clowns
never can be without, to ask more; but she said that a
shilling was enough. We gave her half a crown, and she
offered part of it again. The Macraes were so well pleased
with our behaviour, that they declared it the best day they
had seen since the time of the old Laird of Macleod, who,
I suppose, like us, stopped in their valley, as he was
travelling to Skie.

We were mentioning this view of the Highlander's life
at Macdonald's, and mentioning the Macraes with some
degree of pity, when a Highland lady informed us that we
might spare our tenderness, for she doubted not but the
woman who supplied us with milk was mistress of thirteen
or fourteen milch cows.

. . . Boswell's Troublesome Kindness

I cannot forbear to interrupt my narrative. Boswell, with
some of his troublesome kindness, has informed this family and reminded me that the 18th of September is my
birth-day. The return of my birth-day, if I remember it,
fills me with thoughts which it seems to be the general
care of humanity to escape. I can now look back upon
threescore and four years, in which little has been done,
and little has been enjoyed; a life diversified by misery,
spent part in the sluggishness of penury, and part under
the violence of pain, in gloomy discontent or importunate
distress. But perhaps I am better than I should have been
if I had been less afflicted. With this I will try to be content.

In proportion as there is less pleasure in retrospective

considerations, the mind is more disposed to wander forward into futurity; but at sixty-four what promises, however liberal, of imaginary good can futurity venture to
make? yet something will be always promised, and some
promises will always be credited. I am hoping and I am
praying that I may live better in the time to come, whether
long or short, than I have yet lived, and in the solace of
that hope endeavour to repose. Dear Queeney's day is
next, I hope she at sixty-four will have less to regret.

I will now complain no more, but tell my mistress of
my travels.

. . . uniformity of the Highlands

After we left the Macraes we travelled on through a country like that which we passed in the morning. The Highlands are very uniform, for there is little variety in universal barrenness; the rocks, however, are not all naked,
some have grass on their sides, and birches and alders on
their tops, and in the vallies are often broad and clear
streams, which have little depth, and commonly run very
quick: the channels are made by the violence of the win-
try floods; the quickness of the stream is in proportion
to the declivity of the descent, and the breadth of the
channel makes the water shallow in a dry season.

There are red deer and roebucks in the mountains, but
we found only goats in the road, and had very little entertainment as we travelled either for the eye or ear. There
are, I fancy, no singing birds in the Highlands.

. . . the Inn at Glenelg

Towards night we came to a very formidable hill called
Rattiken, which we climbed with more difficulty than we
had yet experienced, and at last came to Glenelg, a place
on the sea-side opposite to Skie. We were by this time
weary and disgusted, nor was our humour much mended
by our inn, which, though it was built of lime and slate,
the Highlander's description of a house which he thinks
magnificent, had neither wine, bread, eggs, nor any thing
that we could eat or drink. When we were taken up stairs,
a dirty fellow bounced out of the bed where one of us was
to lie. Boswell blustered, but nothing could be got. At
last a gentleman in the neighbourhood, who heard of our
arrival, sent us rum and white sugar. Boswell was now
provided for in part, and the landlord prepared some mutton chops, which we could not eat, and killed two hens,
of which Boswell made his servant broil a limb, with
what effect I know not. We had a lemon and a piece of
bread, which supplied me with my supper. When the repast was ended, we began to deliberate upon bed; Mrs.
Boswell had warned us that we should *catch something*,
and had given us *sheets* for our *security*, for —— and ——,
she said, came back from Skie, so scratching themselves.
I thought sheets a slender defence against the confederacy
with which we were threatened, and by this time our
Highlanders had found a place where they could get
some hay: I ordered hay to be laid thick upon the bed, and
slept upon it in my great coat: Boswell laid sheets upon
his bed, and reposed in linen like a gentleman. The horses
were turned out to grass, with a man to watch them. The
hill Rattiken and the inn at Glenelg were the only things
of which we, or travellers yet more delicate, could find
any pretensions to complain.

. . . a Parsimonious Host

Sept. 2nd, I rose rustling from the hay, and went to tea, which I forget whether we found or brought. We saw the isle of Skie before us, darkening the horizon with its rocky coast. A boat was procured, and we launched into one of the straits of the Atlantick ocean. We had a passage of about twelve miles to the point where —— resided, having come from his seat in the middle of the island to a small house on the shore, as we believe, that he might with less reproach entertain us meanly. If he aspired to meanness, his retrograde ambition was completely gratified, but he did not succeed equally in escaping reproach. He had no cook, nor I suppose much provision, nor had the lady the common decencies of her tea-table: we picked up our sugar with our fingers. Boswell was very angry, and reproached him with his improper parsimony; I did not much reflect upon the conduct of a man with whom I was not likely to converse as long at any other time.

. . . Skye Described

You will now expect that I should give you some account of the isle of Skie, of which, though I have been twelve days upon it, I have little to say. It is an island perhaps fifty miles long, so much indented by inlets of the sea that there is no part of it removed from the water more than six miles. No part that I have seen is plain; you are always climbing or descending, and every step is upon rock or mire. A walk upon ploughed ground in England is a dance upon carpets compared to the toilsome drudgery of wandering in Skie. There is neither town nor village in

the island, nor have I seen any house but Macleod's, that
is not much below your habitation at Brighthelmstone.
In the mountains there are stags and roebucks, but no
hares, and few rabbits; nor have I seen any thing that interested me as a zoologist, except an otter, bigger than I
thought an otter could have been.

You are perhaps imagining that I am withdrawn from
the gay and the busy world into regions of peace and pastoral felicity, and am enjoying the reliques of the golden
age; that I am surveying nature's magnificence from a
mountain, or remarking her minuter beauties on the flowery bank of a winding rivulet; that I am invigorating myself in the sunshine, or delighting my imagination with
being hidden from the invasion of human evils and human
passions in the darkness of a thicket; that I am busy in
gathering shells and pebbles on the shore, or contempla-
tive on a rock, from which I look upon the water, and
consider how many waves are rolling between me and
Streatham.

The use of travelling is to regulate imagination by re-
ality, and instead of thinking how things may be, to see
them as they are. Here are mountains which I should
once have climbed, but to climb steeps is now very laborious, and to descend them dangerous; and I am now content with knowing, that by scrambling up a rock, I shall
only see other rocks, and a wider circuit of barren deso-
lation. Of streams, we have here a sufficient number, but
they murmur not upon pebbles, but upon rocks. Of flow-
ers, if Chloris herself were here, I could present her only
with the bloom of heath. Of lawns and thickets, he must
read that would know them, for here is little sun and no
shade. On the sea I look from my window, but am not
much tempted to the shore; for since I came to this island,
almost every breath of air has been a storm, and what is

worse, a storm with all its severity, but without its magnificence, for the sea is here so broken into channels that there is not a sufficient volume of water either for lofty surges or a loud roar.

... feudal Hospitality at Dunvegan

On the 13th, travelling partly on horseback where we could not row, and partly on foot where we could not ride, we came to Dunvegan, which I have described already. Here, though poor Macleod had been left by his grandfather overwhelmed with debts, we had another exhibition of feudal hospitality. There were two stags in the house, and venison came to the table every day in its various forms. Macleod, besides his estate in Skie, larger I suppose than some English counties, is proprietor of nine inhabited isles; and of his islands uninhabited I doubt if he very exactly knows the number. I told him that he was a mighty monarch. Such dominions fill an Englishman with envious wonder; but when he surveys the naked mountain, and treads the quaking moor, and wanders over the wild regions of gloomy barrenness, his wonder may continue, but his envy ceases. The unprofitableness of these vast domains can be conceived only by the means of positive instances. The heir of *Col,* an island not far distant, has lately told me how wealthy he should be if he could let *Rum,* another of his islands, for twopence halfpenny an acre; and Macleod has an estate, which the surveyor reports to contain eighty thousand acres, rented at six hundred pounds a-year.

While we were at Dunvegan, the wind was high, and the rain violent, so that we were not able to put forth a boat to fish in the sea, or to visit the adjacent islands, which may be seen from the house; but we filled up the time as we could, sometimes by talk, sometimes by reading.

. . . his Mind Too Much at Streatham

You remember the Doge of Genoa, who being asked what struck him most at the French court, answered, " Myself." I cannot think many things here more likely to affect the fancy than to see Johnson ending his sixty-fourth year in the wilderness of the Hebrides. But now I am here, it will gratify me very little to return without seeing, or doing my best to see what those places afford. I have a desire to instruct myself in the whole system of pastoral life; but I know not whether I shall be able to perfect the idea. However, I have many pictures in my mind, which I could not have had without this journey, and should have passed it with great pleasure had you, and Master, and Queeney been in the party. We should have excited the attention and enlarged the observation of each other, and obtained many pleasing topicks of future conversation. As it is, I travel with my mind too much at home, and perhaps miss many things worthy of observation, or pass them with transient notice; so that the images, for want of that re-impression which discussion and comparison produce, easily fade away; but I keep a book of remarks, and Boswell writes a regular journal of our travels, which, I think, contains as much of what I say and do as of all other occurrences together; " for such a faithful chronicler as Griffith."

. . . rain in Mull

Inverary, Oct. 23, 1773

HONOURED MISTRESS,

My last letters to you and my dear master were written from Mull, the third island of the Hebrides in extent. There is no post, and I took the opportunity of a gentleman's passage to the main land.

In Mull we were confined two days by the weather; on the third we got on horse-back, and after a journey difficult and tedious, over rocks naked and valleys untracked, through a country of barrenness and solitude, we came, almost in the dark, to the sea side, weary and dejected, having met with nothing but water falling from the mountains that could raise any image of delight. Our company was the young Laird of Col and his servant. Col made every Maclean open his house where we came, and supply us with horses when we departed; but the horses of this country are small, and I was not mounted to my wish.

At the sea side we found the ferry-boat departed; if it had been where it was expected, the wind was against us, and the hour was late, nor was it very desirable to cross the sea in darkness with a small boat. The captain of a sloop that had been driven thither by the storms, saw our distress, and as we were hesitating and deliberating, sent his boat, which, by Col's order, transported us to the isle of Ulva. We were introduced to Mr. Macquarry, the head of a small clan, whose ancestors have reigned in Ulva beyond memory, but who has reduced himself, by his negligence and folly, to the necessity of selling his venerable patrimony.

. . . a Chieftain's Hut

On the next morning we passed the strait to Inch Kenneth, an island about a mile in length, and less than half a mile broad; in which Kenneth, a Scottish saint, established a small clerical college, of which the chapel walls are still standing. At this place I beheld a scene which I wish you and my master and Queeney had partaken.

The only family on the island is that of Sir Allan, the chief of the ancient and numerous clan of Maclean; the clan which claims the second place, yielding only to Macdonald in the line of battle. Sir Allan, a chieftain, a baronet, and a soldier, inhabits in this insulated desart a thatched hut with no chambers. Young Col, who owns him as his chief, and whose cousin was his lady, had, I believe, given him some notice of our visit; he received us with the soldier's frankness and the gentleman's elegance, and introduced us to his daughters, two young ladies who have not wanted education suitable to their birth, and who, in their cottage, neither forgot their dignity, nor affected to remember it. Do not you wish to have been with us?

Sir Allan's affairs are in disorder by the fault of his ancestors, and while he forms some scheme for retrieving them, he has retreated hither.

. . . a Hasty Return

When our salutations were over, he showed us the island. We walked uncovered into the chapel, and saw in the reverend ruin the effects of precipitate reformation. The floor is covered with ancient grave-stones, of which the inscriptions are not now legible; and without some of the chief families still continue the right of sepulture. The altar is not yet quite demolished; beside it, on the right side, is a bas-relief of the Virgin with her child, and an angel hovering over her. On the other side still stands a hand-bell, which, though it has no clapper, neither Presbyterian bigotry nor barbarian wantonness has yet taken away. The chapel is thirty-eight feet long, and eighteen broad. Boswell, who is very pious, went into it at night to perform his devotions, but came back in haste, for fear of spectres. Near the chapel is a fountain, to which the water, remarkably pure, is conveyed from a distant hill, through pipes laid by the Romish clergy, which still perform the office of conveyance, though they have never been repaired since Popery was suppressed.

We soon after went in to dinner, and wanted neither the comforts nor the elegancies of life. There were several dishes, and variety of liquors. The servants live in another cottage; in which, I suppose, the meat is dressed.

Towards evening, Sir Allan told us that Sunday never passed over him like another day. One of the ladies read, and read very well, the evening service; — and Paradise was opened in the wild.

. . . a Very Uncommon Cave

Next day, 18th, we went and wandered among the rocks on the shore, while the boat was busy in catching oysters, of which there is a great bed. Oysters lie upon the sand, one I think sticking to another, and cockles are found a few inches under the sand.

We then went in the boat to Sondiland, a little island very near. We found it a wild rock, of about ten acres; part naked, part covered with sand, out of which we picked shells; and part clothed with a thin layer of mould, on the grass of which a few sheep are sometimes fed. We then came back and dined. I passed part of the afternoon in reading, and in the evening one of the ladies played on her harpsichord, and Boswell and Col danced a reel with the other.

On the 19th, we persuaded Sir Allan to launch his boat again, and go with us to Icolmkill, where the first great preacher of Christianity to the Scots built a church, and settled a monastery. In our way we stopped to examine a very uncommon cave on the coast of Mull. We had some difficulty to make our way over the vast masses of broken rocks that lie before the entrance, and at the mouth were embarrassed with stones, which the sea had accumulated, as at Brighthelmstone; but as we advanced, we reached a floor of soft sand, and as we left the light behind us, walked along a very spacious cavity, vaulted over head with an arch almost regular, by which a mountain was sustained, at least a very lofty rock. From this magnificent cavern went a narrow passage to the right hand, which we entered with a candle, and though it was obstructed with great stones, clambered over them to a second expansion of the cave, in which there lies a great square stone, which might serve as a table. The air here was very warm, but not oppressive, and the flame of the candle continued pyramidal. The cave goes onward to an unknown extent, but we were now one hundred and sixty yards under ground; we had but one candle, and had never heard of any that went further and came back; we therefore thought it prudent to return.

Going forward in our boat, we came to a cluster of rocks, black and horrid, which Sir Allan chose for the place where he would eat his dinner. We climbed till we got seats. The stores were opened, and the repast taken.

. . . Iona

We then entered the boat again; the night came upon us; the wind rose; the sea swelled; and Boswell desired to be set on dry ground: we, however, pursued our navigation, and passed by several little islands, in the silent solemnity of faint moonshine, seeing little, and hearing only the wind and the water. At last we reached the island; the venerable seat of ancient sanctity; where secret piety reposed, and where fallen greatness was reposited. The island has no house of entertainment, and we manfully made our bed in a farmer's barn. The description I hope to give you another time.

I am, &c.,

SAM: JOHNSON

The Works of God

Mr. Johnson's hatred of the Scotch is so well known, and so many of his *bons mots* expressive of that hatred have been already repeated in so many books and pamphlets, that 'tis perhaps scarcely worth while to write down the conversation between him and a friend of that nation who always resides in London, and who at his return from the Hebrides asked him with a firm tone of voice, What he thought of his country? " That it is a very vile country to be sure, Sir; " (returned for answer Dr. Johnson). "Well, Sir! " replies the other somewhat mortified, " God made it." " Certainly he did (answers Mr. Johnson again); but we must always remember that he made it for Scotchmen, and comparisons are odious, Mr. S——; but God made hell."

(MRS. PIOZZI)

Scotch and Irish Impudence

The account of the Tour to the Western Islands of Scotland, which was undertaken in the autumn of 1773, in company with Mr. Boswell, was not published till some time in the year 1775. This book has been variously received; by some extolled for the elegance of the narrative, and the depth of observation on life and manners; by others, as much condemned, as a work of avowed hostility to the Scotch nation. The praise was, beyond all question, fairly deserved; and the censure, on due examination, will appear hasty and ill-founded. That Johnson entertained some prejudices against the Scotch must not be dissembled. It is true, as Mr. Boswell says, " that he thought their success in England exceeded their proportion of real merit, and he could not but see in them that nationality which no liberal-minded Scotsman will deny." The author of these memoirs well remembers, that Johnson one day asked him, " have you observed the difference between your own country impudence and Scottish impudence? " The answer being the negative: " then I will tell you," said Johnson. " The impudence of an Irishman is the impudence of a fly, that buzzes about you, and you put it away, but it returns again, and flutters and teases you. The impudence of a Scotsman is the impudence of a leech, that fixes and sucks your blood."

(ARTHUR MURPHY)

Mrs. Thrale's Tour in Wales with Dr. Johnson
. . . early Memories

On Tuesday, 5th July, 1774, I began my journey through
Wales. We set out from Streatham in our coach and four
post horses, accompanied by Mr. Johnson and our eldest
daughter. Baretti went with us as far as London, where
we left him, and hiring fresh horses they carried us to the
Mitre at Barnet, a house kept by Lady Lade's Maid, with
whom I left a letter for her quondam mistress. At St. Al-
bans we were hospitably received by Ralph Smith and his
Wife, relations to Mr. Thrale, who gave us a good cold
dinner, and from whom we had much trouble to get away
to a sister of theirs who has another house in the Town,
and detained us to drink tea with her and her son. There I
was first made to observe the apparent degeneration of the
wild pheasant's plumage when rendered domestic. In
the afternoon we drove on to Dunstable, where we spent
the night, after a day in which nothing else had been
learned, seen, done, or known, but the passing through
a space of 40 miles from home with emotions perpetually
changing and perpetually strong, every sign, every bush,
every stone almost, reminding me of times long past but
not forgotten; of incidents not pleasing in themselves perhaps, but delightful from their connection with youthful
gaiety and the remembrance of people now dead, to some
of which I was far more dear than to any now living.
Here I hunted with my Uncle, here I fished or walked
with my Father, here my Grandmother reproved my
Mother for her too great indulgence of me, here poor dear
Lady Salusbury fainted in the coach and charged me not
to tell Sir Thomas of the accident lest it should affect him,

here we were overturned, and on this place I wrote foolish verses which were praised by my foolisher Friends.

. . . Wenlock Edge

This 13th September has been very uncomfortable. We breakfasted with Dr. Adams, a Clergyman of Shrewsbury, whose welcome, and whose breakfast, and whose conversation were so cold that I was most impatient of delay. When we got further it rained pitiably, and we walked up a steep hill they called Wenlock Edge till our feet were very wet and dirty.

. . . Edmund Burke at Beaconsfield

29th September. Last night we were received with open arms by our friends at Beaconsfield; each seemed to contend who should be kindest, but to-day Mr. Burke himself was obliged to go out somewhere about Election matters. There was an old Mr. Lowndes dined with us and got very drunk talking Politics with Will Burke and my Master after dinner. Lord Verney and Edmund came home at night very much flustered with liquor, and I thought how I had spent three months from home among dunces of all ranks and sorts, but had never seen a man drunk till I came among the Wits. This was accidental indeed, but what of that? it was so.

. . . the Drawbacks of Southwark

30th September. When I rose Mr. Thrale informed me that the Parliament was suddenly dissolved and that all the World was to bustle, that we were to go to Southwark, not to Streatham, and canvass away. I heard the first part of this report with pleasure, the latter with pain; nothing but a real misfortune could, I think, affect me so much as the thoughts of going to Town thus to settle for the Winter before I have had any enjoyment of Streatham at all, and so all my hopes of pleasure blow away. I thought to have lived at Streatham in quiet and comfort, have kissed my children and cuffed them by turns, and had a place always for them to play in, and here I must be shut up in that odious dungeon, where nobody will come near me, the children are to be sick for want of air, *and I am never to see a face but Mr. Johnson's.* Oh, what a life that is! and how truly do I abhor it!

(MRS. THRALE)

Johnson and Edmund Burke

An Irish trader at our house one day heard Johnson launch out into very great and greatly deserved praises of Mr. Edmund Burke: delighted to find his countryman stood so high in the opinion of a man he had been told so much of, " Sir (said he), give *me* leave to tell something of Mr. Burke now." We were all silent, and the honest Hibernian began to relate how Mr. Burke went to see the collieries in a distant province; and he would go down into the bowels of the earth (in a bag) and he would examine every thing: " he went in a bag Sir, and ventured his health and his life for knowledge; but he took care of his clothes, that they should not be spoiled, for he went down in a bag." " Well Sir (says Mr. Johnson good-humouredly), if our friend Mund should die in any of these hazardous exploits, you and I would write his life and panegyric together; and your chapter of it should be entitled thus: *Burke in a Bag.*"

He had always a very great personal regard and particular affection for Mr. Edmund Burke, as well as an esteem difficult for me to repeat, though for him only easy to express. And when at the end of the year 1774 the general election called us all different ways, and broke up the delightful society in which we had spent some time at Beaconsfield, Dr. Johnson shook the hospitable master of the house kindly by the hand, and said, "Farewell my dear Sir, and remember that I wish you all the success which ought to be wished you, which can possibly be wished you indeed — *by an honest man.*"

(MRS. PIOZZI)

Johnson's Household

He loved the poor as I never yet saw any one else do, with an earnest desire to make them happy. — What signifies, says some one, giving halfpence to common beggars? they only lay it out in gin or tobacco. "And why should they be denied such sweeteners of their existence (says Johnson)? it is surely very savage to refuse them every possible avenue to pleasure, reckoned too coarse for our own acceptance. Life is a pill which none of us can bear to swallow without gilding; yet for the poor we delight in stripping it still barer, and are not ashamed to shew even visible displeasure, if ever the bitter taste is taken from their mouths." In consequence of these principles he nursed whole nests of people in his house, where the lame, the blind, the sick, and the sorrowful found a sure retreat from all the evils whence his little income could secure them: and commonly spending the middle of the week at our house, he kept his numerous family in Fleet-street upon a settled allowance; but returned to them every Saturday, to give them three good dinners, and his company, before he came back to us on the Monday night — treating them with the same, or perhaps more ceremonious civility, than he would have done by as many people of fashion — making the holy scriptures thus the rule of his conduct, and only expecting salvation as he was able to obey its precepts.

When he spoke of negroes, he always appeared to think them of a race naturally inferior, and made few exceptions in favour of his own; yet whenever disputes arose in his household among the many odd inhabitants of which it consisted, he always sided with Francis against the others, whom he suspected (not unjustly I believe) of greater malignity. It seems at once vexatious and comical to reflect, that the dissensions those people chose to live constantly in, distressed and mortified him exceedingly. He really was oftentimes afraid of going home, because he was so sure to be met at the door with numberless complaints; and he used to lament pathetically to me, and to Mr. Sastres the Italian master, who was much his favourite, that they made his life miserable from the impossibility he found of making theirs happy, when every favour he bestowed on one was wormwood to the rest. If however I ventured to blame their ingratitude, and condemn their conduct, he would instantly set about softening the one and justifying the other; and finished commonly by telling me, that I knew not how to make allowances for situations I never experienced.

. . . When he raised contributions for some distressed author, or wit in want, he often made us all more than amends by diverting descriptions of the lives they were then passing in corners unseen by any body but himself; and that odd old surgeon whom he kept in his house to

tend the out-pensioners, and of whom he said most truly
and sublimely, that

> " In misery's darkest caverns known,
>   His useful care was ever nigh,
>   Where hopeless anguish pours her groan,
>   And lonely want retires to die."

(MRS. PIOZZI)

The Dangers of Solitude

He gave away all he had, and all he ever had gotten, except the two thousand pounds he left behind; and the
very small portion of his income which he spent on himself, with all our calculation, we never could make more
than seventy, or at most fourscore pounds a year, and he
pretended to allow himself a hundred. He had numberless dependents out of doors as well as in, " who," as he
expressed it, " did not care to see him latterly unless he
brought 'em money." For those people he used frequently
to raise contributions on his richer friends; " and this (says
he) is one of the thousand reasons which ought to restrain
a man from drony solitude and useless retirement. Solitude (added he one day) is dangerous to reason, without
being favourable to virtue: pleasures of some sort are necessary to the intellectual as to the corporeal health; and
those who resist gaiety, will be likely for the most part to
fall a sacrifice to appetite; for the solicitations of sense are
always at hand, and a dram to a vacant and solitary person is a speedy and seducing relief. Remember (continued he) that the solitary mortal is certainly luxurious,
probably superstitious, and possibly mad: the mind stag-
nates for want of employment, grows morbid, and is extinguished like a candle in foul air." It was on this principle that Johnson encouraged parents to carry their

daughters early and much into company; for what harm can be done before so many witnesses? " Solitude is the surest nurse of all prurient passions, and a girl in the hurry of preparation, or tumult of gaiety, has neither inclination nor leisure to let tender expressions soften or sink into her heart. The ball, the show, are not the dangerous places: no, 'tis the private friend, the kind consoler, the companion of the easy vacant hour, whose compliance with her opinions can flatter her vanity, and whose conversation can just sooth, without ever stretching her mind, that is the lover to be feared: he who buzzes in her ear at court, or at the opera, must be contented to buzz in vain." These notions Dr. Johnson carried so very far that I have heard him say, " If you would shut up any man with any woman, so as to make them derive their whole pleasure from each other, they would inevitably fall in love, as it is called, with each other; but at six months end if you would throw them both into public life where they might change partners at pleasure, each would soon forget that fondness which mutual dependance, and the paucity of general amusement alone, had caused, and each would separately feel delighted by their release."

(MRS. PIOZZI)

Johnson and the Rev. Charles Congreve

(1. *To the Reverend Dr. Taylor*)

DEAR SIR,

I have upon me in some measure the care of getting a boy into the Bluecoat Hospital, and beg your interest with Mr. Harley or any other man. Our boy is a non-freeman whose parents are both living. We have a presentation for a freeman which we can give in exchange.

Charles Congreve * is here, in an ill state of health, for
advice. How long he has been here I know not. He sent
to me one that attends him as an humble friend, and she
left me a direction. He told me he knew not how to find
me. He is in his own opinion recovering, but has the appearance of a man much broken. He talked to me of theological points, and is going to print a sermon, but I
thought he appeared neither very acute nor very knowing.
His room was disordered and oppressive, he has the appearance of a man wholly sunk into that sordid self-indul-
gence which disease, real or imaginary, is apt to dictate.
He has lived, as it seems, with no great frequency of recollection. He asked me, and told me he had forgot,
whether I was bred at Oxford or at Cambridge. The mind
that leaves things so fast behind it, ought to have gone
forward at no common rate. I believe he is charitable,
yet he seems to have money much in his thoughts; he told
me that this ilness would cost him fifty pound, and told it
with some appearance of discontent: he seemed glad to
see me, and I intend to visit him again. I rather wonder
that he sent to me. I mentioned Hector to him whom I
saw about ten weeks ago, but he heard the name without
emotion or enquiry, nor has ever spoken of any old companions or past occurrences. Is not this an odd frame of
understanding? I asked him how long it was since we had
seen one another, and he answered me roundly, fifty
years. The greatest pleasure that I have had from him is
to find him pious and orthodox; yet he consorts with John
Wesley.

You and I have had ill health, yet in many respects we
bear time better than most of our friends. I sincerely wish
that you may continue to bear it with as little diminution

---

* A schoolfellow of Johnson.

as is possible either of body or mind, and I think, you return the wish to

Dear Sir,

Your most humble servant,

SAM: JOHNSON

London, Dec. 22, 1774
To the Reverend Dr. Taylor in Ashbourn, Derbyshire

(2. *To Edmund Hector*)

March 7, 1776

DEAR SIR,

Some time ago you told me that you had unhappily hurt yourself; and were confined, and you have never since let me hear of your recovery. I hope however that you are grown, at least are growing well. We must be content now to mend very gradually, and cannot make such quick transitions from sickness to health, as we did forty years ago. Let me know how you do, and do not imagine that I forgot you.

I forget whether I told you that at the latter end of the summer I rambled over part of France. I saw something of the vintage, which is all I think that they have to boast above our country, at least, it is their great natural advantage. Their air, I think, is good, and my health mended in it very perceptibly.

Our schoolfellow Charles Congreve is still in town, but very dull, very valetudinary, and very recluse, willing, I am afraid, to forget the world, and content to be forgotten by it, to repose in that sullen sensuality, into which men naturally sink, who think disease a justification of indulgence, and converse only with those who hope to prosper by indulging them. This is a species of Beings with which your profession must have made you much acquainted, and to which I hope acquaintance has made you no friend. Infirmity will come, but let us not invite it; indulgence will allure us, but let us turn resolutely away. Time cannot always be defeated, but let us not yield till we are conquered.

I had the other day a letter from Harry Jackson, who says nothing, and yet seems to have something which he wishes to say. He is very poor. I wish something could be done for him.

I hope dear Mrs. Careless is well, and now and then does not disdain to mention my name. It is happy when a Brother and Sister live to pass their time at our age together. I have nobody to whom I can talk of my first years — when I go to Lichfield I see the old places, but find nobody that enjoyed them with me. May she and you live long together.

I am, dear Sir,
Your affectionate humble servant,
SAM: JOHNSON

To Mr. Hector in Birmingham

(3. *To the Reverend Dr. Taylor*)

March 7, 1776

DEAR SIR,
You will not write to me, nor come to see me, and you will not have me within reach long for We are going to Italy in the spring.

I called the other day upon poor Charles, whom I had not seen for many months. He took no notice of my absence, nor appeared either glad or sorry to see me, but answered everything with monosyllables, and seemed heavy and drowsy, like a man muddled with a full meal; at last I enquired the time, which gave him hopes of being delivered from me, and enabled him to bounce up with great alacrity and inspect his watch. He sits in a room about ten feet square, and though he takes the air every day in his chaise, fancies that he should take cold in any other house, and therefore never pays a visit.

(LETTERS)

The Death of Peyton *

Poor Peyton expired this morning. He probably during many years, for which he sat starving by the bed of a wife, not only useless but almost motionless, condemned by poverty to personal attendance, and by the necessity of such attendance chained down to poverty — he probably thought often how lightly he should tread the path of life without his burthen. Of this thought the admission was unavoidable, and the indulgence might be forgiven to frailty and distress. His wife died at last, and before she was buried he was seized by a fever, and is now going to the grave.

Such miscarriages, when they happen to those on whom many eyes are fixed, fill histories and tragedies; and tears have been shed for the sufferings, and wonder excited by the fortitude of those who neither did nor suffered more than Peyton.

(LETTERS)

Johnson and Mauritius Lowe

(1. *To Viscountess Southwell*)
Bolt Court, Fleet Street, Sept. 9, 1780

MADAM,
Among the numerous addresses of condolence which your great loss must have occasioned, be pleased to re-

* Peyton was one of Johnson's assistants on the Dictionary, and received constant help from Johnson in later years.

ceive this from one whose name perhaps you have never heard, and to whom your ladyship is known only by the reputation of your virtue, and to whom your lord was known only by his kindness and beneficence.

Your ladyship is now again summoned to exert that piety of which you once gave, in a state of pain and danger, so illustrious an example; and your lord's beneficence may be still continued by those who with his fortune inherit his virtues.

I hope to be forgiven the liberty which I shall take of informing your ladyship, that Mr. Mauritius Lowe, a son of your late lord's father, had, by my recommendation to your lord, a quarterly allowance of ten pounds, the last of which, due July 26, he has not received: he was in hourly hope of his remittance, and flattered himself that on October 26, he should have received the whole half-year's bounty, when he was struck with the dreadful news of his benefactor's death.

May I presume to hope, that his want, his relation, and his merit, which excited his lordship's charity, will continue to have the same effect upon those whom he has left behind; and that, though he has lost one friend, he may not yet be destitute. Your ladyship's charity cannot easily be exerted where it is wanted more; and to a mind like yours, distress is a sufficient recommendation.

I hope to be allowed the honour of being,

Madam, &c.,

SAM: JOHNSON

To Viscountess Southwell, Dublin

(2)

On Saturday I dined, as is usual, at the opening of the Exhibition. Our company was splendid, whether more numerous than at any former time I know not. Our tables seem always full. On Monday, if I am told truth, were received at the door one hundred and ninety pounds, for the admission of three thousand eight hundred spectators. Supposing the shew open ten hours, and the spectators staying one with another each an hour, the rooms never had fewer than three hundred and eighty justling against each other. Poor Lowe met some discouragement, but I interposed for him, and prevailed.*

(LETTERS)

A Dancing-Master

Among many others, whom he thus patronized, was a worthless fellow, a dancing-master by profession. . . . This man, notwithstanding the nature of his employment, which was a genteel one, delighted in the company and conversation of marshal's-court attornies, and of bailiffs and their followers, and others of a lower class, sharpers and swindlers, who, when they had made him drunk, would get him to sign notes and engagements of various kinds, which, he not being able to discharge, they had him arrested upon, and this was so frequently the case that much of his time was passed in confinement. His wife, through Mrs. Williams, got at Johnson, and told him her tale, which was that her husband was, at that instant, detained for a small debt in a spunging-house, and he conceiving it to be a piteous one sent her to me for advice. I heard her story, and learned from it that all the merit of the fellow lay in his heels, that he had neither principle

* Johnson persuaded Reynolds, after a picture by Lowe had been rejected for the Exhibition, to admit it. The picture, according to Northcote, was " execrable beyond belief."

nor discretion, and, in short, was a cully, the dupe of ev-
eryone that would make him drunk. I therefore dismissed
her with a message to Johnson to this effect: that her husband made it impossible for his friends to help him, and
must submit to his destiny. When I next saw Johnson, I
told him that there seemed to be as exact a fitness between
the character of this man and his associates, as is between
the wings of a fly, and the web of a spider, and I could not
but think he was born to be cheated. Johnson seemed to
acquiesce in my opinion; but I believe, before that, had
set him at liberty by paying the debt.

(SIR JOHN HAWKINS)

Enemies of His Peace

. . . It is difficult to account for the conduct of Johnson in
the choice of many of his associates, and particularly of
those who, when his circumstances became easy, he suffered to intrude on him. Of these he had some at bed and
board, who had elbowed through the world, and subsisted by lying, begging, and shifting, all of which he
knew, but seemed to think never the worse of them.

His inmates were enemies to his peace, and occasioned
him great disgust: the jealousy that subsisted among them
rendered his dwelling irksome to him, and he seldom ap-
proached it, after an evening's conversation abroad, but
with the dread of finding it a scene of discord, and of having his ears filled with the complaints of Mrs. Williams of
Frank's neglect of his duty and inattention to the interests
of his master, and of Frank against Mrs. Williams, for the
authority she assumed over him, and exercised with an
unwarrantable severity. Even those intruders who had
taken shelter under his roof, and who, in his absence from

home, brought thither their children, found cause to murmur, their provision of food was scanty, or their dinners ill dressed; all which he chose to endure rather than put an end to their clamours, by ridding his house of such thankless and troublesome guests. Nay, so insensible was he of the ingratitude of those whom he suffered thus to hang upon him, and among whom he may be said to have divided an income which was little more than sufficient for his own support, that he would submit to reproach and personal affront from some of them, even Levett would sometimes insult him, and Mrs. Williams, in her paroxysms of rage, has been known to drive him from her presence.

(SIR JOHN HAWKINS)

Strange Customs

At tea-time the subject turned upon the domestic economy of Dr. Johnson's own household. Mrs. Thrale has often acquainted me that his house is quite filled and overrun with all sorts of strange creatures, whom he admits for mere charity, and because nobody else will admit them, — for his charity is unbounded, — or, rather, bounded only by his circumstances.

The account he gave of the adventures and absurdities of the set, was highly diverting, but too diffused for writing, — though one or two speeches I must give. I think I shall occasionally theatricalise my dialogues.

Mrs. Thrale — Pray, sir, how does Mrs. Williams like all this tribe?

Dr. Johnson — Madam, she does not like them at all; but their fondness for her is not greater. She and De Mullin quarrel incessantly; but as they can both be occasionally of service to each other, and as neither of them have any other place to go to, their animosity does not force them to separate.

Mrs. T. — And pray, sir, what is Mr. Macbean?

Dr. J. — Madam, he is a Scotchman: he is a man of great learning, and for his learning I respect him, and I wish to serve him. He knows many languages, and knows them well; but he knows nothing of life. I advised him to write a geographical dictionary; but I have lost all hopes of his ever doing anything properly, since I found he gave as much labour to Capua as to Rome.

Mr. T. — And pray who is clerk of your kitchen, sir?

Dr. J. — Why, sir, I am afraid there is none; a general anarchy prevails in my kitchen, as I am told by Mr. Levat, who says it is not now what it used to be!

Mrs. T. — Mr. Levat, I suppose, sir, has the office of keeping the hospital in health? for he is an apothecary.

Dr. J. — Levat, madam, is a brutal fellow, but I have a good regard for him; for his brutality is in his manners, not his mind.

Mr. T. — But how do you get your dinners drest?

Dr. J. — Why De Mullin has the chief management of the kitchen; but our roasting is not magnificent, for we have no jack.

Mr. T. — No jack? Why how do they manage without?

Dr. J. — Small joints, I believe, they manage with a string, and larger are done at the tavern. I have some thoughts (with a profound gravity) of buying a jack, because I think a jack is some credit to a house.

Mr. T. — Well, but you'll have a spit, too?

Dr. J. — No, sir, no; that would be superfluous; for we shall never use it; and if a jack is seen, a spit will be presumed!

Mrs. T. — But pray, sir, who is the Poll you talk of? She

that you use to abet in her quarrels with Mrs. Williams, and call out, "At her again, Poll! Never flinch, Poll!"

Dr. J. — Why, I took to Poll very well at first, but she won't do upon a nearer examination.

Mrs. T. — How came she among you, sir?

Dr. J. — Why I don't rightly remember, but we could spare her very well from us. Poll is a stupid slut; I had some hopes of her at first; but when I talked to her tightly and closely, I could make nothing of her; she was wiggle waggle, and I could never persuade her to be categorical.

(FANNY BURNEY)

Discord

To-day Mrs. Williams and Mrs. Desmoulines had a scold, and Williams was going away, but I bid her *not turn tail*, and she came back, and rather got the upper hand.

. . . Young Desmoulines thinks he has got something, he knows not what, at Drury-lane; his mother talks little of it. — Sure it is not a *humm*? Mr. Levet, who thinks his ancient rights invaded, stands at bay, *fierce as ten furies*. Mrs. Williams growls and scolds, but Poll does not much flinch.

. . . Discord keeps her residence in this habitation, but she has for some time been silent. We have much malice, but no mischief. Levet is rather a friend to Williams, because he hates Desmoulines more. A thing that he should hate more than Desmoulines, is not to be found.

. . . At home we do not much quarrel; but perhaps the less we quarrel the more we hate. There is as much malignity amongst us as can well subsist, without any thoughts of daggers or poisons.

(LETTERS)

An Irishman's View of Johnson, 1775

Johnson, you are the very man Lord Chesterfield de-
scribes: — a Hottentot indeed, and tho' your abilities are
respectable, you never can be respected yourself. He has
the aspect of an Idiot, without the faintest ray of sense
gleaming from any one feature — with the most awkward
garb, and unpowdered grey wig, on one side only of his
head — he is for ever dancing the devil's jig, and sometimes he makes the most driveling effort to whistle some
thought in his absent paroxisms. He came up to me and
took me by the hand, then sat down on a sofa, and mum-
bled out that he had heard two papers had appeared
against him in the course of this week — one of which was
— that he was to go to Ireland next summer in order to
abuse the hospitality of that place also.

. . . The doctor as he drinks no wine, retired soon after
dinner, and Barretti, who I see is a sort of literary toad
eater to Johnson, told me that he was a man nowise affected by praise or dispraise, and that the journey to the
Hebrides would never have been published but for himself. The Doctor however returned again, and with all the
fond anxiety of an author, I saw him cast out all his nets
to know the sense of the town about his last pamphlet,
"Taxation no Tyranny," which he said did not sell. Mr.
Thrale told him such and such members of both houses
admired it, and why did you not tell me this, quoth Johnson. Thrale asked him what Sir Joshua Reynolds said of
it. Sir Joshua, quoth the Doctor, has not read it. I suppose, quoth Thrale, he has been very busy of late; no, says
the Doctor, but I never look at his pictures, so he won't
read my writings.

. . . Rainy morning. Sat an hour with Dr. Johnson

about noon. He was at breakfast with a Pindar in his
hand, and after saluting me with great cordiality, he, after
whistling in his way over Pindar, layed the book down,
and then told me he had seen my Lord Primate at Sir
Joshua's, and "I believe," says he, "I have not recommended myself much to him, for I differed widely in opinions from him, yet I hear he is doing good things in Ireland." I mentioned Skelton to him as a man of strong
imagination, and told him the story of his selling his library for the support of the poor. He seemed much affected by it, and then fell a rowling and muttering to himself, and I could hear him plainly say after several minutes
pause from conversation, "Skelton is a great good man."
    . . . I went to see Dr. Johnson, found him alone, Bar-
retti came soon after. Barretti (after some pause in conversation) asked me, if the *disturbances* were over in Ireland. I told him I had not heard of any disturbances
there. "What," says he, "have you not been up in arms?"
"Yes, and a great number of men continue so to be."
"And dont you call that disturbance?" returned Barretti.
"No," said I, "the Irish volunteers have demeaned themselves very peaceably, and instead of disturbing the peace
of the country, have contributed much to its preservation." The Doctor, who had been long silent, turned a
sharp ear to what I was saying, and with vehemence said,
"What Sir, dont you call it disturbance to oppose legal
government with arms in your hands, and compel it to
make laws in your favour? Sir, I call it rebellion; rebellion
as much as the rebellion of Scotland." "Doctor," said I,
"I am sorry to hear that fall from you, I must however say
that the Irish consider themselves as the most loyal of His
Majesty's subjects at the same that they firmly deny any
allegiance to a British Parliament. They have a separate
Legislature, and that they have never showed any incli-

nation to resist." " Sir," says the Doctor, " you do owe allegiance to the British Parliament as a *conquered* nation,
and had I been Minister I would have made you submit
to it. I would have done as Oliver Cromwell did; I would
have burned your cities, and wasted you in the fires (or
flames) of them." I, after allowing the Doctor to vent
his indignation upon Ireland, cooly replyed, " Doctor, the
times are altered, and I dont find that you have succeeded
so well in burning the cities, and roasting the inhabitants
of America." " Sir," says he gravely, and with a less vehement tone, " what you say is true, the times are altered, for
power is now nowhere, we live under a government of
influence, not of power; but Sir, had we treated the Americans as we ought, and as they deserved, we should have
at once razed all their towns, — and let them enjoy their
forests — ." After this wild rant, argument would but have
enraged him, I therefore let him vibrate into calmness,
then turning round to me, he, with a smile, says, " After all
Sir, though I hold the Irish to be rebels, I dont think they
have been so very wrong, but you know that you compelled our Parliament, by force of arms, to pass an act in
your favour. That, I call rebellion." " But Doctor," said I,
" did the Irish claim anything that ought not to have been
granted, though they had not made the claim." " Sir, I
wont dispute that matter with you, but what I insist upon
is that the mode of requisition was rebellious." " Well
Doctor, let me ask you but one question, and I shall ask
you no more on this subject, do you think that Ireland
would have obtained what it has got, by any other
means? " " Sir," says he candidly, " I believe it would not.
However, a wise government should not grant even a
claim of justice, if an attempt is made to extort it by
force." I said no more.

(DR. THOMAS CAMPBELL)

The American War of Independence

(1. *To Mrs. Thrale*)

August 1, 1775

DEAR MADAM,

I wonder how it could happen. I forgot that the post went out yesternight, and so omitted to write; I therefore put this by the by-post, and hope it will come, that I may not lose my regular letter.

This was to have been my last letter from this place, but Lucy says I must not go this week. Fits of tenderness with Mrs. Lucy are not common; but she seems now to have a little paroxysm, and I was not willing to counteract it. When I am to go I shall take care to inform you. The lady at Stowhill says, how comes Lucy to be such a sovereign, all the town besides could not have kept you.

America now fills every mouth, and some heads, and a little of it shall come into my letter. I do not much like the news. Our troops have indeed the superiority; five-and-twenty hundred have driven five thousand from their intrenchment; but the Americans fought skilfully; had coolness enough in the battle to carry off their men; and seem to have retreated orderly, for they were not pursued. They want nothing but confidence in their leaders, and familiarity with danger. Our business is to pursue their main army, and disperse it by a decisive battle; and then waste the country till they sue for peace. If we make war by parties and detachments, dislodge them from one place, and exclude them from another, we shall by a local, gradual, and ineffectual war, teach them our own knowledge, harden their obstinacy, and strengthen their confidence, and at last come to fight on equal terms of skill and bravery, without equal numbers.

(LETTERS)

(2. *To the Reverend John Wesley*)

Feb. 6, 1776

SIR,

When I received your Commentary on the Bible, I durst not at first flatter myself that I was to keep it, having so little claim to so valuable a present; and when Mrs. Hall informed me of your kindness, was hindered from time to time from returning you those thanks which I now entreat you to accept. I have thanks likewise to return you for the addition of your important suffrage to my argument on the American question. To have gained such a mind as yours may justly confirm me in my own opinion. What effect my paper has upon the public, I know not; but I have no reason to be discouraged. The lecturer was surely in the right, who, though he saw his audience slinking away, refused to quit the chair while Plato staid.

I am, reverend Sir,

Your most humble servant,

SAM: JOHNSON

A Tour in France with the Thrales, 1775

Notwithstanding the Disgust my last Journey gave me, I have lately been solicitous to undertake another.

So true is Johnson's Observation that any thing is better than Vacuity.

. . . Mr. Johnson has made a little Distich at every Place we have slept at, for example

A Calais	St Omer	Arras	A Amiens
Trop de frais.	Tout est cher.	Hélas!	On n'a rien.
Au Mouton			
Rien de Bon.			

. . . The Banks of the Seine however are surprizingly beautiful, & the whole Country carries an Air of Fertility that is inexpressibly delightful: to see Cherries, Apples, Grapes, Asparagus, Lentils & French Beans planted in large portions all around one, & inviting the Traveller to partake the Bounties of the Nation is so perfectly agreeable that one frets to see so many People *beg,* where one is morally certain nobody can starve.

These Reflexions are interrupted by the Recollection of a Frightful Accident which befel the Carriage in which were Mr Thrale, Baretti and the Girl: their Postillion fell off his Horse on a strong Descent, the Traces were broken, one of the Horses run over and the Chaise carried forwards with a most dangerous Rapidity, which Mr Thrale not being able to endure till somebody came up — jumped out with intent to stop the Horses for Baretti & Queeney — however he only hurt himself & they went on till Sam came up, who had been miserably embarrassed with a vicious Horse which had retarded him so long, and afterwards flung him. This was therefore a day of Distress, & my Master found himself so ill when we arrived at St Germains that the Surgeon he sent for, advised him to go on to Paris & get himself bled & take a good deal of Rest which he hoped would restore him. He left us therefore at St Germains & Mr Baretti kindly went with him to give him Assistance, & get us some Habitation to receive us at Paris. Dr Johnson's perfect unconcern for the Lives of three People, who would all have felt for his, shocked and amaz'd me, — but that, as Baretti says, is true Philosophy; Mrs Strickland did not give it so kind a Name, I soon saw her Indignation towards him prevailing over her Friendship for me.

. . . We have made it up all with Johnson who protests it was not unconcern for Mr Thrale but anger at me that

[made] him sullenly forbear Enquiry, when he found Me unwilling (as he thought it) to give him a ready or rational Answer.

(MRS. THRALE)

Accidents Never Happen

On this account he wished to travel all over the world; for the very act of going forward was delightful to him, and he gave himself no concern about accidents, which he said never happened: nor did the running-away of the horses on the edge of a precipice between Vernon and St. Denys in France convince him to the contrary; "for nothing came of it (he said), except that Mr. Thrale leaped out of the carriage into a chalkpit, and then came up again, looking *as white!*" When the truth was, all their lives were saved by the greatest providence ever exerted in favour of three human creatures; and the part Mr. Thrale took from desperation was the likeliest thing in the world to produce broken limbs and death.

(MRS. PIOZZI)

The French

(*To the Reverend Dr. Taylor*)

DEAR SIR,

I came back last Tuesday from France. Is not mine a kind of life turned upside down? Fixed to a spot when I was young, and roving the world when others are contriving to sit still, I am wholly unsettled. I am a kind of ship with a wide sail, and without an anchor.

Now I am come home, let me know how it is with you.

I hope you are well, and intend to keep your residence this year. Let me know the month, and I will contrive to be about you. Our friendship has now lasted so long, that it is valuable for its antiquity. Perhaps neither has any other companion to whom he can talk of his early years. Let me particularly know the state of your health. I think mine is the better for the journey.

The French have a clear air and fruitful soil, but their mode of common life is gross and incommodious, and disgusting. I am come home convinced that no improvement of general use is to be gained among them.

I am, dear Sir,

Your affectionate servant,

SAM: JOHNSON

London, Nov. 16, 1775

Johnson and Goldsmith

(1)

Dr. Johnson was not grave however because he knew not how to be merry. No man loved laughing better, and his vein of humour was rich, and apparently inexhaustible; though Dr. Goldsmith said once to him, We should change companions oftener, we exhaust one another, and shall soon be both of us worn out. Poor Goldsmith was to him indeed like the earthen pot to the iron one in Fontaine's fables; it had been better for *him* perhaps, that they had changed companions oftener; yet no experience of his antagonist's strength hindered him from continuing the contest. He used to remind me always of that verse in Berni,

> " *Il pover uomo che non sen' erà accorto,*
> *Andava combattendo — ed era morto.*"

Mr. Johnson made him a comical answer one day, when seeming to repine at the success of Beattie's Essay on Truth — " Here's such a stir (said he) about a fellow that has written one book, and I have written many." "Ah, Doctor (says his friend), there go two-and-forty sixpences you know to one guinea."

They had spent an evening with Eaton Graham too, I remember hearing it was at some tavern; his heart was open, and he began inviting away; told what he could do to make his college agreeable, and begged the visit might not be delayed. Goldsmith thanked him, and proposed setting out with Mr. Johnson for Buckinghamshire in a fortnight; " Nay hold, Dr. *Minor* (says the other), I did not invite you."

Many such mortifications arose in the course of their intimacy to be sure, but few more laughable than when the newspapers had tacked them together as the pedant and his flatterer in " Love's Labour lost." Dr. Goldsmith came to his friend, fretting and foaming, and vowing vengeance against the printer, &c. till Mr. Johnson, tired of the bustle, and desirous to think of something else, cried out at last, " Why, what would'st thou have, dear Doctor! who the plague is hurt with all this nonsense? and how is a man the worse I wonder in his health, purse, or character, for being called *Holofernes*? " " I do not know (replies the other) how you may relish being called Holofernes, but I do not like at least to play *Goodman Dull*."

(MRS. PIOZZI)

(2)

When I have told how many follies Dr. Johnson knew of others, I must not omit to mention with how much fidelity he would always have kept them concealed, could they of

whom he knew the absurdities have been contented, in the
common phrase, to keep their own counsel. But returning home one day from dining at the chaplain's table, he
told me, that Dr. Goldsmith had given a very comical and
unnecessarily exact recital there of his own feelings when
his play was hissed; telling the company how he went indeed to the Literary Club at night, and chatted gaily
among his friends, as if nothing had happened amiss; that
to impress them still more forcibly with an idea of his
magnanimity, he even sung his favourite song about an
old woman tossed in a blanket seventeen times as high
as the moon; " but all this while I was suffering horrid tor-
tures (said he), and verily believe that if I had put a bit
into my mouth it would have strangled me on the spot, I
was so excessively ill; but I made more noise than usual to
cover all that, and so they never perceived my not eating,
nor I believe at all imaged to themselves the anguish of
my heart: but when all were gone except Johnson here, I
burst out a-crying, and even swore by —— that I would
never write again." " All which, Doctor (says Mr. Johnson, amazed at his odd frankness), I thought had been a
secret between you and me; and I am sure I would not
have said any thing about it for the world." " Now see
(repeated he when he told the story) what a figure a man
makes who thus unaccountably chuses to be the frigid
narrator of his own disgrace. *Il volto sciolto, ed i pensieri
stretti,* was a proverb made on purpose for such mortals,
to keep people, if possible, from being thus the heralds of
their own shame: for what compassion can they gain by
such silly narratives? No man should be expected to sympathise with the sorrows of vanity. If then you are mortified by any ill usage, whether real or supposed, keep at
least the account of such mortifications to yourself, and

forbear to proclaim how meanly you are thought on by others, unless you desire to be meanly thought of by all."

(MRS. PIOZZI)

Trundle

The little history of another friend's superfluous ingenuity will contribute to introduce a similar remark. He had a daughter of about fourteen years old, as I remember, fat and clumsy: and though the father adored, and desired others to adore her, yet being aware perhaps that she was not what the French call *paitrie des graces,* and thinking I suppose that the old maxim, of beginning to laugh at yourself first where you have anything ridiculous about you, was a good one, he comically enough called his girl *Trundle* when he spoke of her; and many who bore neither of them any ill-will felt disposed to laugh at the happiness of the appellation. " See now (says Dr. Johnson) what haste people are in to be hooted. Nobody ever thought of this fellow nor of his daughter, could he but have been quiet himself, and forborne to call the eyes of the world on his dowdy and her deformity. But it teaches one to see at least, that if nobody else will nickname one's children, the parents will e'en do it themselves."

(MRS. PIOZZI)

Happiness

Mr. Johnson did not like any one who said they were happy, or who said any one else was so. " It is all *cant* (he would cry), the dog knows he is miserable all the time." A friend whom he loved exceedingly, told him on some occasion notwithstanding, that his wife's sister was *really* happy, and called upon the lady to confirm his assertion, which she did somewhat roundly as we say, and with an accent and manner capable of offending Mr. Johnson, if her position had not been sufficient, without anything more, to put him in very ill humour. " If your sister-in-law is really the contented being she professes herself Sir (said he), her life gives the lie to every research of humanity; for she is happy without health, without beauty, without money, and without understanding." This story he told me himself; and when I expressed something of the horror I felt, " The same stupidity (said he) which prompted her to extol felicity she never felt, hindered her from feeling what shocks you on repetition. I tell you, the woman is ugly, and sickly, and foolish, and poor; and would it not make a man hang himself to hear such a creature say, it was happy? "

(MRS. PIOZZI)

An Apology

Neither did he always like to be over-fondled; when a certain gentleman out-acted his part in this way, he is said to have demanded of him — " What provokes your risibility, Sir? Have I said any thing that you understand? — Then I ask pardon of the rest of the company — "

(RICHARD CUMBERLAND)

Johnson Scored Off

(1)

Miss Johnson, one of Sir Joshua's nieces (afterwards Mrs. Deane), was dining one day at her uncle's with Dr. Johnson and a large party: the conversation happening to turn on music, Johnson spoke very contemptuously of that art, and added, " that no man of talent, or whose mind was capable of better things, ever would or could devote his time and attention to so idle and frivolous a pursuit." The young lady, who was very fond of music, whispered her next neighbour, " I wonder what Dr. Johnson thinks of King David." Johnson overheard her, and, with great good humour and complacency, said, " Madam, I thank you; I stand rebuked before you, and promise that, on one subject at least, you shall never hear me talk nonsense again."

(CROKER)

(2)

Dr. Johnson called one morning on Mr. West [the painter] to converse with him on American affairs. After some time Mr. West said that he had a young American [Gilbert Stuart] living with him, from whom he might derive some information, and introduced Stuart. The conversation continued (Stuart being thus invited to take a part in it), when the Doctor observed to Mr. West that the young man spoke very good English; and turning to Stuart rudely asked him where he had learned it. Stuart very promptly replied, " Sir, I can better tell you where I did not learn it — it was not from your dictionary." Johnson seemed aware of his own abruptness, and was not offended.

(GILBERT STUART)

The Death of Harry Thrale

(*To Mrs. Thrale*)

Lichfield, March 25, 1776

DEAR MADAM,

This letter will not, I hope, reach you many days before me; in a distress which can be so little relieved, nothing remains for a friend but to come and partake it.

Poor dear sweet little boy! When I read the letter this day to Mrs. Aston, she said, " Such a death is the next to translation." Yet however I may convince myself of this, the tears are in my eyes, and yet I could not love him as you loved him, nor reckon upon him for a future comfort as you and his father reckoned upon him.

He is gone, and we are going! We could not have enjoyed him long, and shall not long be separated from him. He has probably escaped many such pangs as you are now feeling.

Nothing remains, but that with humble confidence we resign ourselves to Almighty Goodness, and fall down, without irreverent murmurs, before the Sovereign Distributor of good and evil, with hope that though sorrow endureth for a night yet joy may come in the morning.

I have known you, Madam, too long to think that you want any arguments for submission to the Supreme Will; nor can my consolation have any effect but that of showing that I wish to comfort you. What can be done you must do for yourself. Remember first, that your child is happy; and then, that he is safe, not only from the ills of this world, but from those more formidable dangers which extend their mischief to eternity. You have brought into the world a rational being; have seen him happy during the little life that has been granted him; and can have no doubt but that his happiness is now permanent and immutable.

When you have obtained by prayer such tranquillity as nature will admit, force your attention, as you can, upon your accustomed duties and accustomed entertainments. You can do no more for our dear boy, but you must not therefore think less on those whom your attention may make fitter for the place to which he is gone.

I am, dearest, dearest Madam,

Your most affectionate humble servant,

SAM: JOHNSON

The Thrale Babies

(*To Mrs. Thrale*)

[*London*] *May* 11, 1776

DEAR MADAM,

That you may have no superfluous uneasiness, I went this afternoon to visit the two babies at Kensington, and found them indeed a little spotted with their disorder, but as brisk and gay as health and youth can make them. I took a paper of sweetmeats, and spread them on the table. They took great delight to shew their governess the various animals that were made of sugar; and when they had eaten as much as was fit, the rest were laid up for to-morrow.

Susy sends her duty and love with great propriety. Sophy sends her duty to you, and her love to Queeney and Papa. Mr. Evans came in after me. You may set your heart quite at rest, no babies can be better than they appear to be. Dr. Taylor went with me, and we staid a good while. He likes them very much. Susy said her creed in French.

. . . I am, &c.,

SAM: JOHNSON

Boswell Shrinks from the Baltic

(To Mrs. Thrale)

Ashbourne, Sept. 13, 1777

DEAR MADAM,

Now I write again, having just received your letter dated the 10th.

You must not let foolish fancies take hold on your imagination. If Queeney grows tall, she is sufficiently bulky, and as much out of danger of a consumption as nature allows a young maiden to be. Of real evils the number is great, of possible evils there is no end. * * * * * is really to be pitied. Her son in danger; the estate likely to pass not only from her, but to those on whom, I suppose, she would least wish it bestowed, and her system of life broken, are very heavy blows. But she will at last be rich, and will have much gratification in her power, both rational and sensual.

Boswell, I believe, is coming. He talks of being here today. I shall be glad to see him. But he shrinks from the Baltick expedition, which I think is the best scheme in our power. What we shall substitute, I know not. He wants to see Wales, but except the woods of Bachycraigh what is there in Wales? What can fill the hunger of ignorance, or quench the thirst of curiosity? We may perhaps form some scheme or other, but, in the phrase of Hockley in the Hole, it is a pity he has not a better bottom.

Tell my young mistress that this day's letter is too short, and it brings me no news either foreign or domestick.

I am going to dine with Mr. Dyot, and Frank tells sternly, that it is past two o'clock.

I am, dearest Madam,

Your, &c.,

SAM: JOHNSON

Johnson and Queeney Thrale

[*Ashbourne*] *Nov.* 28, 1772

DEAR MISS,

Mamma used us both very sorrily when she hindered
you from writing to me. She dos not know how much
I should love to read your lettters, if they were a little
longer. But we shall soon, I hope, talk matters all over.
I have not had the luck this journey to pick up any curiosities for the cabinet. I would have been glad to bring
you something, if I could have found it.

I hope you go often to see dear Grandmamma. We
must all do what we can to help her and please her, and
take great care now she is so bad, not to make her worse.

You said nothing of Lucy, I suppose she is grown a
pretty good scholar, and a very good playfellow; after dinner we shall have good sport playing all together, and we
will none of us cry.

Make my compliments to Grandmamma, and Papa, and
Mamma, and all the young ones. I am

Dearest Miss,

Your most humble servant,

SAM: JOHNSON

[*London*] 25 *Dec.* 1779

Pray, my dear Love, take the first opportunity of sending
me my watch, which I left at the Bed. I hope there is no
need of telling you, that I wish you all, every good of the
season, and of every Season.

I am, dear Sweet,

Your most humble servant,

SAM: JOHNSON

To Miss Thrale, at Streatham

[London] Wednesday, Dec. 29 [1779]

DEAR LOVE,

I wrote to you some days ago to send me my watch which I forgot; and you have not sent it, which is not kind. Let me have it as soon as ever you can.

> I am, dear Love,
> Your humble servant,
> SAM: JOHNSON

To Miss Thrale

London, 28 Aug. 1780

MY DEAR CHARMER,

I am very obliged to you for your pretty letters. On Saturday I opened my letter with terrour, but soon found that all is mending. Every thing that I have ever proposed for Mr. Thrale has been found right in the event. We must all combine, as propriety shall permit, to impress him with the true opinion of his danger, for without that he will naturally be negligent of himself, and inattentive to his own sensations. Dr. Laurence is of opinion that the tendency to an apoplexy might always be perceived by one who knew how to distinguish it, and if it was perceived at any distance it might be certainly prevented. But if we cannot teach him to watch his own state of body, we must all watch for him as we can.

It is well for me that a Lady so celebrated as Miss Thrale can find time to write to me. I will recompense your condescension with a maxim. Never treat old friends with neglect however easily you may find new. There is a tenderness which seems the meer growth of time, but which is in [fact] the effect [of] many combinations; those with whom we have shared enjoyments, we remember with pleasure, those with whom we have shared sorrow, we remember with tenderness. You must already have begun to observe that you love a book, or a box, or an instrument that you have had a great part of your life, because it brings a great part of your life back to your view. You can never say that your [you love?] a very late acquaintance; you can only like, or only admire. As others stand to you, must you stand to others, and must therefore [know] that no new acquaintance much love you, and therefore if you quit old friends for them, you slight those who love you more in favour of those that love you less. This I hope you will remember, and practice, though far the greater part forget it, and therefore have no friend, as none they deserve.

I have been very grave, but you are a very thinking Lady. We shall now meet in a little time, I hope again, and love each other better and better.

Now am I turning to the second leaf just as if I was writing to your Mamma.

Dr. Burney and Fanny and Sophy are gone to be happy with Mr. Crisp, and Mrs. Burney and Susan are left at home, and I am to go see them; indeed I have no other visit to make hardly, except that blind Mrs. Hervey has sent me a peremptory summons to dine with her on Thursday, and I have promised to go lest she should think me intentionally uncivil; and you know, I am the civillest creature in nature.

Seward called on me two days ago, to get help for a poor woman. This is all the news you can have from

Madam,

Your most humble servant,

SAM: JOHNSON

The Kindness of the Thrales

(To Mrs. Thrale)

[Ashbourne] October 13, 1777

DEAR MADAM,

Yet I do love to hear from you. Such pretty kind letters as you send. But it gives me great delight to find that my master misses me. I begin to wish myself with you more than I should do, if I were wanted less. It is a good thing to stay away till one's company is desired, but not so good to stay after it is desired.

I cannot but think on your kindness and my master's. Life has, upon the whole, fallen short, very short, of my early expectation: but the acquisition of such a friendship, at an age when new friendships are seldom acquired, is something better than the general course of things gives man a right to expect. I think on it with great delight, I am not very apt to be delighted.

I am, &c.,

SAM: JOHNSON

(To Mrs. Thrale)

Lichfield, October 29, 1777

DEAR MADAM,

Though after my last letter I might justly claim an interval of rest, yet I write again to tell you, that for this turn you will hear but once more from Lichfield. This day is Wednesday, on Saturday I shall write again, and on Monday I shall set out to seek adventures; for you know,

None but the brave deserve the fair.

On Monday we hope to see Birmingham, the seat of the mechanick arts; and know not whether our next stage will be Oxford, the mansion of the liberal arts; or London, the residence of all the arts together. The chymists call the world *Academia Paracelsi;* my ambition is to be his fellow-student — to see the works of nature, and hear the lectures of truth. To London therefore — London may perhaps fill me; and I hope to fill my part of London.

In the mean time, let me continue to keep the part which I have had so long in your kindness, and my master's; for if that should grow less, I know not where to find that which may supply the diminution. But I hope what I have been so happy as to gain I shall have the happiness of keeping.

(LETTERS)

Nollekens, the Sculptor

(To Mrs. Porter)

London, Nov. 20, 1777

DEAR LOVE,

You ordered me to write you word when I came home. I have been for some days at Brighthelmstone, and came back on Tuesday night.

You know that when I left you I was not well; I have taken physic very diligently, and am perceptibly better; so much better that I hope by care and perseverance to recover, and see you again from time to time.

Mr. Nollekens, the statuary, has had my direction to send you a cast of my head.* I will pay the carriage when

---

* " Johnson was very much displeased at the manner in which the head had been loaded with hair, which the sculptor insisted upon, as it made him look more like an ancient poet. It had been modelled from the flowing locks of a sturdy Irish beggar, originally a street pavior, who, after he had sat an

we meet. Let me know how you like it; and what the ladies of your rout say to it. I have heard different opinions. I cannot think where you can put it.

I found every body here well. Miss (Queeney) has a mind to be womanly, and her womanhood does not sit well upon her. Please to make my compliments to all the ladies and all the gentlemen to whom I owe them, that is, to a great part of the town.

I am, dear Madam,

Your most humble servant,

SAM: JOHNSON

Fears of a French Invasion

In the year 1777, or thereabouts, when all the talk was of an invasion, he said most pathetically one afternoon, " Alas! alas! how this unmeaning stuff spoils all my comfort in my friends' conversation! Will the people never have done with it; and shall I never hear a sentence again without the *French* in it? Here is no invasion coming, and you *know* there is none. Let the vexatious and frivolous talk alone, or suffer it at least to teach you *one* truth; and learn by this perpetual echo of even unapprehended distress, how historians magnify events expected, or calamities endured; when you know they are at this very moment collecting all the big words they can find, in which to describe a consternation never felt, for a misfortune

hour, refused to take a shilling, stating that he could have made more by begging. * * * Upon hearing the name of an eminent sculptor mentioned Johnson observed: – ' Well, Sir, I think my friend Joe Nollekens can chop out a head with any of them.' " *Nollekens and his Times,* by J. T. Smith.

which never happened. Among all your lamentations, who eats the less? Who sleeps the worse, for one general's ill success, or another's capitulation? "

(MRS. PIOZZI)

Mr. Thrale's Stroke

Mr. Thrale has felt a very heavy blow. He was for some time without reason, and, I think, without utterance. Heberden was in great doubt whether his powers of mind would ever return. He has however perfectly recovered all his faculties and all his vigour. He has a fontanel in his back. I make little doubt but that, notwithstanding your dismal prognostication, you may see one another again.

He purposes this autumn to spend some time in hunting on the downs of Sussex. I hope you are diligent to take as much exercise as you can bear. I had rather you rode twice a day than tired yourself in the morning. I take the true definition of exercise to be labour without weariness.

When I left you, there hung over you a cloud of discontent which is I hope dispersed. Drive it away as fast as you can. Sadness only multiplies self. Let us do our duty, and be cheerful.

Dear Sir, your humble Servant,

SAM: JOHNSON

August 3, 1779
To the Rev^d Dr. Taylor at Ashbourne, Derbyshire

Mr. Thrale Better

(To the Reverend Dr. Taylor)

DEAR SIR,

Mr. Thrale, after whose case you will have a natural curiosity, is with his family at Brighthelmston. He rides very vigorously, and runs much into company, and is very angry if it be thought that any thing ails him. Mrs. Thrale thinks him for the present in no danger. I had no mind to go with them, for I have had what Brighthelmston can give, and I know not they much wanted me.

I have had a little catch of the gout; but as I have had no great opinion of the benefits which it is supposed to convey, I made haste to be easy, and drove it away after two days.

Publick affairs continue to go on without much mending, and there are those still who either fright themselves or would fright others with an invasion; but my opinion is that the French neither have nor had in any part of the Summer a number of ships on the opposite coast equal to the transportation of twenty or of ten thousand Men. Such a fleet cannot be hid in a creek, it must be safely visible and yet I believe no man has seen the man that has seen it. The ships of war were within sight of Plymouth, and only within sight.

I wish, I knew how your health stands. My friends congratulate me upon my looks, and indeed I am very free from some of the most troublesome of my old complaints, but I have gained this relief by very steady use of mercury and purgatives, with some opium, and some abstinence. I have eaten more fruit this summer than perhaps in any since I was twenty years old, but though it certainly did me no harm, I know not that I had any medicinal good from it.

Write to me soon. We are both old. How few of those whom we have known in our youth are left alive! May we yet live to some better purpose.

I am, Sir, your most humble Servant,

SAM: JOHNSON

London, Oct. 19, 1779
To the Rev^d Dr. Taylor in Ashbourne, Derbyshire

Reviewing the Past Year, Easter, 1778

Monday, Apr. 20 [1778]

After a good night, as I am forced to reckon, I rose seasonably, and prayed, using the collect for yesterday.

In reviewing my time from Easter —77, I find a very melancholy and shameful blank. So little has been done that days and months are without any trace. My health has indeed been very much interrupted. My nights have been commonly not only restless but painful and fatiguing. My respiration was once so difficult, that an asthma was suspected. I could not walk but with great difficulty, from Stowhill to Greenhill. Some relaxation of my breast has been procured, I think, by opium, which, though it never gives me sleep, frees my breast from spasms.

I have written a little of the Lives of the poets, I think with all my usual vigour. I have made sermons, perhaps as readily as formerly. My memory is less faithful in retaining names, and, I am afraid, in retaining occurrences. Of this vacillation and vagrancy of mind I impute a great part to a fortuitous and unsettled life, and therefore purpose to spend my time with more method.

This year, the 28th of March passed away without memorial. Poor Tetty, whatever were our faults and failings, we loved each other. I did not forget thee yesterday. Couldest thou have lived! —

I am now, with the help of God, to begin a new life.

(PRAYERS AND MEDITATIONS)

Fanny Burney and Johnson . . . first Impressions

[*Aug.* 1778.] When we were summoned to dinner, Mrs. Thrale made my father and me sit on each side of her. I said that I hoped I did not take Dr. Johnson's place — for he had not yet appeared.

" No," answered Mrs. Thrale, " he will sit by you, which I am sure will give him great pleasure."

Soon after we were seated, this great man entered. I have so true a veneration for him, that the very sight of him inspires me with delight and reverence, notwithstanding the cruel infirmities to which he is subject; for he has almost perpetual convulsive movements, either of his hands, lips, feet, or knees, and sometimes of all together.

. . . Sir John Hawkins

The next name that was started was that of Sir John Hawkins; and Mrs. Thrale said, " Why now, Dr. Johnson, he is another of those whom you suffer nobody to abuse but yourself; Garrick is one, too; for if any other person speaks against him, you browbeat him in a minute! "

" Why, madam," answered he, " they don't know when to abuse him, and when to praise him; I will allow no man to speak ill of David that he does not deserve; and as to Sir John, why really I believe him to be an honest man at the bottom: but to be sure he is penurious, and he is mean, and it must be owned he has a degree of brutality, and a tendency to savageness, that cannot easily be defended."

We all laughed, as he meant we should, at this curious manner of speaking in his favour, and he then related an anecdote that he said he knew to be true in regard to his meanness. He said that Sir John and he once belonged to the same club, but that as he eat no supper after the first night of his admission, he desired to be excused paying his share.

" And was he excused? "

" Oh yes; for no man is angry at another for being inferior to himself! we all scorned him, and admitted his plea. For my part, I was such a fool as to pay my share for wine, though I never tasted any. But Sir John was a most *unclubable* man! "

. . . Bet Flint

" Bet Flint! " cried Mrs. Thrale; " pray who is she? "

" Oh, a fine character, madam! She was habitually a slut and a drunkard, and occasionally a thief and a harlot."

" And, for heaven's sake, how came you to know her? "

" Why, madam, she figured in the literary world, too! Bet Flint wrote her own life, and called herself Cassandra, and it was in verse; — it began:

> ' When Nature first ordained my birth,
> A diminutive I was born on earth,
> And then I came from a dark abode,
> Into a gay and gaudy world.'

So Bet brought me her verses to correct; but I gave her half-a-crown, and she liked it as well. Bet had a fine spirit; she advertised for a husband, but she had no suc⸗ cess, for she told me no man aspired to her! Then she hired very handsome lodgings and a footboy; and she got a harpsichord, but Bet could not play; however, she put herself in fine attitudes, and drummed."

Then he gave an account of another of these geniuses, who called herself by some fine name, I have forgotten what.

" She had not quite the same stock of virtue," continued he, " nor the same stock of honesty as Bet Flint; but I suppose she envied her accomplishments, for she was so little moved by the power of harmony, that while Bet Flint thought she was drumming very divinely, the other jade had her indicted for a nuisance! "

" And pray what became of her, sir? "

" Why, madam, she stole a quilt from the man of the house, and he had her taken up: but Bet Flint had a spirit not to be subdued; so when she found herself obliged to go to jail, she ordered a sedan chair and bid her footboy walk before her. However, the footboy proved refractory, for he was ashamed, though his mistress was not."

" And did she ever get out of jail again, sir? "

" Yes, madam; when she came to her trial, the judge acquitted her. ' So now,' she said to me, ' the quilt is my own, and now I'll make a petticoat of it.' Oh, I loved Bet Flint! "

. . . "And Mrs. Williams," he added, " did not love Bet Flint, but Bet Flint made herself very easy about that."

. . . Mrs. Montagu

Mrs. T. — To-morrow, sir, Mrs. Montagu dines here, and then you will have talk enough.

Dr. Johnson began to see-saw, with a countenance strongly expressive of inward fun, and after enjoying it some time in silence, he suddenly, and with great animation, turned to me and cried,

" Down with her, Burney! — down with her! — spare her not! — attack her, fight her, and down with her at once! You are a rising wit, and she is at the top; and when I was beginning the world, and was nothing and nobody, the joy of my life was to fire at all the established wits! and then everybody loved to halloo me on. But there is no game now; everybody would be glad to see me conquered: but then, when I was new, to vanquish the great ones was all the delight of my poor little dear soul! So at her, Burney — at her, and down with her! "

. . . civil for Four

I have had a thousand delightful conversations with Dr. Johnson, who, whether he loves me or not, I am sure seems to have some opinion of my discretion, for he speaks of all this house to me with unbounded confidence, neither diminishing faults, nor exaggerating praise. Whenever he is below stairs he keeps me a prisoner, for he does not like I should quit the room a moment; if I rise, he constantly calls out, " Don't you go, little Burney! "

Last night, when we were talking of compliments and of gross speeches, Mrs. Thrale most justly said, that nobody could make either like Dr. Johnson. " Your compliments, sir, are made seldom, but when they are made they have an elegance unequalled; but then when you are angry, who dares make speeches so bitter and so cruel? "

Dr. J. — Madam, I am always sorry when I make bitter

speeches, and I never do it but when I am insufferably vexed.

Mrs. T. — Yes, sir; but you suffer things to vex you that nobody else would vex at. I am sure I have had my share of scolding from you!

Dr. J. — It is true, you have; but you have borne it like an angel, and you have been the better for it.

Mrs. T. — That I believe, sir; for I have received more instruction from you than from any man, or any book: and the vanity that you should think me worth instructing always overcame the vanity of being found fault with. And so you had the scolding, and I the improvement.

F. B. — And I am sure both make for the honour of both!

Dr. J. — I think so too. But Mrs. Thrale is a sweet creature, and never angry; she has a temper the most delightful of any woman I ever knew.

Mrs. T. — This I can tell you, sir, and without any flattery — I not only bear your reproofs when present, but in almost everything I do in your absence, I ask myself whether you would like it, and what you would say to it. Yet I believe there is nobody you dispute with oftener than me.

F. B. — But you two are so well established with one another, that you can bear rebuff that would kill a stranger.

Dr. J. — Yes; but we disputed the same before we were so well established with one another.

Mrs. T. — Oh, sometimes I think I shall die no other death than hearing the bitter things he says to others. What he says to myself I can bear, because I know how sincerely he is my friend and that he means to mend me; but to others it is cruel.

Dr. J. — Why, madam, you often provoke me to say

severe things, by unreasonable commendation. If you would not call for my praise, I would not give you my censure; but it constantly moves my indignation to be applied to, to speak well of a thing which I think contemptible.

F. B. — Well, this I know, whoever I may hear complain of Dr. Johnson's severity, I shall always vouch for his kindness, as far as regards myself, and his indulgence.

Mrs. T. — Ay, but I hope he will trim you yet, too!

Dr. J. — I hope not: I should be very sorry to say anything that should vex my dear little Burney.

F. B. — If you did, sir, it would vex me more than you can imagine. I should sink in a minute.

Mrs. T. — I remember, sir, when we were travelling in Wales, how you called me to account for my civility to the people; "Madam," you said, "let me have no more of this idle commendation of nothing. Why is it, that whatever you see, and whoever you see, you are to be so indiscriminately lavish of praise?" "Why, I'll tell you, sir," said I, "when I am with you, and Mr. Thrale, and Queeny, I am obliged to be civil for four!"

. . . family Affairs

As my dear father spent the rest of the day here, I will not further particularise, but leave accounts to his better communication. He probably told you that the P—— family came in to tea; and, as he knows Mrs. P——, pray tell him what Dr. Johnson says of her. When they were gone, Mrs. Thrale complained that she was quite worn out with that tiresome silly woman, who had talked of her family and affairs till she was sick to death of hearing her.

"Madam," said he, "why do you blame the woman for

the only sensible thing she could do — talking of her family and her affairs? For how should a woman who is as empty as a drum, talk upon any other subject? — If you speak to her of the sun, she does not know it rises in the east; — if you speak to her of the moon, she does not know it changes at the full; — if you speak to her of the queen, she does not know she is the king's wife; — how, then, can you blame her for talking of her family and affairs? "

Dr. Johnson has more fun, and comical humour, and love of nonsense about him, than almost anybody I ever saw: I mean when with those he likes; for otherwise, he can be as severe and as bitter as report relates him.

Do you know I have been writing to Dr. Johnson! I tremble to mention it; but he sent a message in a letter to Mrs. Thrale, to wonder why his pupils did not write to him, and to hope they did not forget him. Miss Thrale therefore wrote a letter immediately, and I added only this little postscript: — "P.S. Dr. Johnson's other pupil a little longs to add a few lines to this letter, — but knows too well that all she has to say might be comprised in signing herself his obliged and most obedient servant, F. B.: so that's better than a long rigmarole about nothing."

(Johnson's comment in a letter to Mrs. Thrale — "Queeney sent me a pretty letter, to which —— added a silly short note, in such a silly white hand, that I was glad it was no longer.")

(FANNY BURNEY)

A Quaker Convert

Behold, dear Mrs. Mompessan, the promised minutes of that curious conversation which once passed at Mr. Dilly's, the bookseller, in a literary party, formed by Dr.

Johnson, Mr. Boswell, Dr. Mayo, and others, whom Mrs.
Knowles and myself had been invited to meet, and in
which Dr. Johnson and that lady disputed so earnestly.
It is, however, previously necessary that you should know
the history of the very amiable young woman who was
the subject of their debate.

Miss Jenny Harry that was, for she afterwards married,
and died ere the first nuptial year expired, was the daughter of a rich planter in the East Indies. He sent her over
to England to receive her education, in the house of his
friend, Mr. Spry, where Mrs. Knowles, the celebrated
quaker, was frequently a visitor. Mr. Spry affected wit,
and was perpetually rallying Mrs. Knowles on the subject of her quakerism, in the presence of this young, gentle and ingenuous girl; who, at the age of eighteen, had
received what is called a proper education, one of modern accomplishments, without having been much instructed in the nature and grounds of her religious belief. Upon these visits Mrs. Knowles was often led into a
serious defence of quaker-principles. She speaks with
clear and graceful eloquence on every subject. Her an-
tagonists were shallow theologists, and opposed only idle
and pointless raillery to deep and long-studied reasoning
on the precepts of Scripture, uttered in persuasive ac-
cents, and clothed with all the beauty of language. Without any *design* of making a proselyte she gained one.

Miss Harry grew pensively serious, and meditated perpetually on all which had dropt from the lips of Mrs.
Knowles on a theme, the infinite importance of which she
then, perhaps, first began to feel. At length her imagination pursuing this its primal religious bias, she believed
quakerism the only true Christianity. Beneath such conviction, she thought it her duty to join, at every hazard of
worldly interest, that class of worshippers. On declaring

these sentiments, several ingenious clergymen were commissioned to reason with her; but we all know the force of first impressions in theology. This young lady was argued with by the divines, and threatened by her guardian in vain. She persisted in resigning her splendid expectations for what appeared to her the path of duty.

Her father, on being made acquainted with her changed faith, informed her that she might choose between an hundred thousand pounds and his favour, or two thousand pounds and his renunciation, as she continued a churchwoman or commenced a quaker.

Miss Harry lamented her father's displeasure, but thanked him for the pecuniary alternative, assuring him that it included all her wishes as to fortune.

Soon after she left her guardian's house, and boarded in that of Mrs. Knowles; to her she often observed, that Dr. Johnson's displeasure, whom she had seen frequently at her guardian's, and who had always appeared fond of her, was amongst the greatest mortifications of her then situation. Once she came home in tears, and told her friend she had met Dr. Johnson in the street, and had ventured to ask him how he did; but that he would not deign to answer her, and walked scornfully on. She added, " you are to meet him soon at Mr. Dilly's — plead for me."

Thus far as prefatory to those requested minutes, which I made at the time of the ensuing conversation. It commenced with Mrs. Knowles saying, — " I am to ask thy indulgence, Doctor, towards a gentle female to whom thou usedst to be kind, and who is uneasy at the loss of that kindness. Jenny Harry weeps at the consciousness that thou wilt not speak to her."

" Madam, I hate the odious wench, and desire you will not talk to me about her."

"Yet what is her crime, Doctor?"—"Apostacy, Madam; apostacy from the community in which she was educated."

"Surely the quitting one community for another cannot be a crime, if it is done from motives of conscience. Hadst thou been educated in the Romish church, I must suppose thou wouldst have abjured its errors, and that there would have been merit in the abjuration."

"Madam, if I had been educated in the Roman Catholic faith, I believe I should have questioned my right to quit the religion of my fathers; therefore, well may I hate the arrogance of a young wench, who sets herself up for a judge on theological points, and deserts the religion in whose bosom she was nurtured."

"She has not done so; the name and the faith of Christians are not denied to the sectaries."

"If the name is not, the common sense is."

"I will not dispute this point with thee, Doctor, at least at present, it would carry us too far. Suppose it granted, that, in the mind of a young girl, the weaker arguments appeared the strongest, her want of better judgment should excite thy pity, not thy resentment."

"Madam, it has my anger and my contempt, and always will have them."

"Consider, Doctor, she must be *sincere.*—Consider what a noble fortune she has sacrificed."

"Madam, Madam, I have never taught myself to consider that the association of folly can extenuate guilt."

"Ah! Doctor, we cannot rationally suppose that the Deity will not pardon a defect in judgment (supposing it should prove one) in that breast where the consideration of serving him, according to its idea, in spirit and truth, has been a preferable inducement to that of worldly interest."

" Madam, I pretend not to set bounds to the mercy of the Deity; but I hate the wench, and shall ever hate her. I hate all impudence; but the impudence of a chit's apostacy I *nauseate*."

" Jenny is a very gentle creature. — She trembles to have offended her parent, though far removed from his presence; she grieves to have offended her guardian, and she is sorry to have offended Dr. Johnson, whom she loved, admired, and honoured."

" Why, then, Madam, did she not consult the man whom she pretends to have loved, admired, and honoured, upon her newfangled scruples? If she had looked up to that man with any degree of the respect she professes, she would have supposed his ability to judge of fit and right, at least equal to that of a raw wench just out of her primmer."

" Ah! Doctor, remember it was not from amongst the witty and the learned that Christ selected his disciples, and constituted the teachers of his precepts. Jenny thinks Dr. Johnson great and good; but she also thinks the gospel demands and enjoins a simpler form of worship than that of the established church; and that it is not in wit and eloquence to supersede the force of what appears to her a plain and regular system, which cancels all typical and mysterious ceremonies, as fruitless and even idolatrous; and asks only obedience to its injunctions, and the ingenuous homage of a devout heart."

" The homage of a fool's-head, madam, you should say, if you will pester me about the ridiculous wench."

" If thou choosest to suppose her ridiculous, thou canst not deny that she had been religious, sincere, disinterested. Canst thou believe that the gate of Heaven will be shut to the tender and pious mind, whose *first* consideration has been that of apprehended duty? "

" Pho, pho, Madam, who says it will? "

" Then if Heaven shuts not its gate, shall man shut his heart? — If the Deity accept the homage of such as sincerely serve him under every form of worship, Dr. Johnson and this humble girl will, it is to be hoped, meet in a blessed eternity, whither human animosity must *not* be carried."

" Madam, I am not fond of meeting fools anywhere; they are detestable company, and while it is in my power to avoid conversing with them, I certainly shall exert that power; and so you may tell the odious wench whom you have persuaded to think herself a saint, and of whom you will, I suppose, make a preacher; but I shall take care she does not preach to *me*."

The loud and angry tone in which he thundered out these replies to his calm and able antagonist, frightened us all, except Mrs. Knowles, who gently, not sarcastically, smiled at his injustice. Mr. Boswell whispered me, " I never saw this mighty lion so chafed before."

(ANNA SEWARD)

Easter, 1779

1779, *Good Friday, Apr. 2*

After a night restless and oppressive, I rose this morning somewhat earlier than is usual, and having taken tea which was very necessary to compose the disorder in my breast, having eaten nothing I went to church with Boswel. We came late, I was able to attend the litany with little perturbation. When we came home I began the first to the Thess. having prayed by the collect for the right use of the Scriptures. I gave Boswel Les Pensèes de Pascal that he might not interrupt me. I did not, I believe, read very diligently, and before I had read far, we went to Church again; I was again attentive. At home I read again, then drank tea with a bun and an half, thinking myself less able to fast, than at former times; and then concluded the Epistle. Being much oppressed with drowsiness, I slept about an hour by the fire.

11 p.m.

I am now to review the last year, and find little but dismal vacuity, neither business nor pleasure; much intended and little done. My health is much broken; my nights afford me little rest. I have tried opium, but its help is counterbalanced with great disturbance; it prevents the spasms, but it hinders sleep. O God, have mercy on me.

Last week I published the lives of the poets, written I hope in such a manner as may tend to the promotion of Piety.

In this last year I have made little acquisition, I have scarcely read any thing. I maintain Mrs. Desmoulins and her daughter, other good of myself I know not where to find, except a little Charity.

But I am now in my seventieth year; what can be done ought not to be delayed.

(PRAYERS AND MEDITATIONS)

The Gordon Riots

(*To Mrs. Thrale*)

London, [Friday] June 9, 1780

DEAR MADAM,

To the question, Who was impressed with consternation? it may with great truth be answered, that every body was impressed, for nobody was sure of his safety.

On Friday [June 2] the good Protestants met in St.

George's Fields, at the summons of Lord George Gordon,
and marching to Westminster, insulted the Lords and
Commons, who all bore it with great tameness. At night
the outrages began by the demolition of the mass-house
by Lincoln's Inn.

An exact journal of a week's defiance of government I
cannot give you. On Monday, [June 5], Mr. Strahan, who
had been insulted, spoke to Lord Mansfield, who had I
think been insulted too, of the licentiousness of the popu-
lace; and his Lordship treated it as a very slight irregu-
larity. On Tuesday night they pulled down Fielding's
house, and burnt his goods in the street. They had gut-
ted on Monday Sir George Savile's house, but the building
was saved. On Tuesday [June 6] evening, leaving Fielding's ruins, they went to Newgate to demand their companions who had been seized demolishing the chapel.
The keeper could not release them but by the Mayor's
permission, which he went to ask; at his return he found
all the prisoners released, and Newgate in a blaze. They
then went to Bloomsbury and fastened upon Lord Mansfield's house, which they pulled down; and as for his
goods, they totally burnt them. They have since gone to
Cane-wood, but a guard was there before them. They
plundered some Papists, I think, and burnt a mass-house
in Moorfields the same night.

On Wednesday [June 7] I walked with Dr. Scot to look
at Newgate, and found it in ruins, with the fire yet glow-
ing. As I went by, the Protestants were plundering the
Sessions-house at the Old Bailey. There were not, I believe, a hundred; but they did their work at leisure, in full
security, without sentinels, without trepidation, as men
lawfully employed, in full day. Such is the cowardice of
a commercial place. On Wednesday they broke open the
Fleet, and the King's-bench, and the Marshalsea, and

Woodstreet-counter, and Clerkenwell Bridewell, and released all the prisoners.

At night they set fire to the Fleet, and to the King's-
bench, and I know not how many other places; and one
might see the glare of conflagration fill the sky from many
parts. The sight was dreadful. Some people were threatened; Mr. Strahan advised me to take care of myself.
Such a time of terror you have been happy in not seeing.

The King said in council, that the magistrates had not
done their duty, but that he would do his own; and a proc-
lamation was published, directing us to keep our servants
within doors, as the peace was now to be preserved by
force. The soldiers were sent out to different parts, and
the town is now at quiet.

What has happened at your house you will know, the
harm is only a few butts of beer; and I think you may be
sure that the danger is over. There is a body of soldiers at
St. Margaret's Hill.

Of Mr. Tyson I know nothing, nor can guess to what
he can allude; but I know that a young fellow of little
more than seventy, is naturally an unresisted conqueror
of hearts.

Pray tell Mr. Thrale that I live here and have no fruit,
and if he does not interpose, am not likely to have much;
but I think he might as well give me a little, as give all to
the gardener.

Pray make my compliments to Queeney and Burney.

I am, &c.,

SAM: JOHNSON

(*To Mrs. Thrale*)

London, June 14, 1780

DEAR MADAM,

Every thing here is safe and quiet. This is the first thing
to be told; and this I told in my last letter directed to

Brighthelmstone. There has indeed been an universal panick, from which the King was the first that recovered. Without the concurrence of his ministers, or the assistance of the civil magistrate, he put the soldiers in motion, and saved the town from calamities, such as a rabble's government must naturally produce.

Now you are at ease about the publick, I may tell you that I am not well; I have had a cold and cough some time, but it is grown so bad, that yesterday I fasted and was blooded, and to day took physick and dined: but neither fasting nor bleeding, nor dinner, nor physick, have yet made me well.

No sooner was the danger over, than the people of the Borough found out how foolish it was to be afraid, and formed themselves into four bodies for the defence of the place; through which they now march morning and evening in a martial manner.

I am glad to find that Mr. Thrale continues to grow better; if he is well, I hope we shall be all well: but I am weary of my cough, though I have had much worse.

I am, &c.,

SAM: JOHNSON

Mr. Thrale and Sophy Streatfield

(1)

Jan. 1779. — Mr. Thrale is fallen in love, really and seriously, with Sophy Streatfield; but there is no wonder in that; she is very pretty, very gentle, soft, and insinuating; hangs about him, dances round him, cries when she parts from him, squeezes his hand slyly, and with her sweet eyes full of tears looks so fondly in his face — and all for love of me as she pretends; that I can hardly, sometimes, help laughing in her face. A man must not be a *man* but an *it*, to resist such artillery.

(2)

May, 1781. — Sophy Streatfield is an incomprehensible girl; here has she been telling me such tender passages of what passed between her and Mr. Thrale, that she half frights me somehow, at the same time declaring her attachment to Vyse yet her willingness to marry Lord Loughborough. Good God! what an uncommon girl! and handsome almost to perfection, I think: delicate in her manners, soft in her voice, and strict in her principles: I never saw such a character, she is wholly out of my reach; and I can only say that the man who runs mad for Sophy Streatfield has no reason to be ashamed of his passion; few people, however, seem disposed to take her for life — everybody's admiration, as Mrs. Byron says, and nobody's choice.

(MRS. THRALE)

(3)

We had a large dinner-party at our house; Johnson sat on one side of me, and Burke on the other; and in the company there was a young female to whom I, in my peevishness, thought Mr. Thrale superfluously attentive, to the neglect of me and others; especially of myself, then near my confinement, and dismally low-spirited; notwithstanding which, Mr. T. very unceremoniously begged of me to change place with Sophy ——, who was threatened with a sore throat, and might be injured by sitting near the door. I had scarcely swallowed a spoonful of soup when this occurred, and was so overset by the coarseness of the proposal, that I burst into tears, said something petulant — that perhaps ere long, the lady might be at the head of Mr. T.'s table, without displacing the mistress of the house, &c., and so left the apartment. I retired to the drawing-room, and for an hour or two contended with my vexation, as I best could, when Johnson and Burke came up. On seeing them, I resolved to give a *joba-tion* to both, but fixed on Johnson for my charge, and asked him if he had noticed what passed, what I had suffered, and whether allowing for the state of my nerves, I was much to blame? He answered, "Why, possibly not; your feelings were outraged." I said, "Yes, greatly so; and I cannot help remarking with what blandness and composure you *witnessed* the outrage. Had this transaction been told of others, your anger would have known no bounds; but, towards a man who gives good dinners &c., you were meekness itself!" Johnson coloured, and Burke, I thought, looked foolish; but I had not a word of answer from either.

(MRS. PIOZZI)

Piozzi

13 *August,* 1780. — Piozzi is become a prodigious favourite with me, he is so intelligent a creature, so discerning, one can't help wishing for his good opinion; his singing surpasses everybody's for taste, tenderness, and true elegance; his hand on the forte piano too is so soft, so sweet, so delicate, every tone goes to the heart, I think, and fills the mind with emotions one would not be without, though inconvenient enough sometimes. He wants nothing from us: he comes for his health he says: I see nothing ail the man but pride. The newspapers yesterday told what all the musical folks gained, and set Piozzi down 1200*l.* o' year.

(MRS. THRALE)

New Year Resolutions, 1781

1781

Jan. 2. I was yesterday hindered by my old disease of mind, and therefore begin to day.

Jan. 1. Having sat in my chamber till the year began I used my accommodation of the morning prayer *to the beginning of this year*, and slept remarkably well, though I had supped liberally. In the morning I went to Church. Then I wrote letters for Mrs. Desmoulins, then went to Streatham, and had many stops. At night I took wine, and did not sleep well.

Jan. 2. I rose according to my resolution, and am now to begin another year. I hope with amendment of life. — I will not despair. Help me, help me, O my God. My hope is

1. To rise at eight or sooner.
2. To read the Bible through this year in some language.
3. To keep a Journal.
   To study Religion.
   To avoid Idleness.

(PRAYERS AND MEDITATIONS)

Mr. Thrale's Condition

(*To Mrs. Thrale*)

London, July 10, 1780

DEAR MADAM,

If Mr. Thrale eats but half his usual quantity, he can hardly eat too much. It were better however to have some rule, and some security. Last week I saw flesh but twice, and I think fish once, the rest was pease.

Poor Miss O—— called on me on Saturday, with that fond and tender application which is natural to misery, when it looks to every body for that help which nobody can give. I was melted; and soothed and counselled her as well as I could, and am to visit her to-morrow.

She gave a very honourable account of my dear Queeney; and says of my master, that she thinks his manner and temper more altered than his looks, but of this alteration she could give no particular account; and all that she could say ended in this, that he is now sleepy in the morning. I do not wonder at the scantiness of her narration, she is too busy within to turn her eyes abroad.

(LETTERS)

(To Mrs. Thrale)

London, August 24, 1780

DEAR MADAM,

I do not wonder that you can think and write but of one thing. Yet concerning that thing you may be less uneasy, as you are now in the right way. You are at least doing, what I was always desirous to have you do, and which, when despair put an end to the caution of men going in the dark, produced at last all the good that has been obtained. Gentle purges, and slight phlebotomies, are not my favourites; they are pop-gun batteries, which lose time and effect nothing. It was by bleeding till he fainted, that his life was saved. I would, however, now have him trust chiefly to vigorous and stimulating cathartics. To bleed, is only proper when there is no time for slower remedies.

Does he sleep in the night? if he sleeps, there is not much danger; anything like wakefulness in a man either by nature or habit so uncommonly sleepy, would put me in great fear. Do not now hinder him from sleeping whenever heaviness comes upon him. Quiet rest, light food, and strong purges, will, I think, set all right. Be you vigilant, but be not frighted.

(LETTERS)

Mr. Thrale's Death

(*To Mrs. Thrale*)

London, April 5, 1781

DEAREST MADAM,

Of your injunctions, to pray for you and write to you, I hope to leave neither unobserved; and I hope to find you willing in a short time to alleviate your trouble by some other exercise of the mind. I am not without my part of the calamity. No death since that of my wife has ever oppressed me like this. But let us remember, that we are in the hands of Him who knows when to give and when to take away; who will look upon us with mercy through all our variations of existence, and who invites us to call on him in the day of trouble. Call upon him in this great revolution of life, and call with confidence. You will then find comfort for the past, and support for the future. He that has given you happiness in marriage, to a degree of which, without personal knowledge, I should have thought the description fabulous, can give you another mode of happiness as a mother; and at last the happiness of losing all temporal cares in the thoughts of an eternity in heaven.

I do not exhort you to reason yourself into tranquillity. We must first pray, and then labour; first implore the blessing of God, and [then employ] those means which he puts into our hands. Cultivated ground has few weeds; a mind occupied by lawful business, has little room for useless regret.

We read the will to-day; but I will not fill my first letter with any other account than that, with all my zeal for
your advantage, I am satisfied; and that the other executors, more used to consider property than I, commended
it for wisdom and equity. Yet why should I not tell you
that you have five hundred pounds for your immediate
expenses, and two thousand pounds a-year, with both the
houses and all the goods?

Let us pray for one another, that the time, whether long
or short, that shall yet be granted us, may be well spent;
and that when this life, which at the longest is very short,
shall come to an end, a better may begin which shall
never end.

                    I am, dearest Madam,
                                   Your, &c.,
                                        SAM: JOHNSON

Chapter V

THE LAST YEARS
1781–1784

Learning Italian

A*ugust* 9, 3 p.m., ætat. 72, in the summer-house at Streatham.

After innumerable resolutions formed and neglected, I have retired hither, to plan a life of greater diligence, in hope that I may yet be useful, and be daily better prepared to appear before my Creator and my Judge, from whose infinite mercy I humbly call for assistance and support.

My purpose is,

To pass eight hours every day in some serious employment.

Having prayed, I purpose to employ the next six weeks upon the Italian language, for my settled study.

(PRAYERS AND MEDITATIONS)

Old Friends

Oct. 14, *Sunday,* [1781]
(properly Monday morning)

I am this day about to go by Oxford and Birmingham to Lichfield and Ashbourne. The motives of my journey I hardly know. I omitted it last year, and am not willing

to miss it again. Mrs. Aston will be glad, I think, to see
me. We are both old, and if I put off my visit, I may see
her no more; perhaps she wishes for another interview.
She is a very good woman.

Hector is likewise an old friend, the only companion of
my childhood that passed through the School with me.
We have always loved one another. Perhaps we may be
made better by some serious conversation, of which however I have no distinct hope.

At Lichfield, my native place, I hope to shew a good
example by frequent attendance on publick worship.

At Ashbourne I hope to talk seriously with Taylor.

(PRAYERS AND MEDITATIONS)

The Tediousness of Time

(*To Mrs. Thrale*)

[*Lichfield*], *Oct.* 27, 1781

DEAREST DEAR LADY,

Your Oxford letter followed me hither, with Lichfield
put upon the direction in the place of Oxford, and was
received at the same time as the letter written next after
it. All is therefore well.

Queeney is a naughty captious girl, that will not write
because I did not remember to ask her. Pray tell her
that I ask her now, and that I depend upon her for the
history of her own time.

Poor Lucy's illness has left her very deaf, and, I think,
very inarticulate. I can scarcely make her understand
me, and she can hardly make me understand her. So here
are merry doings. But she seems to like me better than
she did. She eats very little, but does not fall away.

Mrs. Cobb and Peter Garrick are as you left them.

Garrick's legatees at this place are very angry that they receive nothing. Things are not quite right, though we are so far from London.

Mrs. Aston is just as I left her. She walks no worse; but I am afraid speaks less distinctly as to her utterance. Her mind is untouched. She eats too little, and wears away. The extenuation is her only bad symptom. She was glad to see me.

That naughty girl Queeney, now she is in my head again, how could she think that I did not wish to hear from her, a dear sweet. — But he must suffer who can love.

All here is gloomy; a faint struggle with the tediousness of time; a doleful confession of present misery, and the approach seen and felt of what is most dreaded and most shunned. But such is the lot of man.

I am, dearest Madam,

Your, &c.,

SAM: JOHNSON

The Fading World

(To Mrs. Thrale)

Lichfield, Nov. 3, 1781

DEAREST MADAM,

You very kindly remind me of the dear home which I have left; but I need none of your aids to recollection, for I am here gasping for breath, and yet better than those whom I came to visit. Mrs. Aston has been for three years a paralytic crawler; but, I think, with her mind unimpaired. She seems to me such as I left her; but she now eats little, and is therefore much emaciated. Her sister thinks her, and she thinks herself, passing fast away.

Lucy has had since my last visit a dreadful illness, from which her physicians declared themselves hopeless of recovering her, and which has shaken the general fabrick, and weakened the powers of life. She is unable or unwilling to move, and is never likely to have more of either strength or spirit.

I am so visibly disordered, that a medical man, who only saw me at church, sent me some pills. To those whom I love here I can give no help, and from those that love me none can I receive. Do you think that I need to be reminded of home and you?

The time of the year is not very favourable to excursions. I thought myself above assistance or obstruction from the seasons; but find the autumnal blast sharp and nipping, and the fading world an uncomfortable prospect. Yet I may say with Milton, that I do not *abate* much *of heart or hope.* To what I have done I do not despair of adding something, but *what it shall be I know not.*

I am, Madam,
Most affectionately yours,
SAM: JOHNSON

My Piozzi

25th November, 1781. — I have got my Piozzi home at last; he looks thin and battered, but always kindly upon me, I think. He brought me an Italian sonnet written in his praise by Marco Capello, which I instantly translated of course; but he, prudent creature, insisted on my burning it, as he said it would inevitably get about the town how *he* was praised, and how Mrs. Thrale translated and echoed the praises, so that, says he, I shall be torn in pieces, and you will have some *infamità* said of you that

will make you hate the sight of me. He was so earnest
with me that I could not resist, so burnt my sonnet, which
was actually very pretty; and now I repent I did not first
write it into the Thraliana.

(MRS. THRALE)

Johnson Hastens Back

(*To Mrs. Thrale*)

Ashbourne, Nov. 24, 1781

DEAR MADAM,

I shall leave this place about the beginning of next
week, and shall leave every place as fast as I decently
can, till I get back to you, whose kindness is one of my
great comforts. I am not well, but have a mind every
now and then to think myself better, and I now hope to be
better under your care.

It was time to send Kam to another master; but I am
glad that before he went he beat Hector, for he has really
the appearance of a superior species to an animal whose
whole power is in his legs, and that against the most de-
fenceless of all the inhabitants of the earth.

Dr. Taylor really grows well, and directs his compliments to be sent. I hope Mr. Perkins will be well too.

But why do you tell me nothing of your own health?
Perhaps since the fatal pinch of snuff I may have no care
about it. I am glad that you have returned to your meat,
for I never expected that abstinence would do you good.

Piozzi, I find, is coming in spite of Miss Harriet's prediction, or second sight, and when *he* comes and *I* come,
you will have two about you that love you; and I question
if either of us heartily care how few more you have. But
how many soever they may be, I hope you keep your

kindness for me, and I have a great mind to have Queeney's kindness too.

Frank's wife has brought him a wench; but I cannot yet get intelligence of her colour, and therefore have never told him how much depends upon it.

The weather here is chill, and the air damp. I have been only once at the waterfall, which I found doing as it used to do, and came away. I had not you nor Queeney with me.

Your, &c.,

SAM: JOHNSON

(*To Mrs. Thrale*)

Lichfield, Dec. 3, 1781

DEAR MADAM,

I am now come back to Lichfield, where I do not intend to stay long enough to receive another letter. I have little to do here but to take leave of Mrs. Aston. I hope not the last leave. But Christians may [say] with more confidence than Sophonisba

> Avremo tosto lungo lungo spazio
> Per stare assieme, et sarà forse eterno.

My time past heavily at Ashbourne, yet I could not easily get away, though Taylor, I sincerely think, was glad to see me go. I have now learned the inconveniences of a winter campaign; but I hope home will make amends for all my foolish sufferings.

. . . You have got Piozzi again, notwithstanding pretty Harriet's dire denunciations. The Italian translation which he has brought, you will find no great accession to your library, for the writer seems to understand very little English. When we meet we can compare some passages. Pray contrive a multitude of good things for us to do when we meet. Something that may *hold all together;* though if any thing makes *me* love you more, it is going from you.

> I am, &c.,
> SAM: JOHNSON

(*To Mrs. Thrale*)

> *Birmingham, Dec.* 8, 1781

DEAR MADAM,

I am come to this place on my way to London and to Streatham. I hope to be in London on Tuesday or Wednesday, and at Streatham on Thursday, by your kind conveyance. I shall have nothing to relate either wonderful or delightful. But remember that you sent me away, and turned me out into the world, and you must take the chance of finding me better or worse. This you may know at present, that my affection for you is not diminished, and my expectation from you is encreased. Do not neglect me, nor relinquish me. Nobody will ever love you better or honour you more than,

> Madam,
> Your, &c.,
> SAM: JOHNSON

Mrs. Thrale's " If's "

17*th December,* 1781. — Dear Mr. Johnson is at last returned; he has been a vast while away to see his country folks at Litchfield. My fear is lest he should grow paralytick, — there are really some symptoms already discoverable, I think, about the mouth particularly. He will drive the gout away so when it comes, and it must go *somewhere.* Queeny works hard with him at the classicks;

I hope she will be *out* of leading-strings at least before he
gets *into* them, as poor women say of their children.

. . . *January,* 1782. — (after stating her fear of illness
and other ills.) *If* nothing of all these misfortunes, however, befall one; *if* for my sins God should take from me
my monitor, my friend, my inmate, my dear Doctor Johnson; *if* neither I should marry, nor the brew-house people
break; *if* the ruin of the nation should not change the situation of affairs so that one could not receive regular re-
mittances from England: and *if* Piozzi should not pick
him up a wife and fix his abode in this country, — *if,* therefore, and *if* and *if* and *if* again all should conspire to keep
my present resolution warm, I certainly would, at the
close of the four years from the sale of the Southwark estate, set out for Italy, with my two or three eldest girls,
and see what the world could show me.

(In a marginal note, she adds:)

Travelling with Mr. Johnson *I* cannot bear, and leaving
him behind *he* could not bear, so his life or death must
determine the execution or laying aside my schemes. I
wish it were within reason to *hope* he could live four
years.

(MRS. THRALE)

The Death of Levett

(1)

Condemn'd to Hope's delusive mine,
  As on we toil from day to day,
By sudden blast or slow decline
  Our social comforts drop away.

Well tried through many a varying year,
  See Levett to the grave descend;

Officious, innocent, sincere,
Of every friendless name the friend.

Yet still he fills affection's eye,
Obscurely wise and coarsely kind,
Nor, letter'd arrogance, deny
Thy praise to merit unrefin'd.

When fainting Nature call'd for aid,
And hov'ring Death prepar'd the blow,
His vigorous remedy display'd
The power of art without the show.

In misery's darkest caverns known,
His ready help was ever nigh,
Where hopeless anguish pour'd his groan,
And lonely want retir'd to die.

No summons mock'd by chill delay,
No petty gains disdain'd by pride;
The modest wants of every day,
The toil of every day supplied.

His virtues walked their narrow round,
Nor made a pause, nor left a void;
And sure the Eternal Master found
His single talent well employed.

The busy day, the peaceful night,
Unfelt, uncounted, glided by;
His frame was firm, his powers were bright,
Though now his eightieth year was nigh.

Then, with no throbs of fiery pain,
No cold gradations of decay,
Death broke at once the vital chain,
And freed his soul the nearest way.

(JOHNSON)

(2. *To Mrs. Thrale*)

January 28, 1782

DEAREST LADY,

I was blooded on Saturday; I think, not copiously enough, but the Doctor would permit no more. I have however his consent to bleed again to-day. Since I left you I have eaten very little, on Friday chiefly broath, on Saturday nothing but some bread in the morning, on Sunday nothing but some bread and three roasted apples. I try to get well and wish to see you; but if I came, I should only cough and cough. Mr. Steevens who is with me, says that my hearing is returned. We are here all three sick, and poor Levet is gone.

Do not add to my other distresses any diminution of kindness for,

Madam,
Your, &c.,
SAM: JOHNSON

Ill Health, Early 1782

(1)

1st February, 1782. — Here is Mr. Johnson ill, very ill indeed, and — I do not see what ails him; 'tis repelled gout, I fear, fallen on the lungs and breath of course. What shall we do for him? If I lose *him,* I am more than un-

done; friend, father, guardian, confident! — God give me
health and patience. What shall I do?

(MRS. THRALE)

(2)

Poor Dr. Lawrence had long been his friend and confi-
dant. The conversation I saw them hold together in Es-
sex-street one day in the year 1781 or 1782, was a melancholy one, and made a singular impression on my mind.
He was exceedingly ill, and I accompanied him thither
for advice. The physician was however, in some respects,
more to be pitied than the patient: Johnson was panting
under an asthma and dropsy; but Lawrence had been
brought home that very morning struck with the palsy,
from which he had, two hours before we came, strove
to awaken himself by blisters: they were both deaf, and
scarce able to speak besides; one from difficulty of breathing, the other from paralytic debility. To give and receive
medical counsel therefore, they fairly sate down on each
side a table in the Doctor's gloomy apartment, adorned
with skeletons, preserved monsters, &c., and agreed to
write Latin billets to each other: such a scene did I never
see!

(MRS. PIOZZI)

(3)

Poor Johnson is in a bad state of health; I fear his constitution is broken up: I am quite grieved at it, he will not
leave an abler defender of religion and virtue behind him,
and the following little touch of tenderness which I heard
of him last night from one of the Turk's Head Club, en-
dears him to me exceedingly. There are always a great
many candidates ready, when any vacancy happens in
that club, and it requires no small interest and reputation

to get elected; but upon Garrick's death, when numberless
applications were made to succeed him, Johnson was deaf
to them all; he said, No, there never could be found any
successor worthy of such a man; and he insisted upon it
there should be a year's widowhood in the club, before
they thought of a new election. In Dr. Johnson some con-
trarieties very harmoniously meet; if he has too little charity for the opinions of others, and too little patience with
their faults, he has the greatest tenderness for their persons. He told me the other day, he hated to hear people
whine about metaphysical distresses, when there was so
much want and hunger in the world. I told him I supposed then he never wept at any tragedy but "Jane
Shore," who had died for want of a loaf. He called me a
saucy girl, but did not deny the inference.

(HANNAH MORE)

The Papers and Mrs. Thrale

Harley Street, 13th April, 1782. — When I took off my
mourning, the watchers watched me very exactly, "but
they whose hands were mightiest have found nothing:"
so I shall leave the town, I hope, in a good disposition
towards me, though I am sullen enough with the town
for fancying me such an amorous idiot that I am dying
to enjoy every filthy fellow. God knows how distant such
dispositions are from the heart and constitution of H. L. T.
Lord Loughboro', Sir Richard Jebb, Mr. Piozzi, Mr. Sel-
wyn, Dr. Johnson, every man that comes to the house, is
put in the papers for me to marry. In good time, I wrote
to-day to beg the "Morning Herald" would say no more
about me, good or bad.

(MRS. THRALE)

Love and Friendship Distinct Things

Streatham, 17th April, 1782. — I am returned to Streatham, pretty well in health and very sound in heart, notwithstanding the watchers and the wager-layers, who think more of the charms of their sex by half than I who know them better. Love and friendship are distinct things, and I would go through fire to serve many a man whom nothing less than fire would force me to go to bed to. Somebody mentioned my going to be married t'other day, and Johnson was joking about it. I suppose, Sir, said I, they think they are doing me honour with these imaginary matches, when, perhaps the man does not exist who would do me honour by marrying me! This, indeed, was said in the wild and insolent spirit of Baretti, yet 'tis nearer the truth than one would think for. A woman of passable person, ancient family, respectable character, uncommon talents and three thousand a year, has a right to think herself any man's equal, and has nothing to seek but return of affection from whatever partner she pitches on. To marry for love would therefore be rational in me, who want no advancement of birth or fortune, and *till I am in love,* I will not marry, nor perhaps then.

(MRS. THRALE)

Italy for Convenience

22nd August, 1782. — An event of no small consequence to our little family must here be recorded in the " Thraliana." After having long intended to go to Italy for pleasure, we are now settling to go thither for convenience. The establishment of expense here at Streatham is more

than my income will answer; my lawsuit with Lady Salusbury turns out worse in the event and infinitely more costly
than I could have dreamed on; 8000*l.* is supposed necessary to the payment of it, and how am I to raise 8000*l.*?
My trees will (after all my expectations from them) fetch
but 4000*l.*, the money lent Perkins on his bond 1600*l.*, the
Hertfordshire copyholds may perhaps be worth 1000*l.*,
and where is the rest to spring from? I must go abroad
and save money. To show Italy to my girls, and be
showed it by Piozzi, has long been my dearest wish, but
to leave Mr. Johnson shocked me, and to take him appeared impossible. His recovery, however, from an illness
we all thought dangerous, gave me courage to speak to
him on the subject, and this day (after having been let
blood) I mustered up resolution to tell him the necessity
of changing a way of life I had long been displeased with.
I added that I had mentioned the matter to my eldest
daughter, whose prudence and solid judgment, unbiassed
by passion, is unequalled, as far as my experience has
reached; that she approved the scheme, and meant to
partake it, though of an age when she might be supposed
to form connections here in England — attachments of
the tenderest nature; that she declared herself free and
resolved to follow my fortunes, though perfectly aware
temptations might arise to prevent me from ever returning — a circumstance she even mentioned herself.

Mr. Johnson thought well of the project, and wished
me to put it early in execution: seemed less concerned at
parting with me than I wished him: thought his pupil
Miss Thrale quite right in forbearing to marry young, and
seemed to entertain no doubt of living to see us return
rich and happy in two or three years' time. He told Hester
in my absence that he would not go with me if I asked
him. See the importance of a person to himself. I fancied

Mr. Johnson could not have existed without me, forsooth, as we have now lived together for above eighteen years. I have so fondled him in sickness and in health. Not a bit of it. He feels nothing in parting with me, nothing in the least, but thinks it a prudent scheme, and goes to his books as usual. This is philosophy and truth; he always said he hated a *feeler*. . . .

(MRS. THRALE)

Mr. Johnson Cares Nothing

The persecution I endure from men too who want to marry me — in good time — is another reason for my desiring to be gone. I wish to marry none of them, and Sir Philip's teazing me completed my mortification; to see that one can rely on *nobody!* The expences of this house, however, which are quite past my power to check, is the true and rational cause of our departure. In Italy we shall live with twice the respect and at half the expence we do here; the language is familiar to me and I love the Italians; I take with me all I love in the world except my two baby daughters, who will be left safe at school; and since Mr. Johnson cares nothing for the loss of my personal friendship and company, there is no danger of any body else breaking their hearts. My sweet Burney and Mrs. Byron will perhaps think they are sorry, but my consciousness that no one *can* have the cause of concern that Johnson has, and my conviction that he has *no concern at all*, shall cure me of lamenting friends left behind.

. . . I begin to see (now everything shows it) that Johnson's connection with me is merely an interested one; he *loved* Mr. Thrale, I believe, but only wished to find in me a careful nurse and humble friend for his sick and his lounging hours; yet I really thought he could not have *existed* without *my conversation* forsooth! He cares more for my roast beef and plum pudden, which he now devours too dirtily for endurance; and since he is glad to get rid of me, I'm sure I have good cause to desire the getting rid of him.

(MRS. THRALE)

What Care You?

(To Mrs. Thrale)

April [24 *or* 25, 1782]

MADAM,

I have been very much out of order since you sent me away; but why should I tell you, who do not care, nor desire to know? I dined with Mr. Paradise on Monday, with the Bishop of St. Asaph yesterday, with the Bishop of Chester I dined to-day, and with the Academy on Saturday, with Mr. Hoole on Monday, and with Mrs. Garrick on Thursday the 2d of May, and then — what care you? *what then?*

The news run, that we have taken seventeen French transports — that Langton's lady is lying down with her eighth child, all alive — and Mrs. Carter's Miss Sharpe is going to marry a schoolmaster sixty-two years old.

Do not let Mr. Piozzi nor any body else put me quite out of your head, and do not think that any body will love you like

Your, &c.,

SAM: JOHNSON

A Change of Place

(To Mrs. Thrale)

Saturday, June 8, 1782

DEAR MADAM,

Perhaps some of your people may call to-morrow. I have this day taken a passage to Oxford for Monday. Not to frisk as you express it with very unfeeling irony, but to catch at the hopes of better health. The change of place may do something. To leave the house where so much has been suffered affords some pleasure. When I write to you write to me again, and let me have the pleasure of knowing that I am still considered as

Madam,

Your, &c.,

SAM: JOHNSON

Variations of Company

(To Mrs. Thrale)

Oxford, June 12, 1782

DEAR MADAM,

My letter was perhaps peevish, but it was not unkind. I should have cared little about a wanton expression, if there had been no kindness.

I find no particular salubrity in this air, my respiration is very laborious; my appetite is good, and my sleep commonly long and quiet; but a very little motion disables me.

I dine to-day with Dr. Adams, and to-morrow with Dr. Wetherel. Yesterday Dr. Edwards invited some men from Exeter college, whom I liked very well. These variations of company help the mind, though they cannot do much for the body. But the body receives some help from a cheerful mind.

Keep up some kindness for me; when I am with you again, I hope to be less burdensome, by being less sick.

I am, dearest Lady,

Your, &c.,

SAM: JOHNSON

England Sinking

(*To the Reverend Dr. Taylor*)

DEAR SIR,

I have no national news that is not in the papers, and almost all news is bad. Perhaps no nation not absolutely conquered has declined so much in so short a time. We seem to be sinking. Suppose the Irish having already gotten a free trade and an independent Parliament, should say we will have a King, and ally ourselves with the house of Bourbon, what could be done to hinder or to overthrow them?

Poor dear Dr. Lawrence is gone to die at Canterbury. He has lost his speech and the action of his right side, with very little hope of recovering them.

We must all go. I was so exhausted by loss of blood, and by successive disorders in the beginning of this year that I am afraid that the remaining part will hardly restore me. I have indeed rather indulged myself too much, and think to begin a stricter regimen. As it is my friends tell me from time to time that I look better, and I am very willing to believe them. Do you likewise take care of your health, we cannot well spare one another.

I am, dear Sir,

Yours affectionately,

SAM: JOHNSON

London, August 4, 1782

Self-Debates of Mrs. Thrale

August 28th, 1782. — He (Piozzi) thinks still more than he says, that I shall give him up; and if Queeney made herself more amiable to me, and took the proper methods — I suppose I should.

20 *September* 1782, *Streatham.* — and now I am going to leave Streatham (I have let the house and grounds to Lord Shelburne, the expence of it eat me up) for three years, where I lived — never happily indeed, but always easily: the more so perhaps from the total absence of love and ambition —

> " Else these two passions by the way
> Might chance to show us scurvy play."

October 1st. — Now! that dear little discerning creature, Fanny Burney, says I'm in love with Piozzi: very likely; he is so amiable, so honourable, so much above his situation by his abilities, that if

> " Fate had not fast bound her
> With Styx nine times round her,
> Sure musick and love were victorious."

But if he is ever so worthy, ever so lovely, he is *below me* forsooth! In what is he below me? In virtue? I would I were above him. In understanding? I would mine were from this instant under the guardianship of his. In birth? To be sure he is below me in birth, and so is almost every man I know or have a chance to know. But he is below me in fortune: is mine sufficient for us both? — more than amply so. Does he deserve it by his conduct, in which he has always united warm notions of honour with cool attention to œconomy, the spirit of a gentleman with the

talents of a professor? How shall any man deserve fortune, if he does not? But I am the guardian of five daughters by Mr. Thrale, and must not disgrace *their* name and
family. Was then the man my mother chose for me of
higher extraction than him I have chosen for myself? No,
— but his fortune was higher. . . . I wanted fortune then,
perhaps: do I want it now? — Not at all; but I am not to
think about myself; I married the first time to please my
mother, I must marry the second time to please my daughter. I have always sacrificed my own choice to that of
others, so I must sacrifice it again: but why? Oh, because
I am a woman of superior understanding, and must not
for the world degrade myself from my situation in life.
But if I *have* superior understanding, let me at least make
use of it for once, and rise to the rank of a human being
conscious of its own power to discern good from ill. The
person who has uniformly acted by the will of others has
hardly that dignity to boast.

But once again: I am guardian to five girls; agreed:
will this connection prejudice their bodies, souls, or purse?
My marriage may assist *my* health, but I suppose it will
not injure *theirs*. Will his company or companions cor-
rupt their morals? God forbid; if I did not believe him one
of the best of our fellow beings, I would reject him instantly. Can it injure their fortunes? Could he impover-
ish (if he would) five women, to whom their father left
20,000*l*. each, independent almost of possibilities? — To
what then am I guardian? to their pride and prejudice?
and is anything else affected by the alliance? Now for
more solid objections. Is not the man of whom I desire
protection, a foreigner? unskilled in the laws and language of our country? Certainly. Is he not, as the French
say, *Arbitre de mon sort?* and from the hour he possesses
my person and fortune, have I any power of decision how

or where I may continue or end my life? Is not the man, upon the continuance of whose affection my whole happiness depends, *younger* than myself, and is it wise to place one's happiness on the continuance of *any* man's affection? Would it not be painful to owe his appearance of regard more to his honour than his love? and is not my person, already faded, likelier to fade sooner than his? On the other hand, is his life a good one? and would it not be lunacy even to risque the wretchedness of losing all situation in the world for the sake of living with a man one loves, and then to lose both companion and consolation? When I lost Mr. Thrale, every one was officious to comfort and to soothe me; but which of my children or quondam friends would look with kindness upon Piozzi's widow? If I bring children by him, must they not be Catholics, and must not I live among people the *ritual* part of whose religion I disapprove?

These are *my* objections, these *my* fears: not those of being censured by the world, as it is called, a composition of vice and folly, though 'tis surely no good joke to be talked of

" By each affected she that tells my story,
        And blesses her good stars that *she* was prudent."

These objections would increase in strength, too, if my present state was a happy one, but it really is not. I live a quiet life, but not a pleasant one. My children govern without loving me; my servants devour and despise me; my friends caress and censure me; my money wastes in expences I do not enjoy, and my time in trifles I do not approve. Every one is made insolent, and no one comfortable; my reputation unprotected, my heart unsatisfied, my health unsettled. I will, however, resolve on nothing. I will take a voyage to the Continent in spring, enlarge

my knowledge and repose my purse. Change of place
may turn the course of these ideas, and external objects
supply the room of internal felicity.

(MRS. THRALE)

Johnson Leaves Streatham

October 6, 1782

Sunday, went to church at Streatham. *Templo valedixi
cum osculo.*

Oct. 6, *Die Dominica,* 1782

Pransus sum Streathamiæ agninum crus coctum cum
herbis (spinach) comminutis, farcimen farinaceum cum
uvis passis, lumbos bovillos, et pullum gallinæ Turcicæ;
et post carnes missas, ficus, uvas, non admodum maturas,
ita voluit anni intemperies, cum malis Persicis, iis tamen
duris. Non lætus accubui, cibum modicè sumpsi, ne in-
temperantiâ ad extremum peccaretur. Si recte memini,
in mentem venerunt epulæ in exequiis Hadoni celebratæ.
Streathamiam quando revisam?

I dined at Streatham on boiled leg of lamb, with spinach,
the stuffing of flour with raisins, round of beef, and turkey;
and, after the meat course, figs, grapes, not yet ripe in consequence of the bad season, and peaches, also hard. I took
my place in no joyful mood, and eat moderately, avoiding
intemperance. If I remember rightly, the banquet at the
funeral of Hadon came into my mind. When shall I see
Streatham again?

Almighty God, Father of all mercy, help me by thy
Grace that I may with humble and sincere thankfulness
remember the comforts and conveniences which I have
enjoyed at this place, and that I may resign them with

holy submission, equally trusting in thy protection when Thou givest and when Thou takest away. Have mercy upon me, O Lord, have mercy upon me.

To thy fatherly protection, O Lord, I commend this family. Bless, guide, and defend them, that they may so pass through this world as finally to enjoy in thy presence everlasting happiness, for Jesus Christs sake. Amen.

Oct. 7. I was called early. I packed up my bundles, and used the foregoing prayer, with my morning devotions somewhat, I think, enlarged. Being earlier than the family I read St. Pauls farewel in the Acts, and then read fortuitously in the Gospels, which was my parting use of the library.

(PRAYERS AND MEDITATIONS)

A Melancholy Year

(To the Reverend Dr. Taylor)

DEAR SIR,

This, my dear Sir, is the last day of a very sickly and melancholy year. Join your prayers with mine, that the next may be more happy to us both. I hope the happiness which I have not found in this world, will by infinite mercy be granted in another.

I am, dear Sir,
Yours affectionately,
SAM JOHNSON

Dec. 31, 1782
To the Reverend Dr. Taylor in Ashbourne, Derbyshire

A Parting from Piozzi

January 29, 1783. — Adieu to all that's dear, to all that's lovely; I am parted from my life, my soul, my Piozzi. If I can get health and strength to write my story here, 'tis all I wish for now — oh misery! [Four pages missing.] The cold dislike of my eldest daughter I thought might wear away by familiarity with his merit, and that we might live tolerably together, or, at least, part friends — but no; her aversion increased daily, and she communicated it to the others; they treated *me* insolently, and *him* very strangely — running away whenever he came as if they saw a serpent — and plotting with their governess — a cunning Italian — how to invent lyes to make me hate him, and twenty such narrow tricks. By these means the notion of my partiality took air, and whether Miss Thrale sent him word slily or not I cannot tell, but on the 25th January, 1783, Mr. Crutchley came hither to conjure me not to go to Italy; he had heard such things, he said, and by *means* next to *miraculous*. The next day, Sunday, 26th, Fanny Burney came, said I must marry him instantly or give him up; that my reputation would be lost else.

I actually groaned with anguish, threw myself on the bed in an agony which my fair daughter beheld with frigid indifference. She had indeed never by one tender word endeavoured to dissuade me from the match, but said, coldly, that if I *would* abandon my children I *must;* that their father had not deserved such treatment from me; that I should be punished by Piozzi's neglect, for that she knew he hated me; and that I turned out my offspring to chance for his sake, like puppies in a pond to swim or drown according as Providence pleased; that for her part she must look herself out a place like the other servants,

for my face would she never see more. " Nor write to
me? " said I. " I shall not, madam," replied she with a cold
sneer, " easily find out your address; for you are going
you know not whither, I believe."

Susan and Sophy said nothing at all, but they taught
the two young ones to cry " Where are you going, mama?
will you leave us and die as our poor papa did? " There
was no standing *that,* so I wrote my lover word that my
mind was all distraction, and bid him come to me the
next morning, 27th January — my birthday — and spent
the Sunday night in torture not to be described. My false-
hood to my Piozzi, my strong affection for him, the in-
capacity I felt in myself to resign the man I so adored,
the hopes I had so cherished, inclined me strongly to set
them all at defiance, and go with him to church to sanc-
tify the promises I had so often made him; while the idea
of abandoning the children of my first husband, who left
me so nobly provided for, and who depended on my attachment to his offspring, awakened the voice of conscience, and threw me on my knees to pray for *His* direction who was hereafter to judge my conduct. His grace
illuminated me, His power strengthened me, and I flew
to my daughter's bed in the morning and told her my resolution to resign my own, my dear, my favourite purpose,
and to prefer my children's interest to my love.

(MRS. THRALE)

Mrs. Thrale Removes to Bath

April, 1783. — I will go to Bath: nor health, nor strength,
nor my children's affections, have I. My daughter does
not, I suppose, much delight in this scheme [retrench-
ment of expenses and removal to Bath], but why should I

lead a life of delighting her, who would not lose a shilling
of interest or an ounce of pleasure to save my life from
perishing? When I was near losing my existence from the
contentions of my mind, and was seized with a temporary delirium in Argyll Street, she and her two eldest sis-
ters laughed at my distress, and observed to dear Fanny
Burney, that it was *monstrous droll*. *She* could hardly
suppress her indignation.

Sunday Morning, 6th April, 1783. — I have been very
busy preparing to go to Bath and save my money; the
Welch settlement has been examined and rewritten by
Cator's desire in such a manner that a will can revoke it or
charge the estate, or anything. I signed my settlement
yesterday, and, before I slept, wrote my will, charging the
estate with pretty near 3000*l*. But what signifies it? My
daughters deserve no thanks from my tenderness and they
want no pecuniary help from my purse — let me provide
in some measure, for my dear, my absent Piozzi. — God
give me strength to part with him courageously. — I expect him every instant to breakfast with me for the *last
time*. — Gracious Heavens, what words are these! Oh no,
for mercy may we but meet again! and without diminished kindness. Oh my love, my love!

(MRS. THRALE)

The Removal in Retrospect

I was forced to take advantage of my lost lawsuit, and
plead inability of purse to remain longer in London or its
vicinage. I had been crossed in my intentions of going
abroad, and found it convenient, for every reason of
health, peace, and pecuniary circumstances to retire to
Bath, where I knew Mr. Johnson would not follow me,

and where I could for that reason command some little
portion of time for my own use; a thing impossible while I
remained at Streatham or at London, as my hours, carriage, and servants had long been at his command, who
would not rise in the morning till twelve o'clock perhaps,
and oblige me to make breakfast for him till the bell rung
for dinner, though much displeased if the toilet was neglected, and though much of the time we passed together
was spent in blaming or deriding, very justly, my neglect
of œconomy, and waste of that money which might make
many families happy. The original reason of our connection, his *particularly disordered health and spirits,* had
been long at an end, and he had no other ailments than
old age and general infirmity, which every professor of
medicine was ardently zealous and generally attentive to
palliate, and to contribute all in their power for the pro-
longation of a life so valuable. Veneration for his virtue,
reverence for his talents, delight in his conversation, and
habitual endurance of a yoke my husband first put upon
me, and of which he contentedly bore his share for sixteen
or seventeen years, made me go on so long with Mr.
Johnson; but the perpetual confinement I will own to have
been terrifying in the first years of our friendship, and irksome in the last; nor could I pretend to support it without help, when my coadjutor was no more. To the assistance we gave him, the shelter our house afforded to
his uneasy fancies, and to the pains we took to sooth or
repress them, the world perhaps is indebted for the three
political pamphlets, the new edition and correction of his
" Dictionary," and for the Poets Lives, which he would
scarce have lived, I think, and kept his faculties entire, to
have written, had not incessant care been exerted at the
time of his first coming to be our constant guest in the
country; and several times after that, when he found him-

self particularly oppressed with diseases incident to the most vivid and fervent imaginations. I shall for ever consider it as the greatest honour which could be conferred on any one, to have been the confidential friend of Dr. Johnson's health; and to have in some measure, with Mr. Thrale's assistance, saved from distress at least, if not from worse, a mind great beyond the comprehension of common mortals, and good beyond all hope of imitation from perishable beings.

(MRS. PIOZZI)

A Setting Sun

Saturday we had a dinner at home, Mrs. Carter, Miss Hamilton, the Kennicotts, and Dr. Johnson. Poor Johnson exerted himself exceedingly; but he was very ill and looked so dreadfully, that it quite grieved me. He is more mild and complacent than he used to be. His sickness seems to have softened his mind, without having at all weakened it. I was struck with the mild radiance of this setting sun. We had but a small party of such of his friends as we knew would be most agreeable to him, and as we were all very attentive, and paid him the homage he both expects and deserves, he was very communicative, and of course instructive and delightful in the highest degree.

(HANNAH MORE)

Streatham Poplars

London, May 22, 1783

MY DEAREST LOVE,
What a terrible accident! How easily might it have been yet more mischievous. I hope my Mistress's hurt is nei-

ther of any danger nor of much pain. It teaches however, what though every thing teaches, is yet always forgotten, that we are perpetually within the reach of death.

. . . Mrs. Desmoulins left us last week, so that I have only one sick woman to fight or play with instead of two, and there is more peace in the house.

Let me know, my dear Love, how my Mistress goes on, and tell Susy that I shall answer her short letter.

I am writing over the little garden. The poplars, which I have just now watered, grow kindly; they may expect not to be neglected for they came from Streatham.

Crescent illæ, crescetis amores.

I am, dear Madam,
Your most humble servant,
SAM: JOHNSON

To Miss Thrale, at Bath

Pacem Appellant

(*To Mrs. Thrale*)

London, June 5, 1783

DEAR MADAM,

Why do you write so seldom? I was very glad of your letter. You were used formerly to write more, when I know not why you should [have] had much more to say. Do not please yourself with showing me that you can forget me, who do not forget you.

Mr. Desmoulins' account of my health rather wants confirmation. But complaints are useless.

I have, by the migration of one of my ladies, more peace at home; but I remember an old savage chief that says of the Romans with great indignation — *ubi solitudinem faciunt, pacem appellant.*

You give a cheerful account of your way of life. I hope you will settle into tranquillity.

When I can repay you such a narrative of my felicity, you shall see description.

I am, &c.,

SAM: JOHNSON

A Paralytic Stroke

(*To Mrs. Thrale*)

Bolt-court, Fleet-street, June 19,1783

DEAR MADAM,

I am sitting down in no cheerful solitude to write a narrative which would once have affected you with tenderness and sorrow, but which you will perhaps pass over now with the careless glance of frigid indifference. For this diminution of regard however, I know not whether I ought to blame you, who may have reasons which I cannot know, and I do not blame myself, who have for a great part of human life done you what good I could, and have never done you evil.

I have been disordered in the usual way, and had been relieved by the usual methods, by opium and catharticks, but had rather lessened my dose of opium.

On Monday the 16th I sat for my picture, and walked a considerable way with little inconvenience. In the afternoon and evening I felt myself light and easy, and began to plan schemes of life. Thus I went to bed, and in a short time waked and sat up, as has been long my custom, when I felt a confusion and indistinctness in my head, which lasted I suppose about half a minute; I was alarmed, and prayed God, that however he might afflict my body, he would spare my understanding. This prayer, that I might try the integrity of my faculties, I made in

Latin verse. The lines were not very good, but I knew them not to be very good: I made them easily, and concluded myself to be unimpaired in my faculties.

Soon after I perceived that I had suffered a paralytick stroke, and that my speech was taken from me. I had no pain, and so little dejection in this dreadful state, that I wondered at my own apathy, and considered that perhaps death itself when it should come would excite less horrour than seems now to attend it.

In order to rouse the vocal organs I took two drams. Wine has been celebrated for the production of eloquence. I put myself into violent motion, and I think repeated it; but all was vain. I then went to bed, and, strange as it may seem, I think, slept. When I saw light, it was time to contrive what I should do. Though God stopped my speech he left me my hand, I enjoyed a mercy which was not granted to my dear friend Lawrence, who now perhaps overlooks me as I am writing, and rejoices that I have what he wanted. My first note was necessarily to my servant, who came in talking, and could not immediately comprehend why he should read what I put into his hands.

I then wrote a card to Mr. Allen, that I might have a discreet friend at hand to act as occasion should require. In penning this note I had some difficulty, my hand, I knew not how nor why, made wrong letters. I then wrote to Dr. Taylor to come to me, and bring Dr. Heberden, and I sent to Dr. Brocklesby, who is my neighbour. My physicians are very friendly and very disinterested, and give me great hopes, but you may imagine my situation. I have so far recovered my vocal powers, as to repeat the Lord's Prayer with no very imperfect articulation. My memory, I hope, yet remains as it was; but such an attack produces solicitude for the safety of every faculty.

How this will be received by you I know not. I hope you will sympathise with me; but perhaps

> My mistress gracious, mild, and good,
> Cries! Is he dumb? 'Tis time he shou'd.

But can this be possible? I hope it cannot. I hope that what, when I could speak, I spoke of you, and to you, will be in a sober and serious hour remembered by you; and surely it cannot be remembered but with some degree of kindness. I have loved you with virtuous affection; I have honoured you with sincere esteem. Let not all our endearments be forgotten, but let me have in this great distress your pity and your prayers. You see I yet turn to you with my complaints as a settled and unalienable friend; do not, do not drive me from you, for I have not deserved either neglect or hatred.

To the girls, who do not write often, for Susy has written only once, and Miss Thrale owes me a letter, I earnestly recommend, as their guardian and friend, that they remember their Creator in the days of their youth.

O God! give me comfort and confidence in Thee: forgive my sins; and if it be Thy good pleasure, relieve my diseases for Jesus Christ's sake. Amen.

I am almost ashamed of this querulous letter, but now it is written, let it go.

I am, &c.,
SAM: JOHNSON

Mrs. Thrale's Offer

(*To Mrs. Thrale*)

London, June 23, 1783

DEAR MADAM,

Your offer, dear Madam, of coming to me, is charmingly kind; but I will lay up for future use, and then let it not be considered as obsolete; a time of dereliction may come, when I may have hardly any other friend, but in the present exigency I cannot name one who has been deficient in civility or attention. What man can do for man has been done for me. Write to me very often.

I am, Madam,

Your, &c.,

SAM: JOHNSON

The Black Dog

(*To Mrs. Thrale*)

London, June 28, 1783

DEAREST MADAM,

Your letter is just such as I desire, and as from you I hope always to deserve.

The black dog I hope always to resist, and in time to drive, though I am deprived of almost all those that used to help me. The neighbourhood is impoverished. I had once Richardson and Lawrence in my reach. Mrs. Allen is dead. My house has lost Levet, a man who took interest in every thing, and therefore ready at conversation. Mrs. Williams is so weak that she can be a companion no longer. When I rise my breakfast is solitary, the black dog waits to share it, from breakfast to dinner he continues barking, except that Dr. Brocklesby for a little keeps him at a distance. Dinner with a sick woman you may venture to suppose not much better than solitary. After dinner, what remains but to count the clock, and hope for that sleep which I can scarce expect. Night comes at last, and some hours of restlessness and confusion bring me again to a day of solitude. What shall exclude the black dog from an habitation like this? If I were a little richer, I would perhaps take some cheerful female into the house.

. . . I must touch my journal. Last night fresh flies
were put to my head, and hindered me from sleeping. To-
day I fancy myself incommoded by heat.

I have, however, watered the garden both yesterday
and to-day, just as I watered the laurels in the island.

I am, Madam,

Your, &c.,

SAM: JOHNSON

A Visit to Rochester

(*To Mrs. Thrale*)

London, July 8, 1783

Langton and I have talked of passing a little time at
Rochester together, till neither knows well how to refuse,
though I think he is not eager to take me, and I am not
desirous to be taken. His family is numerous, and his
house little. I have let him know, for his relief, that I do
not mean to burden him more than a week. He is however among those who wish me well, and would exert
what power he has to do me good.

(*To Mrs. Thrale*)

London, July 23, 1783

DEAR MADAM,

I have been thirteen days at Rochester, and am just now
returned. I came back by water in a common boat twenty
miles for a shilling, and when I landed at Billingsgate I
carried my budget myself to Cornhill before I could get a
coach, and was not much incommoded.

I have had Miss Susy's and Miss Sophy's letters, and
now I am come home can write and write. While I was
with Mr. Langton we took four little journies in a chaise,

and made one little voyage on the Medway, with four misses and their maid, but they were very quiet.

I am very well, except that my voice soon faulters, and I have not slept well, which I imputed to the heat, which has been such as I never felt before for so long time. Three days we had of very great heat about ten years ago. I infer nothing from it but a good harvest.

Whether this short rustication has done me any good I cannot tell, I certainly am not worse, and am very willing to think myself better. Are you better? Sophy gave but a poor account of you. Do not let your mind wear out your body.

> I am, Madam,
> Your, &c.,
> SAM: JOHNSON

Self-tormenting Solitude

(To Mrs. Thrale)

London, August 13, 1783

DEAR MADAM,

Your letter was brought just as I was complaining that you had forgotten me.

I am now broken with disease, without the alleviation of familiar friendship or domestick society; I have no middle state between clamour and silence, between general conversation and self-tormenting solitude. Levet is dead, and poor Williams is making haste to die: I know not if she will ever more come out of her chamber.

I am now quite alone, but let me turn my thoughts another way.

> I am, Madam,
> Your, &c.,
> SAM: JOHNSON

Miss Williams Perverse

London, Aug. 23, 1783

MY DEAREST LOVE,

The story which Sophy was hindered from telling me, has
not yet been told, though I have now expected it a fortnight. Pray let me have it at last with all its circumstances.

My Mistress lately told me of something said in the papers of Boswel and me. I have heard nothing of it, and
should be [glad] to know what it was. Cut it out and send
it under a cover to Mr. Strahan. There has seldom been
so long a time in which I have had so little to do with Boswel, as since he left London. He has written twice and I
have written once. I remember no more.

Barry, the painter, has just told me what I delight to
tell again, that Ramsay is now walking the streets of Na-
ples in full possession of his locomotive powers.

Poor Mrs. Williams, I am afraid, can expect no such
renovation. I have just been to see her, and I doubt she
gave perverse answer to my enquiries, because she saw
that my tenderness put it in her power to give me pain.
This is hateful and despicable, and yet must not be too
much hated or despised, for strongly entwisted with human nature is the desire of exercising power, however that
power be gained or given. Let us pity it in others, and
despise it in ourselves. Write, my dearest, to

Your humble servant

SAM: JOHNSON

To Miss Thrale, at Weymouth

A Visit to Salisbury

(*To Mrs. Thrale*)

London, August 26, 1783

DEAR MADAM,

Things stand with me much as they have done for some time. Mrs. Williams fancies now and then that she grows better, but her vital powers appear to be slowly burning out. Nobody thinks however that she will very soon be quite wasted, and as she suffers me to be of very little use to her, I have determined to pass some time with Mr. Bowles near Salisbury, and have taken a place for Thursday.

Some benefit may be perhaps received from change of air, some from change of company, and some from mere change of place. It is not easy to grow well in a chamber where one has long been sick, and where every thing seen and every person speaking revives and impresses images of pain. Though it be that no man can run away from himself, he may yet escape from many causes of useless uneasiness. That the *mind is its own place,* is the boast of a fallen angel that had learned to lie. External locality has great effects, at least upon all embodied beings. I hope this little journey will afford me at least some suspense of melancholy.

You give but an unpleasing account of your performance at Portland. Your scrambling days are then over. I remember when no Miss and few Masters could have left you behind, or *thrown you out in the pursuit of honour* or of curiosity. But *tempus edax rerum,* and no way has been yet found to draw his teeth.

I am, dear Madam,

Your, &c.,

SAM: JOHNSON

The Death of Miss Williams

(To Mrs. Thrale)

London, Sept. 22, 1783

DEAR MADAM,

Poor Williams has I hope seen the end of her afflictions. She acted with prudence and she bore with fortitude. She has left me.

> Thou thy weary task hast done,
> Home art gone, and ta'en thy wages.

Had she had good humour and prompt elocution, her universal curiosity and comprehensive knowledge would have made her the delight of all that knew her. She left her little to your charity school.

The complaint about which you enquire is a sarcocele: I thought it a hydrocele, and heeded it but little. Puncture has detected the mistake: it can be safely suffered no longer. Upon inspection three days ago it was determined *extrema ventura.* If excision should be delayed there is danger of a gangrene. You would not have me for fear of pain perish in putrescence. I shall I hope, with trust in eternal mercy, lay hold of the possibility of life which yet remains. My health is not bad; the gout is now trying at my feet. My appetite and digestion are good, and my sleep better than formerly: I am not dejected, and I am not feeble. There is however danger enough in such operations at seventy-four.

Let me have your prayers and those of the young dear people.

I am, dear Madam,

Your, &c.,

SAM: JOHNSON

Write soon and often.

On Old Friends

(To Mrs. Thrale)

DEAR MADAM,

Since you have written to me with the attention and tenderness of ancient time, your letters give me a great part of the pleasure which a life of solitude admits. You will never bestow any share of your good will on one who deserves better. Those that have loved longest love best. A sudden blaze of kindness may by a single blast of coldness be extinguished, but that fondness which length of time has connected with many circumstances and occasions, though it may for a while [be] suppressed by disgust or resentment, with or without a cause, is hourly revived by accidental recollection. To those that have lived long together, every thing heard and every thing seen recals some pleasure communicated, or some benefit conferred, some petty quarrel, or some slight endearment. Esteem of great powers, or amiable qualities newly discovered, may embroider a day or a week, but a friendship of twenty years is interwoven with the texture of life. A friend may be often found and lost, but an *old friend* never can be found, and Nature has provided that he cannot easily be lost.

Lucy Porter has lost her brother. But whom I have lost — let me not now remember. Let not your loss be added to the mournful catalogue. Write soon again to

Madam,

Your most humble servant,

SAM: JOHNSON

London, Nov. 13, 1783
To Mrs. Thrale at Bath

To Fanny Burney

MADAM,

You have been at home a long time, and I have never seen you nor heard from you. Have we quarreled?

I have sent a book which I have found lately, and imagine to be Dr. Burney's. Miss Charlotte will please to examine.

Pray write me a direction of Mrs. Chapone, and pray let me sometimes have the honour of telling you, how much I am,

                                    Madam,
                              Your most humble servant,
                                    SAM: JOHNSON *

Bolt-court, Nov. 19, 1783

At the foot of this letter is written in Miss Burney's hand: — " *F. B. flew to him instantly and most gratefully.*"

Fanny Burney at Bolt Court

Nothing had yet publicly transpired, with certainty or authority, relative to the projects of Mrs. Thrale, who had

---

* Boswell tried to extract this and other letters of Johnson's to Miss Burney, but Miss Burney would not oblige him. She reports his request as follows: " You must give me some of your choice little notes of the Doctor's; we have seen him long enough upon stilts; I want to show him in a new light. Grave Sam, and great Sam, and solemn Sam, and learned Sam, — all these he has appeared over and over. Now I want to entwine a wreath of the graces across his brow; I want to show him as gay Sam, agreeable Sam, pleasant Sam; so you must help me with some of his beautiful billets to yourself."

now been nearly a year at Bath; though nothing was left unreported, or unasserted, with respect to her proceedings. Nevertheless, how far Dr. Johnson was himself informed, or was ignorant on the subject, neither Dr. Burney nor his daughter could tell; and each equally feared to learn.

Scarcely an instant, however, was the latter left alone in Bolt Court, ere she saw the justice of her long apprehensions; for while she planned speaking upon some topic that might have a chance to catch the attention of the Doctor, a sudden change from kind tranquillity to strong austerity took place in his altered countenance; and, startled and affrighted, she held her peace. . . .

Thus passed a few minutes, in which she scarcely dared breathe; while the respiration of the Doctor, on the contrary, was of asthmatic force and loudness; then, suddenly turning to her, with an air of mingled wrath and woe, he hoarsely ejaculated: " Piozzi! "

He evidently meant to say more; but the effort with which he articulated that name robbed him of any voice for amplification, and his whole frame grew tremulously convulsed.

His guest, appalled, could not speak; but he soon discerned that it was grief from coincidence, not distrust from opposition of sentiment, that caused her taciturnity. This perception calmed him, and he then exhibited a face " in sorrow more than anger." His see-sawing abated of its velocity, and, again fixing his looks upon the fire, he fell into pensive rumination.

At length, and with great agitation, he broke forth with: " She cares for no one! You, only — You, she loves still! — but no one — and nothing else! — You she still loves — "

A half smile now, though of no very gay character, softened a little the severity of his features, while he tried

to resume some cheerfulness in adding: " As . . . she
loves her little finger! "

(FANNY BURNEY)

The Ivy Lane Survivors

" What a man am I! " said he to me, in the month of November, " who have got the better of these diseases, the
palsy, the gout, and the asthma, and can now enjoy the
conversation of my friends, without the interruptions of
weakness or pain! " . . .

In this seeming spring-tide of his health and spirits, he
wrote me the following note:

DEAR SIR,
As Mr. Ryland was talking with me of old friends and
past times, we warmed ourselves with a wish, that all who
remained of the club should meet and dine at the house
which once was Horseman's, in Ivy Lane. I have undertaken to solicit you, and therefore desire you to tell us
what day next week you can conveniently meet your old
friends. . . .

Bolt Court, Nov. 22, 1783

Our intended meeting was prevented by a circumstance,
which the following note will explain:

DEAR SIR,
In perambulating Ivy Lane, Mr. Ryland found neither
our landlord Horseman, nor his successor. The old house
is shut up, and he liked not the appearance of any near it:
he, therefore, bespoke our dinner at the Queen's Arms, in
St. Paul's church yard where, at half an hour after three,

your company will be desired to-day, by those who remain of our former society.

> Your humble servant,
> SAM. JOHNSON

Dec. 3

With this invitation I cheerfully complied and met, at
the time and place appointed, all who could be mustered
of our society, namely, Johnson, Mr. Ryland, and Mr.
Payne of the bank. When we were collected, the thought
that we were so few, occasioned some melancholy reflections, and I could not but compare our meeting, at such
an advanced period of life as it was to us all, to that of
the four old men in the " Senile Colloquium " of Erasmus.
We dined, and in the evening regaled with coffee. At ten,
we broke up, much to the regret of Johnson, who proposed staying; but finding us inclined to separate, he left
us, with a sigh that seemed to come from his heart, lamenting that he was retiring to solitude and cheerless
meditation.

> (SIR JOHN HAWKINS)

Familiar and Domestick Companions

(To Mrs. Thrale)

London, Dec. 27, 1783

DEAR MADAM,

You have more than once wondered at my complaint
of solitude, when you hear that I am crowded with visits.
Inopem me copia fecit. Visitors are no proper companions in the chamber of sickness. They come when I could
sleep or read, they stay till I am weary, they force me to
attend when my mind calls for relaxation, and to speak
when my powers will hardly actuate my tongue. The

amusements and consolations of languor and depression are conferred by familiar and domestick companions, which can be visited or called at will, and can occasionally be quitted or dismissed, who do not obstruct accommodation by ceremony, or destroy indolence by awakening effort.

Such society I had with Levet and Williams; such I had where — I am never likely to have it more.

I wish, dear Lady, to you and my dear girls many a cheerful and pious Christmas.

I am
Your, &c.,
SAM: JOHNSON

The Approbation of Mankind

(To Mrs. Thrale)

London, Dec. 31, 1783

DEAR MADAM,

In the mean time I am well fed; I have now in the house pheasant, venison, turkey and ham, all unbought. Attention and respect give pleasure, however late or however useless. But they are not useless when they are late; it is reasonable to rejoice, as the day declines, to find that it has been spent with the approbation of mankind.

The ministry is again broken, and to any man who extends his thoughts to national consideration the times are dismal and gloomy. But to a sick man what is the publick?

The new year is at hand; may God make it happy to me, to you, to us all, for Jesus Christ's sake! Amen.

I am, Madam,
Your, &c.,
SAM: JOHNSON

All the World against England

(To the Reverend Dr. Taylor)

DEAR SIR,

I am still confined to the house, and one of my amusements is to write letters to my friends, though they, being busy in the common scenes of life, are not equally diligent in writing to me. Dr. Heberden was with me two or three days ago, and told me that nothing ailed me, which I am glad to hear, though I knew it not to be true. My nights are restless, my breath is difficult, and my lower parts continue tumid.

The struggle, you see, still continues between the two sets of ministers: those that are *out* and *in* one can scarce call them, for who is *out* or *in* is perhaps four times a day a new question. The tumult in government is, I believe, excessive, and the efforts of each party outrageously violent, with very little thought on any national interest, at a time when we have all the world for our enemies, when the King and parliament have lost even the titular dominion of America, and the real power of Government every where else. Thus Empires are broken down when the profits of administration are so great, that ambition is satisfied with obtaining them, and he that aspires to greatness needs do nothing more than talk himself into importance. He has then all the power which danger and conquest used formerly to give; he can raise a family and reward his followers.

Mr. Burke has just sent me his Speech upon the affairs of India, a volume of above a hundred pages closely printed. I will look into it; but my thoughts seldom now travel to great distances.

I would gladly know when you think to come hither, and whether this year you will come or no. If my life be continued, I know not well how I shall bestow myself.

I am, Sir,

Your affectionate &c.,

SAM: JOHNSON

" London, Jan. 24, 1784 "
" To the Rev. Dr. Taylor in Ashbourne, Derbyshire "

Piozzi Recalled from Italy

Bath, Jan. 27th, 1784. — On this day twelvemonths . . . oh dreadfullest of all days to me! did I send for my Piozzi and tell him we must part. The sight of my countenance terrified Dr. Pepys, to whom I went into the parlour for a moment, and the sight of the agonies I endured in the week following would have affected anything but interest, avarice, and pride personified, . . . with such, however, I had to deal, so my sorrows were unregarded. Seeing them continue for a whole year, indeed, has mollified my strong-hearted companions, and they *now* relent in earnest and wish me happy: I would now therefore be *loath to dye,* yet how shall I recruit my constitution so as to live? The pardon certainly did arrive the very instant of execution — for I was ill beyond all power of description, when my eldest daughter, bursting into tears, bid me call home the man of my heart, and not expire by slow torture in the presence of my children, who had my life in their power. "You are dying *now,*" said she. "I know it," replied I, "and I should die in peace had I but seen him *once again.*" "Oh send for him," said she, "send for him quickly! " "He is at Milan, child," replied I, "a thousand miles off! " "Well, well," returns she, "hurry him back, or I myself will send him an express." At these words I revived, and have been mending ever since. This was the first time that any of us had named the name of Piozzi to each other since we had put our feet into the coach to come to Bath.

(MRS. THRALE)

Sitting Up at Night

(To Mrs. Thrale)

London, Feb. 9, 1784

DEAR MADAM,

The remission of the cold did not continue long enough to afford me much relief. You are, as I perceive, afraid of the opium; I had the same terrour, and admitted its assistance only under the pressure of insupportable distress, as of an auxiliary too powerful and too dangerous. But in this pinching season I cannot live without it; and the quantity which I take is less than it once was.

My physicians flatter me, that the season is a great part of my disease; and that when warm weather restores perspiration, this watery disease will evaporate. I am at least willing to flatter myself.

I have been forced to sit up many nights by an obstinate sleeplessness, which makes the time in bed intolerably tedious, and which continues my drowsiness the following day. Besides, I can sometimes sleep erect, when I cannot close my eyes in a recumbent posture. I have just bespoke a flannel dress, which I can easily slip off and on, as I go to bed, or get out of it. Thus pass my days and nights in morbid wakefulness, in unseasonable sleepiness, in gloomy solitude, with unwelcome visitors, or ungrateful exclusions, in variety of wretchedness. But I snatch every lucid interval, and animate myself with such amusements as the time offers.

One thing which I have just heard, you will think to surpass expectation. The Chaplain of the factory at Petersburg relates, that the Rambler is now, by the command of the Empress, translating into Russian; and has promised when it is printed to send me a copy.

Grant, O Lord, that all who shall read my pages, may become more obedient to thy laws; and when the wretched writer shall appear before thee, extend thy mercy to him, for the sake of Jesus Christ. Amen.

I am, Madam,

Your, &c.,

SAM: JOHNSON

Hawkins Visits Johnson

In a visit, which I made him in a few days, in consequence of a very pressing request to see me, I found him labouring under great dejection of mind. He bade me draw near him, and said, he wanted to enter into a serious conversation with me; and, upon my expressing a willingness to join in it, he, with a look that cut me to the heart, told me, that he had the prospect of death before him, and that he dreaded to meet his Saviour. I could not but be astonished at such a declaration, and advised him, as I had done once before, to reflect on the course of his life, and the services he had rendered to the cause of religion and virtue, as well by his example, as his writings; to which he answered, that he had written as a philosopher, but had not lived like one. In the estimation of his offences, he reasoned thus — " Every man knows his own sins, and also, what grace he has resisted. But, to those of others, and the circumstances under which they were committed, he is a stranger: he is, therefore, to look on

himself as the greatest sinner that he knows of." At the
conclusion of this argument, which he strongly enforced,
he uttered this passionate exclamation — " Shall I, who
have been a teacher of others, myself be a castaway? "

(SIR JOHN HAWKINS)

A Relief from the Dropsy

. . . On the Saturday following, I made him a visit, and,
upon entering his room, observed in his countenance such
a serenity, as indicated that some remarkable crisis of his
disorder had produced a change in his feelings. He told
me that . . . he had spent the previous day in an abstraction from all worldly concerns; that, to prevent interruption, he had, in the morning, induced Frank not to
admit any one to him, and had added these awful words
" For your master is preparing to die." He then mentioned
to me, that, in the course of this exercise, he found himself
relieved from the disorder which had been growing on
him, and was becoming very oppressing, the dropsy, by a
gradual evacuation of water to the amount of twenty
pints. . . . Several times he cried out — " It is wonderful,
very wonderful! "

(SIR JOHN HAWKINS)

Futurity

(To Mrs. Thrale)
London, March 10, 1784

MADAM,
    You know I never thought confidence with respect to
futurity any part of the character of a brave, a wise, or a
good man. Bravery has no place where it can avail noth-

ing; wisdom impresses strongly the consciousness of those faults, of which it is itself perhaps an aggravation; and goodness, always wishing to be better, and imputing every deficience to criminal negligence, and every fault to voluntary corruption, never dares to suppose the condition of forgiveness fulfilled, nor what is wanting in the crime supplied by penitence.

This is the state of the best, but what must be the condition of him whose heart will not suffer him to rank himself among the best, or among the good? Such must be his dread of the approaching trial, as will leave him little attention to the opinion of those whom he is leaving for ever; and the serenity that is not felt, it can be no virtue to feign.

The sarcocele ran off long ago, at an orifice made for mere experiment.

The water passed naturally, by God's mercy, in a manner of which Dr. Heberden has seen but few examples. The chirurgeon has been employed to heal some excoriations; and four out of five are no longer under his cure. The physician laid on a blister, and I ordered, by their consent, a salve; but neither succeeded, and neither was very easily healed.

I have been confined from the fourteenth of December, and know not when I shall get out; but I have this day dressed me, as I was dressed in health.

Your kind expressions gave me great pleasure; do not reject me from your thoughts. Shall we ever exchange confidence by the fireside again?

I hope dear Sophy is better; and intend quickly to pay my debt to Susy.

> I am, Madam,
> Your, &c.,
> SAM: JOHNSON

The Consequences of Death

Some person in a company at Salisbury, of which Dr. Johnson was one, vouched for the company that there was nobody in it afraid of death. "Speak for yourself, Sir," said Johnson, "for indeed I am." "I did not say of dying," replied the other; "but of death, meaning its consequences." "And so I mean," rejoined the Doctor; "I am very seriously afraid of the consequences."

(RICHARD GREEN)

The Irrevocable Sentence

(*To Mrs. Thrale*)

London, March 20, 1784

MADAM,

Your last letter had something of tenderness. The accounts which you have had of my danger and distress were I suppose not aggravated. I have been confined ten weeks with an asthma and dropsy. But I am now better. God has in his mercy granted me a reprieve; for how much time his mercy must determine.

On the 19th of last month I evacuated twenty pints of water, and I think I reckon exactly; from that time the tumour has subsided, and I now begin to move with some freedom. You will easily believe that I am still at a great distance from health; but I am, as my chirurgeon expressed it, amazingly better. Heberden seems to have great hopes.

Write to me no more about *dying with a grace;* when you feel what I have felt in approaching eternity — in fear of soon hearing the sentence of which there is no revocation, you will know the folly; my wish is, that you may know it sooner. The distance between the grave and the remotest point of human longevity, is but a very little; and of that little no path is certain. You knew all this, and I thought that I knew it too; but I know it now with a new conviction. May that new conviction not be vain!

I am now cheerful; I hope this approach to recovery is a token of the Divine mercy. My friends continue their kindness. I give a dinner to-morrow.

Pray let me know how my dear Sophy goes on. I still hope that there is in her fits more terrour than danger. But I hope, however it be, that she will speedily recover. I will take care to pay Miss Susy her letter. God bless you all.

I am, Madam,
Your, &c.,
SAM: JOHNSON

Approaching Nuptials

28th May, 1784. — Here is the most sudden and beautiful spring ever seen after a dismal winter: so may God grant me a renovation of comfort after my many and sharp afflictions. I have been to London for a week to visit Fanny Burney, and to talk over my intended (and I hope approaching) nuptials, with Mr. Borghi: a man, as far as I can judge in so short an acquaintance with him, of good sense and real honour: — who loves my Piozzi, *likes* my conversation, and wishes to serve us sincerely. He has recommended Duane to take my power of attorney, and Cator's loss will be the less felt. Duane's name is as high as the Monument, and his being known familiarly to Borghi will perhaps quicken his attention to our concerns.

Dear Burney, who loves me *kindly* but the world *reverentially*, was, I believe, equally pained as delighted with my visit: ashamed to be seen in my company, much of her fondness for me must of course be diminished; yet she had not chatted freely so long with anybody but Mrs. Philips, that my coming was a comfort to her. We have told all to her father, and he behaved with the utmost propriety.

Nobody likes my settling at Milan except myself and Piozzi; but I think 'tis nobody's affair but our own: it seems to me quite irrational to expose ourselves to unnecessary insults, and by going straight to Italy all will be avoided.

(MRS. THRALE)

To Oxford with Boswell

(To Mrs. Thrale)

London, May 31, 1784

DEAR MADAM,

Why you expected me to be better than I am I cannot imagine: I am better than any that saw me in my illness ever expected to have seen me again. I am however at a great distance from health, very weak and very asthmatick, and troubled with my old nocturnal distresses; so that I am little asleep in the night, and in the day too little awake.

I have one way or other been disappointed hitherto of that change of air, from which I think some relief may possibly be obtained; but Boswel and I have settled our resolution to go to Oxford on Thursday. But since I was at Oxford, my convivial friend Dr. Edwards and my learned friend Dr. Wheeler are both dead, and my probabilities of pleasure are very much diminished. Why, when so many are taken away, have I been yet spared! I hope that I may be fitter to die.

How long we shall stay at Oxford, or what we shall do when we leave it, neither Bozzy nor I have yet settled; he is for his part resolved to remove his family to London and try his fortune at the English bar: let us all wish him success.

Think of me, if you can, with tenderness.

I am, Madam,

Your, &c.,

SAM: JOHNSON

Piozzi's Return

10th June, 1784. — I sent these lines to meet Piozzi on his return. They are better than those he liked so last year at Dover:

> " Over mountains, rivers, vallies,
> See my love returns to Calais,
> After all their taunts and malice,
> Ent'ring safe the gates of Calais,
> While delay'd by winds he dallies,
> Fretting to be kept at Calais,
> Muse, prepare some sprightly sallies
> To divert my dear at Calais,
> Say how every rogue who rallies
> Envies him who waits at Calais
> For her that would disdain a Palace
> Compar'd to Piozzi, Love, and Calais."

28th June. — I am not *yet sure* of seeing him again — not *sure* he lives, not *sure* he loves me *yet.* . . . Should anything happen now!! Oh, I will not trust myself with such a fancy: it will either kill me or drive me distracted.

Bath, 2nd July, 1784. — The happiest day of my whole

life, I think — Yes, quite the happiest: my Piozzi came home yesterday and dined with me; but my spirits were too much agitated, my heart was too much dilated. I was too *painfully* happy *then;* my sensations are more quiet to-day, and my felicity less tumultuous.

. . . We shall go to London about the affairs, and there be married in the Romish Church.

(MRS. THRALE)

Breaking the News

(Mrs. Piozzi to Dr. Johnson)

Bath, June 30

MY DEAR SIR,

The enclosed is a circular letter which I have sent to all the guardians, but our friendship demands somewhat more; it requires that I should beg your pardon for concealing from you a connexion which you must have heard of by many, but I suppose never believed. Indeed, my dear Sir, it was concealed only to save us both needless pain; I could not have borne to reject that counsel it would have killed me to take, and I only tell it you now because all is irrevocably settled, and out of your power to prevent. I will say, however, that the dread of your disapprobation has given me some anxious moments, and though, perhaps, I am become by many privations the most independent woman in the world, I feel as if acting without a parent's consent till you write kindly to

Your faithful servant.

CIRCULAR

SIR,

As one of the executors of Mr. Thrale's will and guardian to his daughters, I think it my duty to acquaint you

that the three eldest left Bath last Friday for their own
house at Brighthelmstone in company with an amiable
friend, Miss Nicholson, who has sometimes resided with
us here, and in whose society they may, I think, find some
advantages and certainly no disgrace. I waited on them
to Salisbury, Wilton, &c., and offered to attend them to
the seaside myself, but they preferred this lady's company
to mine, having heard that Mr. Piozzi is coming back
from Italy, and judging perhaps by our past friendship
and continued correspondence that his return would be
succeeded by our marriage.

I have the honour to be, Sir, your obedient servant.
Bath, June 30, 1784

Johnson's Reply

MADAM, — If I interpret your letter right, you are igno-
miniously married; if it is yet undone, let us once more
talk together. If you have abandoned your children and
your religion, God forgive your wickedness: if you have
forfeited your fame and your country, may your folly do
no further mischief. If the last act is yet to do, I who have
loved you, esteemed you, reverenced you, and served you,
I who long thought you the first of humankind, entreat
that, before your fate is irrevocable, I may once more see
you. I was, I once was, — Madam, most truly yours,

SAM. JOHNSON.

I will come down, if you permit it.

Mrs. Thrale Defends Herself

SIR, — I have this morning received from you so rough
a letter in reply to one which was both tenderly and

respectfully written, that I am forced to desire the conclusion of a correspondence which I can bear to continue
no longer. The birth of my second husband is not meaner
than that of my first; his sentiments are not meaner; his
profession is not meaner, and his superiority in what he
professes acknowledged by all mankind. It is want of fortune then that is ignominious; the character of the man
I have chosen has no other claim to such an epithet. The
religion to which he has always been a zealous adherent
will, I hope, teach him to forgive insults he has not deserved; mine will, I hope, enable me to bear them at once
with dignity and patience. To hear that I have forfeited
my fame is indeed the greatest insult I ever yet received.
My fame is as unsullied as snow, or I should think it un-
worthy of him who is henceforth to protect it.

I write by the coach the more speedily and effectually
to prevent your coming hither. Perhaps by my fame (and
I hope it is so) you mean only that celebrity which is a
consideration of a much lower kind. I care for that only
as it may give pleasure to my husband and his friends.

Farewell, dear Sir, and accept my best wishes. You
have always commanded my esteem, and long enjoyed
the fruits of a friendship never infringed by one harsh
expression on my part during twenty years of familiar
talk. Never did I oppose your will, or control your wish;
nor can your unmerited severity itself lessen my regard;
but till you have changed your opinion of Mr. Piozzi let
us converse no more. God bless you.

His Last Letter

DEAR MADAM, — What you have done, however I may
lament it, I have no pretence to resent, as it has not been

injurious to me: I therefore breathe out one sigh more of tenderness, perhaps useless, but at least sincere.

I wish that God may grant you every blessing, that you may be happy in this world for its short continuance, and eternally happy in a better state; and whatever I can contribute to your happiness I am very ready to repay, for that kindness which soothed twenty years of a life radically wretched.

Do not think slightly of the advice which I now presume to offer. Prevail upon Mr. Piozzi to settle in England: you may live here with more dignity than in Italy, and with more security: your rank will be higher, and your fortune more under your own eye. I desire not to detail all my reasons, but every argument of prudence and interest is for England, and only some phantoms of imagination seduce you to Italy.

I am afraid, however, that my counsel is vain, yet I have eased my heart by giving it.

When Queen Mary took the resolution of sheltering herself in England, the Archbishop of St. Andrew's, attempting to dissuade her, attended on her journey; and when they came to the irremeable stream that separated the two kingdoms, walked by her side into the water, in the middle of which he seized her bridle, and with earnestness proportioned to her danger and his own affection pressed her to return. The Queen went forward — If the parallel reaches thus far, may it go no further. The tears stand in my eyes.

I am going into Derbyshire, and hope to be followed by your good wishes, for I am, with great affection, — Your, etc.,

SAM. JOHNSON

Mrs. Thrale's Reply

Not only my good Wishes but most fervent Prayers for
your Health and Consolation shall for ever attend and
follow my dear Mr. Johnson. Your last letter is sweetly
kind, and I thank you for it most sincerely. Have no Fears
for me, however; no *real* Fears. My Piozzi will need few
Perswasions to settle in a Country where he has succeeded
so well; but he longs to shew me to his Italian Friends,
and he wishes to restore my Health by treating me with a
Journey to many Places I have long wish'd to see. . . .
He is a religious Man, a sober Man, a Thinking Man — he
will not injure me, I am sure he will not, let nobody injure
him in your good Opinion, which he is most solicitous to
obtain and preserve, and the harsh Letter you wrote to me
at first grieved him to the very heart. Accept his Esteem,
my dear Sir, do; and his Promise to treat with long continued Respect and Tenderness the Friend whom you
once honoured with your Regard and who will never
cease to be, my dear Sir,
Your truly affectionate and faithful serv^t.

*The signature to this letter was violently erased by John-
son.*

Mrs. Thrale Marries Piozzi

25th July, 1784. — I am returned from church the happy
wife of my lovely faithful Piozzi . . . subject of my prayers, object of my wishes, my sighs, my reverence, my
esteem. — His nerves have been horribly shaken, yet he
lives, he loves me, and will be mine for ever. He has
sworn, in the face of God and the whole Christian Church;
Catholics, Protestants, all are witnesses.

(MRS. THRALE)

A Stone for His Wife's Grave

(To John Ryland)

DEAR SIR,

Mr. Payne will pay you fifteen pounds towards the stone of which you have kindly undertaken the care. The Inscription is in the hands of Mr. Bagshaw, who has a right to inspect it before he admits it into his Church.

Be pleased to let the whole be done with privacy, that I may elude the vigilance of the papers.

I am going for a while into Derbyshire in hope of help from the air of the country.

I hope your journey has benefited you. The Club prospers; we meet by ten at a time.

God send that you and I may enjoy and improve each other.

I am, dear Sir,
Your most humble servant,
SAM: JOHNSON

July 12, 1784
To Mr. Ryland
  in Muscovy Court
    Tower hill

On Dictionaries

(To Francesco Sastres)

Ashbourne, August 21, 1784

DEAR SIR,

I am glad that a letter has at last reached you; what became of the two former, which were directed to *Morti-*

mer instead of *Margaret* Street, I have no means of know-ing, nor is it worth the while to enquire; they neither enclosed bills, nor contained secrets.

My health was for some time quite at a stand, if it did not rather go backwards; but for a week past it flatters me with appearances of amendment, which I dare yet hardly credit. My breath has been certainly less ob-structed for eight days; and yesterday the water seemed to be disposed to a fuller flow. But I get very little sleep; and my legs do not like to carry me.

You were kind in paying my forfeits at the club; it can-not be expected that many should meet in the summer, however they that continue in town should keep up ap-pearances as well as they can. I hope to be again among you.

I wish you had told me distinctly the mistakes in the French words. The French is but a secondary and subor-dinate part of your design; exactness, however, in all parts is necessary, though complete exactness cannot be at-tained; and the French are so well stocked with diction-aries, that a little attention may easily keep you safe from gross faults; and as you work on, your vigilance will be quickened, and your observation regulated; you will bet-ter know your own wants, and learn better whence they may be supplied. Let me know minutely the whole state of your negotiations. Dictionaries are like watches, the worst is better than none and the best cannot be expected to go quite true.

The weather here is very strange summer weather; and we are here two degrees nearer the north than you. I was I think loath to think a fire necessary in July, till I found one in the servants' hall, and thought myself entitled to as much warmth as them.

I wish you would make it a task to yourself to write to
me twice a week; a letter is a great relief to

Dear Sir,

Your, &c.,

SAM: JOHNSON

Sastres was the Italian master with whom Johnson became acquainted when he hoped to go to Italy with the
Thrales. He attended Johnson regularly during his last
days, and has recorded how shortly before the end Johnson
burnt his mother's letters — " They drew from him a flood
of tears. When the paper they were written on was all con-
sumed he . . . cast a melancholy look upon their ashes,
which he took up and examined to see if a word was still
legible."

His Last Visit to Lichfield

I have lately been in the almost daily habit of contemplating a very melancholy spectacle. The great Johnson
is here, labouring under the paroxysms of a disease, which
must speedily be fatal. He shrinks from the consciousness
with the extremest horror. It is by his repeatedly expressed desire that I visit him often: yet I am sure he
neither does, nor ever did feel much regard for me; but he
would fain escape, for a time, in any society, from the terrible idea of his approaching dissolution. I never would
be awed by his sarcasms, or his frowns, into acquiescence
with his general injustice to the merits of *other* writers;
with his national, or party aversions; but I feel the truest
compassion for his present sufferings, and fervently wish
I had power to relieve them.

A few days since I was to drink tea with him, by his
request, at Mrs. Porter's. When I went into the room, he

was in deep but agitated slumber, in an arm-chair. Opening the door with that caution due to the sick, he did not
awaken at my entrance. I stood by him several minutes,
mournfully contemplating the temporary suspension of
those vast intellectual powers, which must so soon, as to
this world, be eternally quenched.

Upon the servant entering to announce the arrival of a
gentleman of the university, introduced by Mr. White, he
awoke with convulsive starts, — but rising, with more
alacrity than could have been expected, he said, " Come,
my dear lady, let you and I attend these gentlemen in the
study." He received them with more than usual compla-
cence; but whimsically chose to get astride upon his chair-
seat, with his face to its back, keeping a trotting motion
as if on horseback; but, in this odd position, he poured
forth streams of eloquence, illumined by frequent flashes
of wit and humour, without any tincture of malignity.
That amusing part of this conversation, which alluded to
the learned Pig, and his demi-rational exhibitions, I shall
transmit to you hereafter.

(ANNA SEWARD)

His Wife's Tombstone

(*To John Ryland*)

DEAR SIR,

I have just received a letter in which you tell me that
you love to hear from me, and I value such a declaration
too much to neglect it. To have a friend, and a friend
like you, may be numbered amongst the first felicities of
life; at a time when weakness either of body or mind loses
the pride and the confidence of self-sufficiency, and looks
round for that help which perhaps human kindness can-

not give, and which we yet are willing to expect from one another.

I am at this time very much dejected. The water gains fast upon me, but it has invaded me twice in this last half year, and has been twice expelled: it will, I hope, give way to the same remedies.

My Breath is tolerably easy, and since the remission of asthma about two months ago, has never been so strait and so much obstructed as it once was.

I took this day a very uncommon dose of squills, but hitherto without effect, but I will continue their use very diligently. Let me have your prayers.

I am now preparing myself for my return, and do not despair of some more monthly meetings. To hear that dear Payne is better gives me great delight.

I saw the draught of the stone. I am afraid the date is wrong. I think it should be 52. We will have it rectified. You say nothing of the cash but that you have paid it. My intention was that Mr. Payne should have put into your hands fifteen pounds which he received for me at Midsummer. If he has not done it, I will order you the money which is in his hands.

Shall I ever be able to bear the sight of this stone? In your company I hope I shall. You will not wonder that I write no more. God bless you for Christ's sake.

> I am, dear Sir,
>
> Your most humble servant,
>
> SAM: JOHNSON

Lichfield, Nov. 4, 1784

Hurrying Back to London

(To Sir John Hawkins)

Lichfield, November 7, 1784

I am relapsing into the dropsy very fast, and shall make such haste to town that it will be useless to write to me; but when I come, let me have the benefit of your advice, and the consolation of your company.

(LETTERS)

Doctor and Patient

He had scarce arrived in town, before it was found to be too true, that he was relapsing into a dropsy; and farther, that he was at times grievously afflicted with an asthma. Under an apprehension that his end was approaching, he enquired of Dr. Brocklesby, with great earnestness indeed, how long he might probably live, but could obtain no other than unsatisfactory answers: and, at the same time, if I remember right, under a seeming great pressure of mind, he thus addressed him, in the words of Shakespeare:

> " Canst thou not minister to a mind diseas'd;
> Pluck from the memory a rooted sorrow,
> Raze out the written troubles of the brain,
> And with some sweet oblivious antidote,
> Cleanse the full bosom of that perilous stuff,
> Which weighs upon the heart? " —
> *Macbeth* [Act v. sc. 3]

To which the doctor, who was nearly as well read in the above author as himself, readily replied,

> — " Therein the patient
> Must minister to himself."

Upon which Johnson exclaimed — " Well applied: — that's
more than poetically true."

(SIR JOHN HAWKINS)

"I Drive Her Quite from My Mind"

Last Thursday, Nov. 25th, my father set me down at Bolt-
court, while he went on upon business. I was anxious to
again see poor Dr. Johnson, who has had terrible health
since his return from Lichfield. He let me in, though very
ill. He was alone, which I much rejoiced at; for I had a
longer and more satisfactory conversation with him than
I have had for many months. He was in rather better
spirits, too, than I have lately seen him; but he told me he
was going to try what sleeping out of town might do for
him.

" I remember," said he, " that my wife, when she was
near her end, poor woman, was also advised to sleep out
of town; and when she was carried to the lodgings that
had been prepared for her, she complained that the stair-
case was in very bad condition — for the plaster was
beaten off the wall in many places. ' Oh,' said the man
of the house, ' that's nothing but by the knocks against it
of the coffins of the poor souls that have died in the lodgings! ' "

He laughed, though not without apparent secret anguish, in telling me this. I felt extremely shocked, but,
willing to confine my words at least to the literal story, I
only exclaimed against the unfeeling absurdity of such a
confession.

" Such a confession," cried he, " to a person then coming

to try his lodging for her health, contains, indeed, more absurdity than we can well lay our account for."

I had seen Miss T. the day before.

" So," said he, " did I."

I then said, — " Do you ever, sir, hear from her mother? "

" No," cried he, " nor write to her. I drive her quite from my mind. If I meet with one of her letters, I burn it instantly. I have burnt all I can find. I never speak of her, and I desire never to hear of her more. I drive her, as I said, wholly from my mind."

. . . The good Mr. Hoole, and equally good Mr. Sastres attend him, rather as nurses than friends, for they sit whole hours by him, without even speaking to him. He will not, it seems, be talked to — at least very rarely. At times, indeed, he re-animates; but it is soon over, and he says of himself, " I am now like Macbeth, — question enrages me."

My father saw him once while I was away, and carried Mr. Burke with him, who was desirous of paying his respects to him once more in person. He rallied a little while they were there; and Mr. Burke, when they left him, said to my father — " His work is almost done; and well has he done it! "

(FANNY BURNEY)

On Reading the Bible

Saturday, Nov. 20, 1784. — This evening, about eight o'clock, I paid a visit to my dear friend Dr. Johnson, whom I found very ill and in great dejection of spirits. We had a most affecting conversation on the subject of religion, in which he exhorted me, with the greatest warmth of kindness, to attend closely to every religious duty, and particularly enforced the obligation of private prayer and receiving the Sacrament. He desired me to stay that night and join in prayer with him; adding, that he always went to prayer every night with his man Francis. He conjured me to read and meditate upon the Bible, and not to throw it aside for a play or a novel. He said he had himself lived in great negligence of religion and worship for forty years; that he had neglected to read his Bible, and had often reflected what he could hereafter say when he should be asked why he had not read it.

(JOHN HOOLE)

Rays of Hope

I saw him about noon; he was dozing; but waking, he found himself in a circle of his friends. Upon opening his eyes, he said, that the prospect of his dissolution was very terrible to him, and addressed himself to us all, in nearly these words: " You see the state in which I am; conflicting with bodily pain and mental distraction: while you are in health and strength, labour to do good, and avoid evil, if ever you hope to escape the distress that now oppresses me." — A little while after, — " I had, very early in my life, the seeds of goodness in me: I had a love of virtue, and a reverence for religion; and these, I trust, have brought forth in me fruits meet for repentance; and, if I have repented as I ought, I am forgiven. I have, at times, entertained a loathing of sin and of myself, particularly at the beginning of this year, when I had the prospect of death before me; and this has not abated when my fears of death have been less; and, at these times, I have had such rays of hope shot into my soul, as have almost persuaded me, that I am in a state of reconciliation with God."

(SIR JOHN HAWKINS)

Provision for Francis Barber

Tuesday, December 7th. Ten minutes past two, p.m.

After waiting some short time in the adjoining room, I was admitted to Dr. Johnson in his bedchamber, where, after placing me next him on the chair, he sitting in his usual place on the east side of the room (and I on his right hand), he put into my hands two small volumes (an edition of the New Testament), as he afterwards told me, saying, "*Extremum hoc munus morientis habeto.*" He then proceeded to observe that I was entering upon a life which would lead me deeply into all the business of the world; that he did not condemn civil employment, but that it was a state of great danger; and that he had therefore one piece of advice earnestly to impress upon me — that I would set apart every seventh day for the care of my soul; that one day, the seventh, should be employed in repenting what was amiss in the six preceding, and fortifying my virtue for the six to come; that such a portion of time was surely little enough for the meditation of eternity. He then told me that he had a request to make to me; namely, that I would allow his servant Frank to look up to me as his friend, adviser, and protector, in all difficulties which his own weakness and imprudence, or the force or fraud of others, might bring him into. He said that he had left him what he considered an ample provision, viz. 70l. per annum; but that even that sum might not place him above the want of a protector, and to me, therefore, he recommended him as to one who had will, and power, and activity to protect him. Having obtained my assent to this, he proposed that Frank should be called in; and desiring me to take him by the hand in token of the promise, repeated before him the recommendation he had just made of him, and the promise I had given to attend to it.

(WILLIAM WINDHAM)

"Don't Compliment Now"

Wednesday, Dec. 8. — Went with Mrs. Hoole and my son, by appointment: found him very poorly and low, after a very bad night. Mr. Nichols the printer was there. My son read the Litany, the Doctor several times urging him to speak louder. After prayers Mr. Langton came in: much serious discourse: he warned us all to profit by his situation; and, applying to me, who stood next him, exhorted me to lead a better life than he had done. " A better life than you, my dear Sir! " I repeated. He replied warmly, " Don't compliment now."

(JOHN HOOLE)

A Male Nurse

10th. This day at noon I saw him again. He said to me, that the male nurse to whose care I had committed him, was unfit for the office. " He is," said he, " an idiot, as aukward as a turnspit just put into the wheel, and as sleepy as a dormouse."

(SIR JOHN HAWKINS)

The Last Night

December 13. — In the morning meant to have met Mr. Cruikshank in Bolt Court; but while I was deliberating about going, was sent for by Mr. Burke. Went to Bolt Court about half-past three. Found Dr. Johnson had been almost constantly asleep since nine in the morning, and heard from Mr. Des Moulins an account of what had passed in the night. He had compelled Frank to give him a lancet, and had besides concealed in the bed a pair of scissors, and with one or the other of these had scarified himself in three places, two in the leg, &c. On Mr. Des Moulins making a difficulty of giving him the lancet, he said, " Don't you, if you have any scruples; but I will compel Frank ": and on Mr. Des Moulins attempting afterwards to prevent Frank from giving it to him, and at last to restrain his hands, he grew very outrageous, so as to call Frank scoundrel, and to threaten Mr. Des Moulins that he would stab him. He then made the three incisions above mentioned, of which one in the leg, &c. were not unskilfully made; but the other in the leg was a deep and ugly wound from which, with the others, they suppose him to have lost nearly eight ounces of blood. Upon Dr. Heberden expressing his fears about the scarification, Dr. Johnson told him he was *timidorum timidissimus.*

(SIR JOHN HAWKINS)

A Calm Sleep

Monday, Dec. 13. — Went to Bolt Court at eleven o'clock in the morning; met a young lady coming down stairs from the Doctor, whom, upon inquiry, I found to be Miss Morris (a sister to Miss Morris, formerly on the stage). Mrs. De Moulins told me that she had seen the Doctor; that by her desire he had been told she came to ask his blessing, and that he said, " God bless you! " I then went up into his chamber, and found him lying very composed in a kind of doze: he spoke to nobody. Sir John Hawkins, Mr. Langton, Mrs. Gardiner, Rev. Mr. Strahan and Mrs.

Strahan, Doctors Brocklesby and Butter, Mr. Steevens, and Mr. Nichols the printer, came; but no one chose to disturb him by speaking to him, and he seemed to take no notice of any person. While Mrs. Gardiner and I were there, before the rest came, he took a little warm milk in a cup, when he said something upon its not being properly given into his hand: he breathed very regular, though short, and appeared to be mostly in a calm sleep or dozing. I left him in this state, and never more saw him alive.

(JOHN HOOLE)

"Jam Moriturus"

13*th.* At noon, I called at the house, but went not into his room, being told that he was dozing. I was further informed by the servants, that his appetite was totally gone, and that he could take no sustenance. At eight in the evening, of the same day, word was brought me by Mr. Sastres, to whom, in his last moments, he uttered these words "Jam moriturus," that, at a quarter past seven, he had, without a groan, or the least sign of pain or uneasiness, yielded his last breath.

(SIR JOHN HAWKINS)

BIBLIOGRAPHY

Johnsonian Miscellanies. 2 vols. Edited by George Birkbeck Hill. (Clarendon Press)

These two volumes, from which, together with the Letters, by far the greater part of this book is taken, are invaluable to anyone interested in Johnson. In addition to numerous small anecdotes, they contain Johnson's Annals (his reminiscences of his childhood); His Prayers and Meditations; Mrs. Piozzi's Anecdotes; Arthur Murphy's biography; Extracts from Sir John Hawkins's Life; Dr. Thomas Campbell's Diary of a Visit to England in 1775; and the fascinating Recollections of Dr. Johnson by Miss Reynolds, Sir Joshua's sister.

Letters of Samuel Johnson. 2 vols. Edited by George Birkbeck Hill. (Clarendon Press).

Autobiography, Letters and Literary Remains of Mrs. Thrale. Edited by Abraham Hayward

Diary and Letters of Madame d'Arblay. (Fanny Burney)

Dr. Johnson and Mrs. Thrale, by A. M. Broadley. Containing the Journal of the Welsh Tour, and letters of Mrs. Thrale. (John Lane)

French Journals of Mrs. Thrale and Dr. Johnson. Edited by Moses Tyson and Henry Guppy. (The Manchester University Press)

The Queeney Letters. Edited by the Marquis of Lansdowne. (Cassell & Co.)

The Swan of Lichfield (Letters of Anna Seward). Edited by Hesketh Pearson. (Hamish Hamilton)

Samuel Johnson:
   The Lives of the Poets *Poems*
   The Rambler   *Preface to the Dictionary*
   Rasselas

INDEX

A NOTE ON THE TYPE

The text of this book is set in Caledonia, a Linotype face designed by W. A. Dwiggins. Caledonia belongs to the family of printing types called " modern face " by printers — a term used to mark the change in style of type-letters that occurred about 1800. Caledonia is in the general neighborhood of Scotch Modern in design, but is more freely drawn than that letter.

The book was composed, printed, and bound by The Plimpton Press, Norwood, Massachusetts. The paper was made by S. D. Warren Company, Boston. Typography by W. A. Dwiggins.